Orgsm: A Memoir
Inside the Matriarchal Cult of OneTaste
Ruwan Meepagala

Subversalist Publishing

Contents

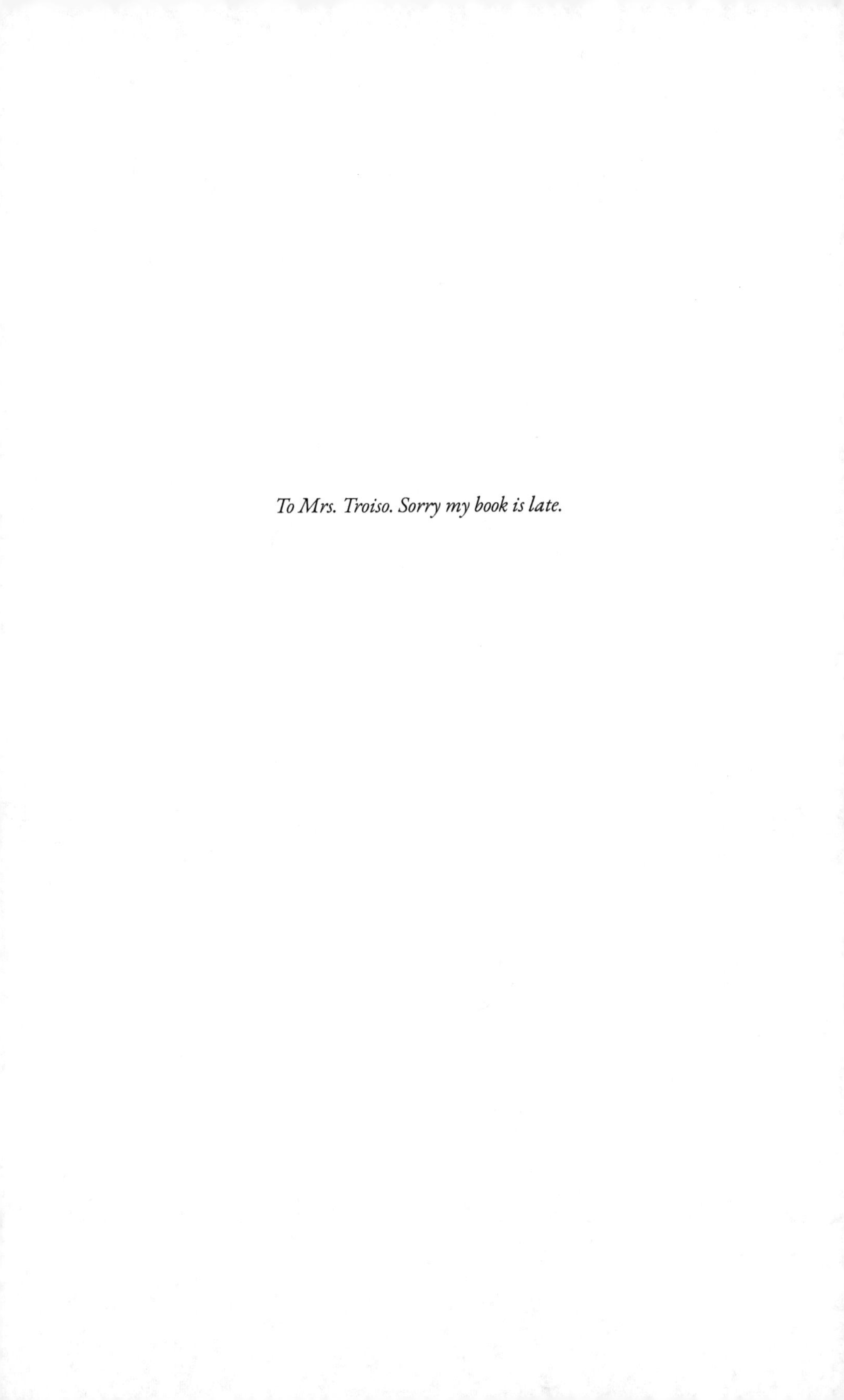

To Mrs. Troiso. Sorry my book is late.

Disclaimer

All the events in this book are real. Except for public figures and those who gave consent to use their full name, all other characters are fictionalized. Names have been changed, dialogue has been re-attributed, many people have been composited, and some have been omitted completely to both conceal identities and make the story more readable. So if you think you recognize someone, you're wrong.

Not a single sentence of this book was written by AI. Read human.

Pre-sentencing Edition

This is the limited first edition. It will be updated to include the pending criminal sentencing.

To receive the final version of the book, drop in your email at

<u>orgsmbook.com/prerelease</u>

You will also receive the following bonuses promised to pre-orderers:

1. Advance reader copy of Ruwan's next book, *Anima: The Five Aspects of Feminine Unconscious*

2. *How To Brainwash Yourself* mini-course

3. Free access to Ruwan's paywall meditations

PROLOGUE

My heart was pounding and my throat was dry.

"TurnON" some call those sensations. I used to too.

I entered the courthouse of the Eastern District of New York for *USA vs Rachel Cherwitz and Nicole Daedone.* I handed in my phone and passed through the metal detectors. I was early. Knowing nothing about the legal system, I sat on the "defense" side of the gallery. I didn't mean to take a side. But in federal court, as in that of public opinion, you're expected to choose.

It's not that I was indifferent to the outcome. The verdict of this trial would have a great emotional impact on the life stories of many people I cared about, myself included. It would set a legal precedent for how cults and "brainwashing" could be criminalized in the future. But it wasn't as simple as the 'Good vs. Evil' morality that the opposing ends liked to frame it in.

Was OneTaste built on good intentions, then was tempted wayward by money, sex, and power? Or was it designed from the beginning to farm hearts, minds, and loins, but wrapped in a facade of female empowerment? Only one person could know for sure.

Nicole Daedone entered the courtroom wearing a grey pantsuit and tan shawl. Thirteen years ago I saw her in person for the first time. That time I was in awe. Those were very different circumstances.

She made a startled face when she saw me. So did her attorney, Jennifer Bonjean, who also represented Harvey Weinstein and Bill Cosby. Two young paralegals from the government kept whispering and looking back at me. I assumed they recognized me from the documentary.

I had appeared or been quoted in every piece about the "Orgasm Cult" since I left in 2014. I received plenty of threats from OneTaste loyalists for criticizing the organization.

And hate mail from strangers for crediting OneTaste for changing my life. I even received a clandestine message from Nicole that she would pay me not to publish this book.

A part of me wished I took the deal. It would have saved me a lot of trouble.

For two years in the cult, I wrote down every detail and dialogue. I had almost a hundred dusty notebooks at home, many stained with lube. For over ten years, I had been sifting through these scenes that defined the end of my innocence.

Nicole's co-defendant entered the court. I swelled with conflicting feelings upon seeing Rachel Cherwitz. She walked with her head turned so we couldn't make eye contact. *Everything is a communication.*

Both sides of the gallery filled in. Their expressions revealed their affiliation before they sat. Hyperbolic smiles over tired eyes sat near me on the defense side. Cold cynicism sat on the side of the prosecution. Those who recognized me, gave me a look.

Court is a ritual space. Its formalities and gravity trigger the release of neurochemicals that create an altered state that most would call "surreal." Heightened attention changes perception. Seconds feel like minutes. Minutes feel like hours.

There are many ways to trigger similar altered states—enchantment, terror, rapture, ecstasy. Group vulnerability is one. Being in a room where a hundred women enter *Orgasm* together is another. Living in a reality where such things are normal is the most sustaining.

"All rise," the bailiff said.

Judge Diane Gujarati entered and sat on the bench.

"Good morning, all," she said and proceeding to get into 'housekeeping.'

But all I could hear was *"Welcome to TurnON New York."*

It was fitting that the judge and lead prosecutor were both women. OneTaste's primary media narrative was that they were being persecuted for alternative views on sexuality and female empowerment. They compared this indictment to the witch trials.

In another setting all the roles could have been reversed. With the right vulnerabilities exploited, any person in this room— judge, jury, attorneys— could have been sitting in an audience whose authority was held by Nicole. In such an environment, she would have been the judge and jury of reality, the collective belief of right and wrong.

"Reality" is a set of agreements.

The verdict of this trial would determine more than the futures of two women who ran a global movement around female sexuality. It would be a state-mandated decision around the nature of free will.

Nicole did advertise that this was a "path best not started." In that respect, she was honest. It even was part of the allure. Odysseus couldn't help listening to the Sirens' song of forbidden knowledge and untold pleasures, despite knowing the consequences. In my two years on the path, I got an education in *The Feminine*— women, emotions, and the darker truths of human consciousness— that I couldn't have gotten anywhere else.

I remembered what Om Rupani said about how "karma is a web of causes and effects." How did I end up sitting in federal court today?

I watched a TED Talk. I read a self-help book. And I attended an event that wasn't at all what I expected...

STAGE 1: CLIMAX

Involuntary contraction followed by explosive release. The subject is ejected into a new reality.

THE POSTCARD READ "COME to The Meetup on Female Orgasm."

I double-checked the address on the back. The meetup was held at a second story event space south of Union Square. I was early. I considered doing a lap around the block to kill time, but did that last week and ended up chickening out.

"Hi, are you here for TurnON?" a melodic voice said.

There was a young woman standing next to the table at the top of the stairs. She was wearing a bright pink dress and a smile that was all eyes and teeth.

"Yeah haha."

My dating coach said I needed to stop fake laughing after I spoke. He said I did that because I couldn't handle tension. My calves clenched in my sweatpants.

"Great, just sign your name here," she said.

She had emerald green eyes that sparkled even in the fluorescent light. She said her name was Abby Shakti.

"Nice to meet you, Ruwan. That will be ten dollars," Abby said.

"Oh I paid online. For two tickets actually."

My chest sunk in. It was stupid to buy two tickets.

"Oh that was you. Okay go right on in," she said. "You can put your rollerblades in the cubby."

The event room was some sort of dance studio. The walls were mirrored but had dark curtains over them. The floor was padded. The lighting was clinical. There were ten chairs in a circle, eight black and two white. There was only one person here, an old Indian guy in a starched white shirt. He resembled my dad. I didn't want to be here anymore.

I sat in the seat next to him anyway. Normally I would have sat as far away as possible, but my normal behavior hadn't been working for me lately.

"Um, hey so have you been to this thing before?" I asked.

He looked at me over his nose. "Yes, last week I attended," he said in a slight accent. "It is very interesting what they do here. I want to learn the *Orgasmic Meditation*."

"Cool. Me too."

"Do you have a girlfriend?"

"What?"

"Do you have a woman that you make love to?"

"Well, kind of, yeah..."

My voice trailed off. My stomach was knotted. I had felt winded all week. Lisa hadn't returned my texts for six days. I had been holding on to hope that she was just sick or hit by a car or something. But it is harder to believe your own lie when spoken out loud. I knew she was about to dump me.

"When I was a young man I had many girlfriends," the old Indian man said. "I made love to many women."

"Oh, okay."

"I am sixty-six years old now. But I still have the energy of a much younger man. I can still satisfy many women."

"That's cool, I guess."

My calves clenched again. I didn't like that I always did that, but it was better than balling up my fists. At least people couldn't see it.

More people came in and filled the seats. Some seemed to know each other already. There was a young woman wearing leg warmers and her hair in a bun. A heavyset Asian guy walked in wearing a cowboy hat. A lanky bearded hipster sat down next to me and rolled up the sleeves of his green flannel shirt. Everyone began small talking. I wanted to go home.

"Okay everyone," said Abby Shakti while entering the room. "We're going to get started now."

She sat in one of the white chairs. A Latino man with deep set eyes sat in the other one.

"My name is Abby," she said.

"And I'm Sergio," he said.

"And welcome to TurnON New York," they said together.

"We're from OneTaste," Abby continued. "OneTaste is an organization that teaches about female orgasm through a practice called Orgasmic Meditation."

I already knew about OneTaste. They were a wellness company based in San Francisco. I discovered them five years ago through their founder's TEDx Talk titled, "Orgasm: The Cure to the Hunger in the Western Woman."

Lisa and I were supposed to learn this OM thing together. Sex was the only thing that kept her attention more than drugs. And I liked that it had something to do with spirituality. My favorite self-help author Tim Ferriss featured it in his latest book, *The Four Hour Body*, calling it 'The Fifteen Minute Orgasm.' I tried following the technique with the book open, but Lisa didn't come for one minute let alone fifteen. We were saving up to fly out to San Francisco to take a class on it. I had to find out what I was doing wrong.

"So tonight," Sergio said, "we're going to play three communication games to give you the feeling of Orgasm in your bodies."

"The first game is called Inside Outs," Abby said. "I will say a prompt, and you will fill in the blank with whatever pops into your head. The first one is easy: My name is..."

Starting from Abby's left we went around saying our names.

"This feels like AA," the bearded hipster said under his breath.

"Okay, now the first real prompt," Abby said. "This is why I'm here tonight..."

The event wasn't what I expected.

Most of the evening was spent on the second game called 'Hot Seats'. One person was the focus of attention, and anyone could ask them any question about anything. Someone asked the leg warmers girl if she would scream at the top of her lungs and she did so without hesitation. People asked the Indian man why he was trying to hide his loneliness with bravado. The bearded hipster was asked about his lack of purpose and need for father's approval. He broke down and cried. I had never seen a man with a beard cry before. I was embarrassed for him.

I didn't understand how the question-askers could know how to ask the exact question that would get an emotional response. And I didn't understand what any of this had to do with women's orgasms.

In the third and final game, we were supposed to pick someone and say something we wouldn't normally share out loud. Many people commended the bearded hipster for his vulnerability. I shared with Abby that I didn't believe her smile could possibly be real. Sergio shared with me that he was disappointed that I declined to participate in the HotSeat game.

Abby closed with a sales pitch for the next Orgasmic Meditation class that was happening in December. I still had no idea what this event and clitoris-stroking had to do with each other.

This was weird. I felt weird. But I did learn something. I had always thought of truth as binary— Either something was true or it wasn't. But I could see now how there were degrees of truth. I had never seen people, let alone strangers, be so emotionally open.

For all the *I love you*'s we exchanged, Lisa and I never were that truthful. We didn't lie to each other outright, but we were never vulnerable with each other. She never knew how I really felt, and I had never had a clue what was going on inside her. Today I witnessed a greater magnitude of truth with this group of strangers than in all the nights she and I spent in each other's arms.

Abby Shakti caught up with me at the cubby.

"Hey, I appreciated your communication to me," she said. "I didn't realize I was smiling so hard. I guess that's how I deal with tumescence."

"What's *tumescence*?"

"It's any kind of overwhelming sensation. Some people deal with it by becoming dramatic. Others deal with it by shutting down. Some people try to control it by…"

"Clenching their muscles?"

"Yeah, that could be one way."

The Indian man walked up and spoke to Abby as if I wasn't there.

"Hello Abigail Shakti," he said. "I find you to be a beautiful goddess."

"Oh, well thank you, Kumar."

"I would like to give you manual pleasure. I would like to give you *the Orgasmic Meditation*."

"Um, Kumar, that's not how you ask. And you really should receive training before you..."

"I saw Nicole's TED Talk and I have read *The Four Hour Body*. I know how it's done. You only undress from the waist, I keep my clothes on. You butterfly your legs, and I..."

"Kumar, you need to take the class first," Abby said through a smile full of tumescence.

I sidled away. Near the exit, Sergio had just finished enrolling the bearded guy to the OM class. I had been afraid to speak up the entire event. Now was my chance.

"Hey, um, Sergio, can I ask you a question?"

"Yes?" His voice was deep yet gentle.

"I had a question about OM... I heard you say something about how it makes men more sensitive..."

"Yes."

"Um, well, would it help a guy, you know hypothetically, if he has, like, erectile... um, you know, a problem getting it up?"

Sergio had soft grey eyes that hid under thick brows. For some reason it wasn't hard to make eye contact with him. If anything, it was hard not to.

"Yes, it can, Ruwan."

"How does that work exactly?"

"You see, the pleasure she feels, that's her Orgasm... But OM teaches a man to stroke for *his* pleasure. That's your Orgasm... But then there's also a third Orgasm that is created between the two of you."

I had no idea what he was talking about.

"So do you want to take the How to OM class?" he said.

"Um, I'm not sure yet. A hundred-fifty dollars seems like a lot."

"Hey, what are we talking about here?" Abby said.

It seemed like she was following me.

"I was just telling this gentleman about *the Third*," Sergio said.

"There's no third Orgasm, Sergio," she said.

"Yes there is. Yours, mine, and ours."

"No. There's only one Orgasm and it's between us."

"No. Nicole said..."

"Nicole said that *the Third* is just an alchemical concept..."

I slinked away as the orgasm people argued. If they were confused, then there really was no hope for me. This was a dead end just like everything else.

LISA DUMPED ME, AS expected.

She said she realized that "we were different people." I knew what that really meant. But by then I had adjusted my expectations so I didn't feel any pain. I didn't really feel anything at all. She cried and cried. She wanted to do it one more time. Of course. I had to double up on dick pills to get it up. It made my face flush and my lips swell. Bad side effect, I guess.

In five months of dating, I had sex with Lisa almost never without pharmaceutical aid. I could only go natural if we did it first thing in the morning before my anxiety kicked in.

I had started taking Viagra shortly before meeting Lisa. Following my dating coach's early guidance, I brought a few women home a few weekends in a row, but each time I couldn't getting it up. My dating coach said this was because I had lost my virginity kind of late— therefore my self-concept still hadn't caught up to my reality. He suggested I take Viagra till I had enough experience. But before then I fell in love with Lisa.

We met at a Skrillex concert. Her friend asked my roommate Roger to buy her a drink. Lisa tried talking to me, but I mostly ignored her because she was clearly out of my league. She and all her glamorous friends were from upper crust families. She mistook my silence for confidence. I always felt out of place in her world. Apparently, my anatomy did too.

Luckily, my roommates were already taking the blue pill. Roger had gotten a doctor to write him a prescription. Brad had found a way to order them in bulk from India. Most of the guys we partied with took *sildenafil citrate* for those nights when we drank too hard.

"They lead to comical erections," Brad often said.

I told Lisa that I took them to counteract all the cocaine we were doing. But the truth was, I really did coke so I'd have an excuse to take Viagra.

She had her own blue pills. A month into our relationship she confessed that she was addicted to Percocet, *blues,* as the kids called them. But we got her off that. Since then, we stuck to softer stuff, like cocaine.

Viagra does as advertised. It turns your member into a tool. It rises regardless of your emotional state. No more humiliation. No more performance anxiety. But it also takes away the range of sensations. You can only feel pleasure when you go hard and fast. For our breakup sex, Lisa wanted it tender and slow. So I didn't feel any pleasure. I didn't feel anything at all.

"So, I guess I'll see you around then," I said as she dressed up in my room for the last time.

"No, Ruwan."

"You don't want to be friends?"

"No, Ruwan. I'm going to rehab."

"Oh. But you stopped taking blues months ago. And we had the coke under control…"

Lisa sighed. "How are you so smart but such an idiot at the same time?"

I sent a letter to the address she left me but never got a response. As months passed, I returned to my old way of life. I visited my folks in Queens and had our typical cold interactions. I worked at my part-time writing job. I went to the gym with Roger. I attended Meetup events. But I almost didn't care if they happened or not. I hated to admit it, but Lisa had become my source of direction. With her there was always a crisis to fix, a problem to solve. It always felt important. *I* always felt important. Without her, I wasn't sure why I did anything at all.

Hurricane Sandy was the most exciting thing to happen that fall. The Category Three storm wiped out all the power south of Fortieth Street. The roommates and I stayed up the first night smoking pot and philosophizing by candlelight.

Roger and I went outside to watch the storm. The rain was flying horizontally down 7th Street. It matched the rage in my soul. I wanted to tell Roger how I had been feeling but wasn't sure how to put it into words.

"You know what we should do?" he said. "Let's sell all our things and live in an RV. All we really need to live is a laptop and some clothes. We can shower at the gym, and park in a different neighborhood every day…"

"Yes! We'll be completely off grid!"

"That was the problem with *Occupy*," he said. "You can't change a system while inside it. You need to unplug first…. Buckminster Fuller said that. *You can't change things by fighting the existing reality. But you can make a new one that makes the old one obsolete.*"

I thought that was a brilliant idea. Once the storm passed, I began downsizing my belongings. I brought up the van idea to Roger a few weeks later.

"Oh dude, that was just a high thought," he said.

"Oh."

"You actually thought I wanted to live with you in a van on the street? It's fucking cold out. Winter is coming."

"Right."

It was almost December. The Mayan calendar said the world was supposed to end in a few weeks. I didn't really mind if it did.

So one afternoon, when I got a random call from Abby Shakti, the bright smiling girl from OneTaste, I picked up. When she asked me to buy the How-to OM class, I said "yes." When she told me they had a sale where it was fifty bucks off, I said "cool". And it was being held in Alphabet City, just a few blocks away from my apartment.

I still didn't get what OneTaste or their clitoris-stroking thing was about, but it was something to do, I guessed.

Why do we fuck?

In each of our cells are these pseudo-intelligent strands of protein called "genes." These microscopic slave drivers are responsible for all our behaviors and urges. That we smell and taste, love and fear is all to serve their agenda of endless replication. We exist not for ourselves, but as a vehicle of our genes' immortality.

And what do we get for all this hard work?

Five to eight seconds of pleasurable contraction.

"When people think of Orgasm, they think of Climax," the teacher said.

Her name was Nicole Daedone. She was much taller and blonder in person. Nicole was the founder of OneTaste. I had watched her TEDx Talk over thirty times. Now, she was sitting right in front of me on a barstool-height chair, so close that she could stab me with her stiletto heel.

"Orgasm," she continued, "is a great fire. And climax is an ember that shoots off that fire." She tilted her head and smiled. "Hey that's pretty good... Rachel! Write that one down!"

In the back of the classroom, a much smaller auburn-haired woman nodded and typed into her phone. There were four other staff members there, all wearing grey t-shirts with words, 'Powered by Orgasm' in black.

The How-to OM class was held in a community center in Alphabet City. The room was long and narrow with a single pane window at the far end. There was a thick grey blanket taped over it, I assumed to stop the draft. I was shivering. It was the first of December. I should have worn a sweater or something.

There were thirty students in all, seated in two rows. We were a complete cross section of middle-class New York; intellectuals in pea coats, burners in sustainably made parkas. The Asian guy wearing the black Stetson sat just behind me. A hyper-flexible contortionist woman chose to sit cross-legged on the floor instead of one of the provided chairs. When she leaned forward her breasts tumbled over her shins. Before the day was over, half of the people in this room would have their pants off. But right now, our eyes were glued on the teacher.

"Most of the world uses the *male* definition for orgasm," she continued. She drew a line in the air sloping up, followed by a quick drop off. "That works for the male mind, because it works for the male body. We want to introduce the female definition of Orgasm." She drew a wavy up and down curve. "It's more unpredictable. Like women."

A couple of people chuckled.

Nicole had an unusual cadence when she spoke, pausing and re-routing sentences as if reading off a fast-action teleprompter. She sat with her spine perfectly straight and still, but her eyes and hands animated. Every so often she'd uncross and recross her legs, revealing an isosceles of white panties under her silver-sequined skirt.

"Okay, let's do check-ins!" Nicole said. She pointed to the first person in the back row of students. "What brought you here today?"

The first student to answer was a preppy-looking guy in a blazer and scarf. "I'm not really sure why I'm here," he said. "I guess I just want to learn the OM thing."

"Thank you," Nicole said.

The next student down the line was a fair-skinned woman with crystal jewelry and henna tattoos on her hands. She said something about 'source energy' guiding her to this class to connect with the 'divine feminine.' The preppy guy next to her groaned and crossed his arms.

"Thank you," Nicole said.

A bearded hipster guy checked in. "I just want to get over my..."

"Hold on," Nicole interrupted. "No *just*. The word 'just' negates the importance of whatever comes after it. Don't you ever negate your desire. Speak in the affirmative. Try again."

"Uh, okay. I... want...um, to be able to satisfy my wife in bed."

"Thank you," Nicole said.

The hipster man's hipster wife checked in. She wore his green oversized flannel. "I want to feel something," she said. "I don't feel anything down there, you know..."

"In your *pussy*?" Nicole said.

"Ohh I don't like that word," said the hipster woman.

"There's a reason we use charged words like *'pussy'* and *'cock'*," Nicole said. "Most of the world is trying to reduce charge. We don't. The truth carries the most sensation."

"Um okay, I want to feel something in my... pussy."

"Thank you," Nicole said.

That's what she said to end every interaction. To some students that's all she said. To others she entered a dialogue that resembled impromptu therapy. I didn't understand the point of all of this. At this rate, 'check ins' were going to take all damn day.

"I want to be a master stroker," said the Asian guy with the cowboy hat.

"You can have that," Nicole said. "Thank you."

Why was *I* here?

Guys like Roger and Brad never did personal development. The last couple years I had been doing everything the self-help books said. I left my job to "follow my bliss" and now I was broke. I'd spent every penny I had on workshops, seminars, and coaching and what did I have to show for it? More anxiety. More dysphoria.

Maybe all this self-help shit was a scam. Maybe status and well-being are predetermined at birth. Maybe that's why I had erectile dysfunction. Nature was telling me to stay in my league. The whole world seemed to be.

Even my roommate Brad went out of his way to fuck with me. Last night I had a date over and right when I was walking her to the door, he barged out of the bathroom naked and flexing. He said he didn't hear us, but I know he did it as a power play. I wanted to scream at him, but I let it go as always. Maybe he can't help it. Maybe he's just fulfilling his role in the mammalian dominance hierarchy...

"Hi, are you here with us?"

I looked up to see Nicole smiling at me. She rocked her stiletto heel on the rung of her chair. It was my turn to answer.

"Oh, well, um, uh, I'm here because anything to do with sex is interesting..." my voice trailed off. My calves clenched. There was a lump in my throat.

Nicole's attention turned to the next student leaving a cold draft in its wake. The tip of her tongue reached the back of her teeth as if to say 'thank...'

"I want to connect with people better!" I spat out.

Nicole flashed a smile that lit up the room. Her body turned to face me again. Her light brown eyes squinted while getting bigger in the way that only the photogenic know how to do.

"*I* know why you don't connect with people. You only stay in this tonal range," she said, holding her palms six inches apart. "It's a nice range, but you're denying everyone the full spectrum." She spread her palms to full wingspan and her smile got bigger and brighter. The lump in my throat dropped to my stomach.

"Uhm..."

"You see, you're trying to play 'super cute frat boy' who says everything is 'cool' all the time. But everything isn't cool with you all the time. You're not a cool frat boy... You're a *dark, dangerous man.*"

"Uh..." My thighs began to tremble. I clenched them still.

"Is this okay, are you *dying*?" She squinted and lowered her head towards me.

I didn't understand the question, but I shook my head no. She nodded and continued.

"You're trying to be nice and be liked when what you really want to say is 'Move bitch or I'll cut your throat!'" she said miming a shank.

The class laughed.

I was blinking more than usual. The room seemed brighter. They must have turned up the overhead lights. My calves unclenched and my toes wiggled in argyle-patterned wool. I exhaled.

I made sure to inflect my voice and said "I think I get what you're saying..."

"There he is! That was a quick turnaround!" Nicole grinned and turned to the rest of the class. "Do you feel the difference in him?"

Affirmative female sounds came from the audience. I didn't understand. All I did was inflect my tone of voice. Nicole let the rest of the class check in, ending with the busty contortionist sitting on the floor.

But I did feel different. I felt solid and relaxed. I couldn't remember what I was just thinking about. Maybe it was just placebo. Maybe it didn't matter.

I wiggled my toes in my socks. They sloshed around in sweat.

THE HIGHLIGHT OF THE class was the live demonstration.

"Tightness in my chest!" a voice yelled from the back of the room.

"Heat in my head!"

"My pussy is wet!"

I stood on one leg on a creaky plastic folding chair too afraid to put my other foot down for the noise it might make. Too afraid to even breathe lest I disrupt whatever it was that was making the air so thick. I leaned over, trembling, to get a good look. I needed to see the stroking technique of *the* Nicole Daedone.

"Rumbling in my stomach!"

"Sweat on my forehead!"

It was one p.m. We were at the midway point of the class. Nicole was stroking the upper left-hand quadrant of the clitoris of the auburn-haired woman who lay spread-eagle on a white sheet on a massage table. Her name was Rachel and her bare vagina, I mean, *pussy*, was pointed directly at the center of the class.

"Rapid heartbeat!"

"Tingly balls!"

People kept shouting out things they were feeling. Before the demonstration started, Nicole said this is called 'Sharing Frames.'

"A Frame is a sensory snapshot of something you're feeling," she had said. "Naming the feeling and body part will keep you in your body when the sensation gets high and you want to check out. It also gives feedback to Rachel on the table. It lets her know you feel her orgasm."

As if watching a woman coming could make you feel things, whatever. Yet, it seemed like everyone in the room was shouting something. I felt as if I was in one of those improv mystery theater shows where they planted actors in the audience, only everyone was an actor except me.

"Chills down my neck!"

"Swelling in my cock!"

I didn't feel anything, did I? I mean, my knee was trembling, but that was just because I was balancing on one leg. My stomach was feeling butterflies, but I could attribute that to only having butter coffee for breakfast. Sweaty palms? They probably cranked up the heat. Yes, it was hot wasn't it? I felt light-headed too. That must have been from the altitude. I *was* standing on a chair.

"I'm bringing her up now," Nicole said. Her fingertip stroked quickly. Rachel's moans got faster and higher pitched. Her big toes began to wiggle.

"Tingles in my spine!" said the henna-tattooed woman.

"Electricity in my thighs!" said the busty contortionist lady.

"Electric shudders in my spine too!" the cowboy stammered.

It didn't seem like Nicole was doing anything special. She went through the same steps that were listed in Tim Ferriss's book.

"Now I'm bringing her down," Nicole said. She made slower strokes with the pad of her finger. "Ooooh yeah, uh-huh. Can you feel that?"

Head nods all around. I felt dizzy. Nicole wiped the lube off Rachel's nether region and helped her sit up.

"Now look at how Rachel's face has changed," Nicole said. "That's the Orgasm mask. It's like the pregnancy mask, but prettier. Makeup was designed to replicate a woman in orgasm: flushed cheeks, red lips, darkened eyelids."

More affirmative sounds came from the audience.

Everyone shared more Frames. Rachel put her pants back on. Sergio told the class that we had a ninety-minute break for lunch.

I finally put my right foot down on the chair. I was completely off balance.

THERE ISN'T A COOL way to hold three pillows and a yoga mat.

I tried to, but the girth of it all made it impossible without the appearance of struggling.

It was six p.m. We were at the final portion of the How-to OM class, 'The Lab.' This was where we partnered up with someone in the class and did the practice under supervision. I didn't have a partner yet, but I had my 'Nest' supplies.

Orgasmic Meditation occurred in a *Nest*. An OM Nest consisted of one yoga mat, one blanket, three pillows— one for the woman's head and two for each thigh, and a firm meditation cushion or yoga block to sit on. The men in today's class were instructed to bring a complete nest. Some brought their nests in rolling suitcases. I opted out of some of the objects because I didn't know how to carry it all.

Luckily, I only lived three blocks away. I grabbed them from home during the lunch break. I was surprised that OneTaste New York would choose such an out-of-the-way location as Alphabet City. Avenue C of all places! Roger and Brad called it 'Avenue Crumb.'

I wondered what this building's purpose was when not being used for female orgasm classes. The vestibule had fliers for community programs, meditation sessions, and concerts. The walls had been hand-painted with Hebrew writing and pictures of multicultural children holding hands.

"This place is a private community center," said a ginger-haired man over my shoulder. He was a fellow student, with his nest supplies in an IKEA bag. He had a hypertrophic smile and intense eyes.

"Oh," I said.

"Yeah man..." he said through a grin. "And the owner of this place got it *for free*. Back in the eighties Alphabet City was a ghost town, all boarded up homes and crack houses. Squatters would come and live in them, and if they stayed long enough they claimed it as their property. Because in New York State, if you physically occupy land for ninety days..."

"Adverse possession?"

"Yeah man! Only suckers pay rent."

He introduced himself. Then he told me he was an anarchist.

"Anarchy is the purest form of capitalism," he said. "The less Uncle Sam meddles with the market, the more it can reflect the needs of the people."

"What about the Tragedy of the Commons?" I said.

"You're assuming the market is made up of selfish *con*sumers," the ginger-haired anarchist said. "But I don't consume anymore. I *prosume*."

"You presume..."

"I PROsume."

"Pro-sume?"

"Yes," he said. "A prosumer takes an active role in the marketplace to keep creating value as he prosumes. I'm prosuming this OM class right now."

I was not sure I understood what Prosumerism was. I was sure it was something I would someday make fun of.

"So what had you prosume this class?" he asked.

"Well, honestly... I don't know what I'm doing with my life. And I thought... I thought maybe I could make a career out of sex education or personal development or something like that."

"How old are you?"

"Twenty-four."

"You don't need to know what you're doing yet," he said. "Life is like a diamond." He put his two index fingers together. "You start by branching out and trying everything." He moved his fingers diagonally up and away from each other. "Then you figure out what you like, and what you don't like, and you focus back in," He moved his fingers up and together, completing the shape.

"That makes sense. How old are you?"

"Twenty-six."

He told me he was a stockbroker. He worked at the New York Stock Exchange.

"Really?"

"Yeah man. As far as I know, I was the only broker at *Occupy*. Now I sleep in Central Park in a tent. I shower and change at the gym, then I take the train down to the exchange. Like I said, only suckers pay rent."

"That sounds... awesome."

I wanted to tell him about my plan to live in an RV. I wanted to ask him what he thought about society being a Prisoner's Dilemma. But his attention was already turning away.

A young woman with librarian glasses sidled up to us.

"Hey, meet my friend Elma," he said.

Elma nudged him and pointed to another woman across the room. He sighed.

"Ah okay. Hey, I gotta go talk to my girlfriend," the ginger anarchist stockbroker said. "Well, ex-girlfriend... but we signed up for the class as a couple."

The How-to OM class was open to both couples and singles. Most of the room seemed to be single. They gender-balanced the class so that people could find partners more easily.

The anarchist left me with Elma. She said she used to work with the anarchist guy on Wall Street but quit a few months ago.

"It paid well, but I always felt empty," she said. "All day I'd just look at the clock waiting for the market to close. I didn't want to live like that anymore. I decided I don't want to spend the rest of my life waiting for time to pass."

"I lost my job too recently," I said. I was a sales manager at a marketing firm. Each month I'd try to hit my sales quota in the first week, then spend the rest of the month attempting to write a novel. Once my boss noticed the pattern, I was canned.

"Cool," she said. "Would you like to OM?"

"Okay."

Sergio opened the door to the classroom and cleared his throat. "Please enter the space quietly and mindfully. We're starting the lab in five minutes," he said.

The other staff instructed us to set up our nests in two long rows with an aisle in the middle for staff to walk through. Rachel transitioned from demo object to lab instructor.

She directed the male staff members with the tone one would use with a misbehaved dog. The men followed her orders with tails between their legs.

We all set up our nests and stood next to them. She guided us through the ten steps of OM that we had learned in the afternoon portion of the class:

Step 1: Ask your partner to OM.

Moot step given that we've already arranged partners, but it was part of the formality of the OM Container. The Container was the ritual-aspect of the OM that must occur in the same way every time. This is allowed OMers from all over the world to OM with each other with the same exact expectations. OMs always occurred in a nest, it was always fifteen minutes, and the steps were always done in order.

Uniformity is necessary to create a common culture and therefore perception of reality.

How you asked for an OM was also regimented to make it easy to ask, and easy to say no. This way no one ever had to fear rejection, nor feel pressure to consent when they didn't want to.

"Ask the way you would offer someone a cup of tea," Rachel reminded us.

Elma and I exchanged the words, "Would you like to have an OM?" followed by awkward head nods.

Step 2: Get in the nest.

"Strokees! Get in the nest!" Rachel said.

The *strokee* was the woman getting stroked. That was Elma. The *stroker* is the person doing the stroking. That was me.

We both took off our shoes. My sweat-soaked argyle socks released a terribly pungent odor. Elma thought it was her.

"I'm sorry, my feet never smell this bad," she said.

"Really, it's no big deal," I said.

Step 3: Safeport.

Nicole had told us that in the brain there is a mechanism called the *vigilance center*, corresponding with the amygdala, whose function is to assess potential danger. She said it's four times bigger in women than in men because mothers have evolved to watch out for their offspring.

To *safeport* her was to tell her what I was going to do before I did it. Safeporting allowed her to not be surprised, so her vigilance center could relax. I'd later learn that 'safeporting' was originally a nautical term that L. Ron Hubbard, the founder of Scientology, repurposed as communication jargon.

I safeported Elma that I was about to touch her thighs for Step 4. She safeported me that she was on her period but had a diva cup in so not to worry. I was not worried. I didn't know what a diva cup was.

Step 4: Apply Grounding pressure.

The stroker was supposed to massage the strokee's thighs before genital contact. It was called *grounding* as in grounding an electrical current to prevent surges.

"You are grounding her, but you're also grounding yourself" Rachel said.

Step 5: Do the 'Noticing' step.

I was supposed to make three observations of her ladybits. It was a way to train our attention on her genitals.

"Make value-neutral statements. Just say what's there, no judgments. Only color, texture, and shape," Rachel instructed.

I told Elma that her hood was covering her clit, and that her labia were crumpled into each other. I wondered if 'crumpled' was still value-neutral. Oh, and that they were a light brownish pink.

"Your pubic hair is frizzy and black" I heard from across the aisle. I sneaked a peek. It was the cowboy. He was OMing with the contortionist.

Step 6: Put on latex gloves, and apply lube to finger.

The gloves were for sanitary purposes. I fingered a dollop of *OneStroke*, OneTaste's in-house lubricant that I had to purchase during lunchtime for fifteen dollars.

Step 7: Do the lube stroke, and start stroking.

I placed my finger between Elma's crumpled labia and reached up trying to find her clit. It was harder than I thought. We were supposed to not only find her clit, but find the 'one-o'clock' position on it. That's where the most nerve endings are, they said. Eight thousand nerve endings. Or eighty thousand. Or eight hundred thousand. I'm pretty sure Rachel said all of those numbers.

I glanced again at the contortionist and the cowboy. He seemed to really be having a hard time. He was dripping sweat all over her thighs and was hyperventilating. Three staff members came over to coach him through it. One of them was Abby Shakti, who sold me the class.

Step 8: Make adjustments through Offers and Requests.

We were supposed to work together to try to find the resonant stroke: the speed, pressure, and location that allowed the most sensation.

I made *Offers* which were yes or no questions to get a read on her such as 'Would you like more pressure?'. She made *Requests* which were also asked as yes or no questions, but I had to do whatever it was.

"Would you move further left?" she asked.

I moved my finger left.

"Would you move more left?" she asked.

I moved more left.

"No, too much left!" she said.

She didn't phrase it as a yes or no question, but I adjusted anyway.

Step 9: Apply direct Grounding pressure and do the towel stroke.

Rachel announced that the fifteen minutes were up. Thank God. My back ached from the quasi-yoga position we were told to sit in. My wrist hurt. My neck has a crick in it. I was not doing nearly as bad as the cowboy though. He looked like he just missed a heart-attack.

I applied firm pressure with my palms on to her vulva to 'push the blood back into her body.' It seemed unnecessary. The diva cup must already be doing that, whatever that was.

I took the washcloth we were given and wiped the excess lube off Elma's labia in the prescribed fashion.

Step 10: Share Frames and pack up the nest.

"A *Frame* is a sensory snapshot of something you experienced," Rachel reminded us.

Normally you were supposed to share Frames privately between partners. But this time we were going to share our sensory snapshots as a group. The women put their pants back on and we all sat in a big oval taking up the entire space of the room.

One by one, students shared their Frames with the room. Most people had a hard time describing their sensations. Rachel would jump in to correct them.

"We're not writing poetry here!" she said. "A Frame is a sensation in your BAH-dy: There was a moment when you felt... *hot, cold, tingling, buzzing,* in your... *finger, clit, belly, forehead.* The purpose of sharing frames is to build your vocabulary when it comes to sensation. That way it sticks in your brain's language center, and you can start your next OM from there."

That made sense. I never really remembered what I was feeling. It's a lot easier to remember what you're thinking because thoughts are usually in words.

On my turn I said, "It felt like hot tea was being poured up my arm."

That was quite a big exaggeration, but not a total lie. My shoulder probably felt warm for a second. Maybe.

I expected Rachel to correct me. She didn't. She either liked me or just wanted to get this class over with.

After everyone was done with sharing Frames, Rachel did a sales pitch for their Coaching Program, a yearlong program where they trained you to become an Orgasm Coach, which was some sort of life coach, but who taught OM too. The next one was their sixth one, 'Coaching Program 6'. She didn't say the price which meant it must be expensive. Spending the hundred bucks on this class was already a stretch for me.

Elma and I packed up the nest together.

"Maybe we can OM again sometime," she said.

"Yeah, maybe."

I left the room before we could exchange contact info.

The sun set as I walked home carrying the three pillows and the yoga mat. I couldn't help feeling disappointed. I wasn't sure what to expect, but I was hoping the class would point me in some direction.

When I got to the apartment Brad was sprawled on the couch watching college football. I remembered him embarrassing me in front of my date last night. My heart began to pound. My skin tightened. Sensation flooded my body.

You're a dark, dangerous man.

"Roopadoop!" he said. "How was the diddling class?"

I turned to him with cold eyes and said with extra inflection my voice, "If you ever pull that naked shit again, I'll break your fucking nose."

That was a bit excessive, I thought. But it felt good.

THEY SAID TO TRY OMing ten times before you decide if you like it or not.

OMing was like yoga or lifting weights, they said. You would only get the benefits from repetition. They claimed the increased sensitivity had downstream effects in feeling better in your body, greater intuition, more authentic expression, better sex, and better connection with others, just to name a few. But you wouldn't notice the effects after one time.

I could buy that. And I did spend a hundred bucks on the class. I might as well get my money's worth.

OneTaste made it easy for new OMers to continue practicing. Twice a week there was a secret free event for people who had taken the How-to OM class, called an 'OM Circle.' Like the lab portion of the class, an OM Circle was a group OM guided by a staff member, usually Sergio.

"And begin!" he said as his meditation timer app made a gong sound.

Strokers brought the nest supplies. Strokees brought the pussies. By my third OM Circle, I had found a better way to transport my nest. I duct taped a yoga block to a yoga mat and velcro-ed pillows in the right places. My entire nest could now be rolled up, rolled out, and easily carried without feeling awkward. Sergio recorded a video of me demonstrating my invention after an OM Circle and posted it to The OM Hub.

The OM Hub was a secret Facebook group for OMers. To be invited you had to have been OM trained and vetted by a OneTaste staff member. This allowed everyone to feel safe to freely ask for someone to touch their vulva.

"Hey I'm looking for a stroker for #2 for the New York OM Circle on Wednesday. Would anyone like to OM?" would read a typical OM Hub post.

There were OM Circles in all the cities with a OneTaste presence: New York, San Francisco, Los Angeles, London, Boulder, and Austin. Every OM Circle had two OMs so one had to specify their "number one" versus "number two" partners. Most people switched partners between OMs. The women would stay in the nests, while the strokers would switch positions. The whole thing lasted about an hour.

OneTaste provided latex gloves and clean hand towels for each OM. Strokers were strictly instructed to never 'double dip' into their lube jar with the same gloves. That way everything stayed sanitary.

"OneTaste is a clean, well-lit place for Orgasm," read their marketing materials.

I felt creepy posting to the OM Hub for the first time. I almost deleted my public offer to stroke a random clitoris. But before I could, my inbox was flooded with responses. Within an hour, I was fully booked for every OM Circle for three weeks out.

My dating coach always said, "men are hunters, women are choosers." Women take a bigger risk when having sex, therefore must be more guarded. But that's only true in a conventional "patriarchal" society— one that runs on male assumptions.

In the OM Community, the sexual marketplace was different. OneTaste's "clean, well-lit space" allowed women to feel safe to take their pants off with a stranger. Unlike in the real world where women are incentivized to be guarded, in the OM Community they could really let their desires out.

Years later, OneTaste would be celebrated for being a "female-led" organization, but that labeling glossed over what really made the group interesting. OneTaste was a matriarchy. The culture was built around female assumptions. Feelings were more important than logic. Connection was valued over competition. No one ever spoke about their jobs. There was no small talk. OMers shared their deepest desires and fears the way most people talked about the weather.

"May I share a desire with you?" I overheard an older Latino man say as I rolled up my nest.

"Yes, you may," said a woman.

"I have a desire to massage you from head to toe."

"No thank you. But thank you for expressing your desire."

"Thank you for hearing it."

After one OM Circle, I was rolling up my nest when a pair of yoga pants plopped down beside me.

"Hey, I saw Sergio's video of your nest on the OM Hub," said the owner of the yoga pants who was also inside of them.

She had wild blonde hair, Egyptian-looking jewelry, and a girl-next-door smile.

"Oh haha," I said, which is to say I said nothing.

Her name was Xena. She was a yoga teacher, chakra healer, and somatic experiencing therapist. I only knew what two of those things were. She said she had been OMing since June.

"Oh I thought they said December was their first New York class," I said.

"It was the first class for the public," she said. "But over the summer Nicole did a special class just for the *Sister Goddesses*."

"For the who?"

"Have you heard of Mama Gena's School of Womanly Arts?"

I squinted at her. She laughed.

"It's a school taught by this woman Regena on... Womanly Arts. Regena and Nicole go way back. Over the summer, Nicole came to one of our classes to teach OM. Anyway, a lot of the Sister Goddesses, that's what we call ourselves, a lot of us OM now. Some of the women here are SG's."

She pointed out the most radiant women in the room. Each Sister Goddess seemed to be perpetually laughing, flirting, or charming.

"Would you like to OM sometime?" Xena said.

"Yes, but I'm kind of booked for the next few Circles."

"You can come to my apartment. I prefer private OMs," she said. "Honestly I just came here to find a new stroker. I had one last summer, but then he became more than just an OM partner, and... well you know how it goes."

I didn't at all know how it goes.

"Opening doors in two minutes!" Sergio yelled. "If your pants are off, please put them on. You can continue flirting later."

AFTER EVERY OM CIRCLE was a TurnON.

The OM Circle was for the OMers. TurnON was for newcomers.

"We fill the room with Orgasm during the OM Circle, so that new people at TurnON can feel it when they walk in," Sergio explained.

Another way to put it was that newcomers would hear female vocalizations of pleasure from the hallway. If "sex sells," then OneTaste had broken the marketing game.

Regardless, they had done something right. Their TurnON event had grown from the awkward eight person one I attended back in September to regularly bringing in over fifty people twice per week. Nicole's recent best-seller, *Slow Sex*, a play off the "Slow Food" movement, along with the "15 Minute Orgasm" chapter in Tim Ferriss's *Four Hour Body* had brought in a lot of mainstream attention.

"Everyone's pants on? Opening doors!" Sergio yelled.

"Yeeoo," Roger said as he walked in with the wide-eyed crowd. I finally convinced him to check out a TurnON. He brought a date.

"Oh my god," his date said. "Were those women actually having orgasms just now?"

"Yeah, I told you. They were doing the fingering thing," Roger said.

"It's not fingering," I said. "It's a *meditative practice*."

TurnON New York, now held on Mondays and Wednesdays, was the only moment in my life that I got to be real— really real. It took me a couple weeks to gather the courage to get up on the Hot Seat, but now it was my favorite thing. Vulnerability is a drug. After a lifetime of suppressed emotions, I was quickly addicted to my only fix.

I saved seats for Roger and his date next to me. I was excited for him to have an experience like mine.

"Welcome to TurnON New York," Rachel said with a beaming smile. "We're from an organization called OneTaste who teach about female Orgasm through a practice called Orgasmic Meditation... Everyone in the right place? No one came here for underwater basket-weaving?"

The group laughed.

"Orgasmic Meditation, or OM for short, is a partnered practice, where a woman lies down, butterflies her legs open, and then a man— well it can be a man or a woman, but for simplicity's sake I'll describe it as a man, sits to her right and strokes the upper left quadrant of her clitoris, up-down, up-down, up-down, with no goal other than to experience sensation in their bodies. Right Jane?"

"Right Rachel!" said the co-facilitator.

OneTaste had moved staff members from around the country to New York, which was to be the next big hub. Rachel was the Head of New York. Jane, from the San Francisco office, was her second-in-command. She was a tall woman with a perpetual smirk and often made sarcastic comments. Both Rachel and Jane sat on the edges of their seats with their legs spread wide open.

"So tonight, we're going to have an OM," Rachel said, "...but we're not going to take our pants off. We're going to play three communication games to get turned on. Turn On is any activation of your involuntary nervous system. You know, like butterflies in your stomach..."

"Flushed cheeks..." Jane added.

"Sweaty palms..."

"Tingles..."

"Chills up your spine..."

"Chills down your spine...

"You know, that kind of thing... Jane will explain the first game."

"The first game is called *Inside-Outs*," Jane said. "The goal is to get you out of your head and into the room. I will say a prompt, and you say the first thing that pops into your head. First thought, best thought. Got it? Okay the first one is easy. My name is..."

The audience chairs were set up in a circle, as before, but had to be in three rows to accommodate the crowd. The first few chairs were always filled by OneTaste staff or experienced OMers. You could tell because they were always young women with bright sparkly eyes who sat with a straight back and legs spread apart.

"Bonnie," said the first person. Bonnie was a petite woman with curly chestnut hair who had founded OneTaste Austin. OneTaste moved her here to grow the New York Community.

"Tanisha," said the next woman. Tanisha was a doctor. I knew this because OneTaste staffers always introduced her by saying, "This is Tanisha. She's a doctor."

"Abby," said Abby Shakti, the emerald-eyed young woman who signed me up for the How-to OM class.

Jane gave a few more prompts for everyone to answer. Some were funny. Some were serious. As they progressed, everyone seemed to become more relaxed and open.

"Okay, this next game is called *HotSeats*," Rachel said. "One person will volunteer to get on the HotSeat, then everyone else can ask them any question on any topic at any level of intensity. If you're on the HotSeat, you can choose to lie, to tell the truth, or refuse to answer. But we invite you to tell the truth. The truth carries the most sensation."

Rachel scanned the room.

"Okay, who's first? How about... Lila?"

A young woman with silver-dyed hair got up on the HotSeat. She had a slight southern twang with certain words when she spoke. She didn't work for OneTaste but seemed to know all the OneTaste staff well. She wore a black dress under a black turtleneck over black stockings with knee-high combat boots that didn't reflect any light.

"What's changed in your life since you started OMing?" Tanisha asked her.

"It feels like time has slowed down," Lila said. "It's like being on a light mushroom trip. Like, I get more *day* in every day."

"Huh," said Roger to himself.

"Thank you," said Tanisha.

"How does it feel to have moved to New York for the Coaching Program?" Bonnie asked.

"Exciting. Crazy. It's like y'all say, *Rapid Changing Reality*."

"Why are you dressed like that?" someone else asked.

"Because I felt like it. And I'm a witch."

"Thank you."

"We'll take you off the HotSeat," Rachel said.

Abby Shakti got on the HotSeat next.

"How do you feel about CP5 going on without you?" Bonnie asked.

Abby got emotional. I wondered what the question meant.

"I feel like my friends are graduating and I got left behind," Abby said.

"Thank you."

"Okay, we'll take you off the HotSeat," Rachel said then shot daggers at Bonnie.

Sometimes HotSeats went on for a long time. Sometimes they only lasted one question. It seemed totally random.

Roger went on next. He responded to the first question jovially and made the audience laugh. He was taken off after two questions. I was disappointed that they didn't keep him on longer.

"Our final game is called *Intimacies*," Rachel said. "We humans are judgment-making machines. The problem with judgments is that when we have one, we can no longer interact with that person directly. In this game you get to share your judgment, positive or negative, so that you can let it go and see the real person in front of you. If you're the one receiving the Intimacy, remember their judgments are not about you. Just let it roll off like water on a duck's back. I'll give an example..."

She looked at me. "Ruwan, you look like a player who is looking for a game."

"Um, thank you."

Bonnie had one for Roger. "Roger, every time you open your mouth I think, 'Oh great, here's another typical dude who is trying to deflect intimacy with humor.'"

"Thanks?"

Most people seemed to use Intimacies to flirt with each other. Roger's date had one for the room.

"This was interesting," she said. "But I don't like being forced to say, 'thank you.'"

"Thank you," said Rachel.

Tanisha, the doctor, had another one for me. "Ruwan," she said, "when I look at you I think, 'Little Brother'."

Roger only partially restrained his laughter.

Rachel gave a sales pitch for the next How to OM class and for the yearlong Coaching Program again. My body buzzed when she described how it would teach people to incorporate Orgasm into their lives and eventually train other people to do so, too. Anyone who was interested could book a free two hour 'Exploratory Session'. That must have meant it was super expensive.

Roger wanted to get drinks after the event. I told them I'd catch up with them. I found Rachel standing by the door with her nose in her phone.

"Hi Rachel."

She took a moment before responding, then looked up with a smile.

"Hi RU-wan."

"I was wondering how much that Coaching Program costs."

"Oh you're interested... let's set up an Exploratory Session."

"Well, I probably can't afford it. I was just wondering about the price."

"That's alright. If there's desire, there's a way. Are you free tomorrow at one p.m.?"

"Um, yeah. But how much does it cost?"

She held eye contact with me, rather, she held me in her eyes. I had the flash memory that just a few weeks ago I watched her orgasming in the OM class.

"Fifteen thousand dollars," she said.

"I definitely can't afford that."

"That's okay. Let's just have a conversation."

"Uh, okay. As long as it's clear that I'm not buying anything."

"Great. Give me your number and I'll text you my address."

"That's a TurnON folks!" Sergio yelled. "You don't have to go home, but you can't stay here!"

I CAUGHT UP WITH Roger and his date at a bar on Sixth Avenue.

Roger's date was gender studies major from Barnard, Columbia University's all-women school. She had a lot of questions about OneTaste and OM. Her arms were crossed and she had an accusatory tone when she asked. But she also kept leaning in and wouldn't let Roger change the subject.

I didn't know how to respond to most of her questions. But since she was so critical, I became defensive and exaggerated the benefits. I used many of OneTaste's explanations even though I didn't know if they were true.

"Wait, so what do men get out of it?" she asked.

"OM trains a guy to feel more. He learns to feel what she's feeling, so he can also feel more pleasure in his own body."

"But if you feel more pleasure, won't you also feel more pain?"

"That's a good question."

The server came by and took our orders. I decided not to drink. Most OMers abstained from substances to heighten their sensitivity. Brad joined us a few minutes later. He was coming from the gym. There was some tension after I threatened to punch him, but we squashed it. We chalked it up to me having let a lot of things build up between us. Both Brad and Roger did note that I had been behaving a little differently since going to TurnON events.

"What did you think of Roo's orgasm thing?" Brad said.

"It was interesting..." Roger's date said.

Brad asked her critical questions similar to the ones she had just asked me. She uncrossed her arms and basically regurgitated the answers I had just given her, but with enthusiasm. Apparently, the best way to make someone defend a position is to attack them there.

"So Roo," Brad turned to me. "These OM girls, they're easy right?"

My calves clenched. I explained to him that women who OMed weren't any 'easier' than other women. If anything, they were harder because they had a better bullshit detector. But because they were sexually empowered, they didn't need to play games and could directly ask for what they wanted.

"There's a word for it, bro," Roger chimed, "it's called *polyamory.*"

"Like the bonobo apes," his date added. "Patriarchal chimpanzees fight all the time. But the matriarchal bonobos maintain cohesion through sex... and keep the males in line."

Brad shook his head. "Doesn't work. My dad said they tried that in the sixties. People got jealous."

"But that's just because of perceived scarcity," I said. "Like if the four of us were on an island, women would be a scarce resource. So we would probably fight over them, right?"

Roger's date re-crossed her arms.

"But imagine there were three girls and three guys. Then we'd probably pair off."

"Or the one alpha male would take them all," Brad said.

"Yeah maybe. But then the other two would gang up on him... But now imagine there were now six women but still only three dudes. Or sixty women and three dudes. At a certain point of abundance there would be no reason to ever be jealous or compete. In fact, the three of us would probably be so worn out that we'd be happy when another guy took one off our hands."

Roger nodded and stroked his beard. His date glared at him and he stopped.

"It's like that with money too," I said. "The economy would be a lot more efficient if we pooled resources. But instead we perceive that there's not enough to go around. So we all hoard selfishly, which then creates real scarcity."

"I told you Roo is becoming a communist," Brad muttered.

"No, it's about redesigning society so it's not a Prisoner's Dilemma."

"What's that?" Roger's date asked.

"Oh here we go…" Roger said.

"So the scenario is two of us rob a bank together and get caught," I said. "The cops hold us in different cells and give us each the choice: rat each other out or stay silent. If we both stay silent, we each serve a normal jail sentence. If we both rat, we each get penalized with a slightly longer sentence. But if one of us rats, and the other stays silent, the rat gets off free and the silent one does a double sentence for both, the *Sucker's Payoff*."

Roger yawned extra loud.

"What would you guys do?" Brad asked. "Can we all agree if we're in that situation we stay silent? Ratting is a total dick move."

"There's no right decision, that's why it's a dilemma," I said. "What's good for the group is always at odds with what's good for the individual. That's the problem with society. It's not that people are inherently good nor bad, it's the incentives of the game that make us so."

"Word," Roger jumped in. "You hear the Jets might get Tebow?"

"Yeah, but they won't play him," Brad said. "They tried communes in the sixties. They didn't work. Because in the end it's all about status. My dad always says it always comes down to the Haves and Have Nots."

"I'm just saying, if we had a more cooperative society, we'd all have a better quality of life. We wouldn't need to do all these things we hate just to experience a few things we like. Wouldn't it be great if we all could do whatever we feel like all the time?"

"People do do that, Roo," Brad said. "They're called drug addicts."

I thought of Lisa in rehab. I wondered if she would ever respond to my letter.

Roger finally succeeded in changing the subject. I was mostly silent the rest of the evening. Something had gotten me wound up. I no longer had an interest in football, or politics, or any of these low sensation subjects. I wanted to be vulnerable. I wanted to feel. The bartender called last call and we got ready to leave.

"Be careful with these people, Roo," Roger said. "You know, when you Google 'One-Taste' the third thing that pops up is 'OneTaste cult'?"

"Yeah, well. What's a cult other than a couple of like-minded individuals?"

"IF THERE'S DESIRE, THERE'S a way," Rachel had said.

The Exploratory with Rachel was in a small Upper East Side walkup. She gave me a warm hug that made my body relax. She took my coat and offered me a cup of tea as if it was a cup of tea. I reminded her that I wasn't going to buy anything.

"That's okay, we're just going to talk," she said.

That's what we did for the next two hours. Rather, I talked. Rachel asked incredibly precise questions, like a personal Hot Seat, that got me opening up about everything.

I grew up with debilitating shyness. By middle school this meant being treated like a non-person, especially by the opposite sex. Feelings were never discussed in my household let alone desires. My one and only conversation with my mom about girls was me being shamed for receiving a love letter on Valentine's Day. I was five. My dad's sex talk to me was "don't have sex. And if any of your friends ever have sex, you better tell me so I can tell their parents."

At fifteen, I was so anxious and inhibited that I decided to kill myself. My little brother almost walked in on me, and I became even more ashamed. This led me to spirituality and self-help. Since then, I compulsively read psychology books and watched TED Talks to try to "fix myself."

In college, I became an officer candidate for the Marine Corps because I figured being "hard" was the solution to my dysphoria. I earned my commission as a Second Lieutenant but then read a psychology book said modern military training causes PTSD—I didn't want to end up *more* anxious, so I decided not to serve. After college, I hired a dating coach to attack my social anxiety head on. I was already getting the sense that the false "pickup" persona was counterproductive when Nicole confirmed it to me in the How to OM class.

I was two years out of college now. Since then I had attempted all sorts of things— being a youth motivational speaker, writing an erotica novel to catch the "50 Shades" hype. I even took the FDNY firefighter exam but couldn't finish the test because I ate a bad shawarma that morning and had to rush to the toilet. It felt like the whole world was conspiring against me. I settled for a part-time job managing the blog for a scammy pop-up ad company. I was just making ends meet.

I almost cried sharing this with Rachel. I had never shared this with anybody. While speaking, it dawned on me that I had been slow playing my whole life. All my attempts to improve myself seemed to bring me back to the same place. It was like swimming around inside of a fishbowl. I wanted to leave the bowl. Sometimes you need to make a bold move.

"I just realized I spend a lot of my life waiting for time to pass," I said.

"That's interesting," Rachel said. "So, what do you want?"

I listed some goals that I had recently written down for some productivity book I was reading. But it felt empty. I remembered my interaction with Nicole.

"I want to feel... alive," I said.

"Well, it sounds like the Coaching Program makes the most sense for you," she said.

The Coaching Program was ten months, with a three-day immersion every month with Nicole and the senior faculty. Every week there was also an OM lab with local faculty in each major city. The New York labs would be held at the New York OM Residence in Harlem which would open in January. Each student was also assigned a mentor. Mine would be Sergio. Normally it was fifteen thousand, but Rachel would discount it to eleven for me. And I could make it in payments of just a thousand per month.

I did say I wasn't going to buy anything today. But that was my fear speaking, I thought. Lots of people carry credit card debt. And this was an investment in my future. My heart was beating hard as I handed her my credit card. That was just Turn On, I remembered. It was just sensation.

I would treat this as a life experiment. CP6 was just ten months. I had to take a chance. How fucked up could my life possibly get in a year?

THERE WERE LAYERS TO the OM Community.

TurnON events were the surface. Being a regular at OM Circles was another. Each layer gave you more access. By joining CP6, I had gone a layer deeper.

OneTaste hosted a New Year's Day party for Coaching Program students and serious OMers. It was at the Upper East Side apartment where I had my Exploratory with Rachel. Sergio hugged me when I walked in.

He and I did our first coaching session at a cafe a few days earlier. It was very different than what I was used to. I had been working with my dating coach for almost a year prior. Those coaching sessions always involved psychological theories and step-by-step formulas.

Sergio did none of that. He just asked me about my feelings and quoted Nicole a few times. The only insight he shared was that he believed my erectile dysfunction and anxiety both came from suppressing my emotions.

"Feel your desire," was the only advice he gave.

I thought it was a ridiculous waste of time till last night when Roger and I went out for New Year's. Instead of approaching women with my dating coach's formulas, I stood in the middle of the bar "feeling my desire." Out of nowhere, a young woman came up to me and ended up inviting me home with her before the ball even dropped. Nothing like that had ever happened to me before. I tried not to make too much meaning of it. It would be easy to get caught in confirmation bias. But I couldn't help feeling like something magical had just happened.

Maybe this was what OM had to do with life. Every moment was a "stroke." If you put your full attention on feeling the moment, it would show you how to engage to create more sensation for the next moment. Continue this indefinitely and you enter *nirvana* on earth, an "orgasmic life."

But now I felt anxious again. A group of OMers were laughing and flirting on the other side of the room. I recognized most of them. There was Abby Shakti and the guy who wore the cowboy hat. There was the busty contortionist who casually sat with her knee behind her shoulder. Everyone seemed to be at a level of energy far beyond my range.

"Hi Ruwan, are you shy?" Jane said.

"Uh, um, well..."

"You don't have to be shy here. We're all good people."

I didn't know why I felt so awkward now after being so confident last night. I tried feeling my desire, but nothing was coming. Most of the party had now piled on to the couch. Abby's head poked out the top. She was covered by multiple bodies.

"I'm so happy right now," she said.

Bonnie burst out of the kitchen with an idea.

"Hey let's play Blow Your Cover!" she said.

"Yeah!" said multiple voices.

Blow Your Cover was a communication game similar to Hot Seats. We focused on one person at a time, but instead of asking them questions, the audience told them what they really thought of them. As in all OneTaste games, the other person simply responded with 'Thank you.'

"Blow Your Cover can get intense," Jane said. "The first time I played, Rachel looked me in the eyes and said, 'You look to me like a dominatrix hiding in a fat suit.'"

I noticed Rachel wasn't here.

Blow Your Cover was intense. They went right after each other saying things you would never hear people, let alone strangers, say to each other. But none of it was mean. The most surprising statements were the kind ones, the incredibly specific compliments, the ones that showed the recipient how precisely they were being seen.

There was a certain kind of face each person made by the end of their turn. It was a face that said, 'Wow I can't believe you could tell that about me'. In OneTaste they called this being *nailed*.

"Ruwan," Bonnie said. "You look to me like someone who is sick and tired of being normal."

I immediately felt funny. I couldn't hear what the next person said to me. Nor the next. I didn't quite understand what Bonnie meant, but something in it felt important enough to spend the next ten minutes thinking about it. I had been nailed.

"Hey what's going on?" a sleepy voice said from the back bedroom. Rachel appeared. She was in a spaghetti strap top and pajama bottoms.

"We're just playing Blow Your Cover, Rachel," Bonnie said.

"Blow Your Cover is a very advanced game. You should not be playing it with new OMers."

"I'm sorry Rachel."

"Janey," Rachel said. "It's getting late. We need to move early tomorrow."

It was eight-thirty p.m.. Rachel returned to the bedroom leaving a lull in the party.

"Okay, I think we've Peaked," Jane said.

"Yep, the party definitely Peaked," Bonnie said.

"That's a Peak folks," Sergio yelled. "You don't have to go home but you can't stay here!"

Everybody laughed.

Within two minutes, everyone got on their coats and began to exit. I had never seen a party close so abruptly.

"That's the thing with these Orgasm people," the contortionist lady said under her breath. "Everything is like an OM to them. They listen to the 'stroke' like it's God. Once there's a slight drop in sensation, they change everything."

Before I could walk out the door, something made me turn my head around quickly. Bonnie was standing there as if she was waiting for me to look. Her chestnut curls were tucked into a beanie.

"Hey you have a car right?"

I nodded.

Among my financial strains was a car I purchased last year to get to my job at a marketing firm up in Westchester. I was fired after six months but had forty-five left on the note. I meant to sell it over the summer, but Lisa really liked that I could drive her around, so I squeezed every penny to keep it.

"Would you like to drive me and T to our new house?" Bonnie asked as if offering a cup of tea.

"Sure."

This apartment was just a temporary sublet for new staff arrivals, Bonnie explained. OneTaste had just acquired a permanent residence uptown for its New York staff and dedicated students. Every major OneTaste city had a OneTaste residence that was the core of the community. I heard the one in San Francisco had sixty residents and one big bathroom where they all showered together. The New York residence was a penthouse in a brand-new high rise in Harlem.

I pulled into a parking spot right in front of their building. It was a modern high rise that sharply contrasted the old brownstones and run down apartments around it. The lobby had glass doors with the building's name, 'The Morellino' frosted vertically onto it.

"Do you want to see our place?" Tanisha said.

"Yeah! Come see our place!" Bonnie said.

"Okay."

OneTaste rented two of the eight units on the top floor, *Penthouse A* and *Penthouse C.*

"We're hoping whoever is in *B* moves out so we can connect them all," Tanisha said.

The hydraulic elevator brought us to the top floor. Bonnie entered the door labeled *PHA* without looking up from her phone. Tanisha showed me into the door labeled *PHC.*

Her high heels clacked on the hardwood floor as she walked in. The apartment opened into a long hallway with exposed brick on the left and three doors on the right— two bedrooms and a bathroom. At the end of the hallway was a big open space that included a California kitchen and a single white couch. Tanisha assured me there would be more furniture eventually. On the far end of the open area was a staircase to another big bedroom. The upstairs room opened to a private rooftop courtyard, which opened to a public courtyard. She said that PHA was a mirror image of PHC.

"So, that makes six bedrooms total... How many people live here?" I asked.

"So far just me, Bonnie, Rachel, Jane, and Sergio," she said.

She shut off the lights. The moon was almost full and made her dark skin glow purplish. She began down the stairs. I followed.

I wanted to know what it was like to live in an orgasm commune. I bet they lived in the cooperative utopian abundance I had only theorized about. Meanwhile I lived in a windowless underground room in the East Village in an illegally converted one bedroom. I had to walk through Roger's bedroom to get to mine and shared a thin wall with the building's garbage room. I deserved better.

"So, uh, just out of curiosity, what's the criteria for moving into a place like this?"

"Oh, so you're interested!" she said and spun around two steps below me. Her face was exactly at my crotch level. She looked up and batted her lashes.

This would be a huge lifestyle upgrade. But I was already going a little deep with these people.

"Uhhh, umm, well I... I don't think I can."

Real smooth, little brother.

"Okay," she said. "Come over and OM with me tomorrow."

TANISHA ANSWERED THE DOOR in a towel.

Penthouse C looked much different in the daylight. The exposed brick shimmered with the morning sun. Tanisha's toweled silhouette was a dark hourglass surrounded by white glow.

"I'm going to take a shower first. OM with Bonnie in the meantime," she said.

"Okay."

Sergio was walking out of PHC as I came in. He hugged me.

"Welcome brother," he whispered. "It's good to have another man in the house. I could use the backup."

Bonnie and I OMed on the floor of the upstairs bedroom, overlooking the private courtyard. Unlike previous OMs, I felt like varying the stroke. Bonnie's big toes wiggled throughout the OM.

"You were on my Spot the whole time," Bonnie said. The *Spot* was the location on the clit with the highest sensation in each moment.

"Yeah I don't know what I was doing. My finger just went there..."

"Like a magnet," she said as if an explanation. She looked over my shoulder at someone behind me. "Are you OMing with him too?"

I turned and saw Jane towering over me with her pants already off.

"Yeah," Jane said. She and Bonnie switched places in the nest.

I thought I was supposed to be asked for an OM. Maybe this was what Sergio was referring to.

The OM with Jane was different. Jane was a bigger woman so I needed to sit on extra cushions to get my leg over her. Her big toes also wiggled. Neither of these OMs felt particularly sexual, though my body felt great after, like I was charging up.

"I think I get OMing now," I said to Jane after we shared frames. "I'm starting to feel how there was more sensation when I got to a precise spot and a certain level of pressure."

Jane smirked. "You're dialing into *limbic resonance*," she said.

"Limbic what?"

"It's when the limbic systems in our brains get into sync with each other," Jane said. "When you find that perfect stroke it's like running your finger on a wine glass to make it sing. When you match the frequency of the glass, it causes it to resonate. When you stroke at the exact frequency of my body it causes resonance and we both feel it as higher sensation."

"Oh. Cool."

Tanisha was still in the bathroom when I went back down. My belly felt full. Weird. All I had for breakfast that morning was butter coffee. I number-two'ed in the hallway bathroom. Diarrhea.

The toilet wouldn't flush. Shit. But my body felt great. Maybe OMing was in fact filling me with 'Orgasm.' Maybe it was healing my libido. I wondered if I could have sex without a dick pill right now. I'd better find a plunger.

I opened the door to see Tanisha. She was leaning against the brick wall with one foot up as if she had been waiting.

"Hey, do you want to have sex instead?" she said.

All the heat from my nether regions rushed back into my body. My calves tensed.

"Uh sure," I croaked. "But, uh, I just clogged your toilet so I need to get a plunger first."

I ran outside the Morellino and shot a text to Sergio: "Do you have a plunger?? I need a plunger! I'm clogged!"

Fuck. Shit. Fuck and shit. The lower half of my body was numb. I got this deadness feeling every time sex was on the table. I already knew I wouldn't work down there. Why would I leave my home without dick pills? This was the worst. If only there was a dick pill store. And I needed to unclog the toilet.

I walked up Frederick Douglass Boulevard to the closest hardware store on Google Maps. It was closed or out of business. Across the street however, was an unmarked store with Caribbean flags in the window. A hand-written sign advertised herbal remedies. Inside were five muscular black men speaking patois.

The man behind the counter asked me what I wanted. When I stuttered, he cut me off.

"I got da pills and I got da shots and I got da drinks" he said. "Err'ting all natural herbs. Err'ting here is all natural. Not like 'dem pharmaceuticals."

One of the muscular men slapped a ten on the counter and the shopkeeper gave him a shot in a plastic container. The man popped the lid and swallowed it in one gulp.

"What does it do?" I asked.

"It give you *energy* mon," he said as if I asked the stupidest question. "Energy. *Energy*, ya know. And not like 'dem pharmaceuticals that go hard for only four hours. This one lasts twenty-four hours, this one fifty hours, this one lasts one hundred hours."

"One hundred hours?"

"Yah, mon. But depends on your metabolism. I have a fast metabolism so I take a lot." He flexed and veins inflated on his arms. Everyone in here was wearing a tank top despite it being a cold January morning.

I bought a drink for seven dollars. It tasted like homemade cola with a familiar medicinal flavor. My face flushed and my lips swelled a little. It must've been working.

Sergio texted me back that he had a plunger and he would handle it. I felt better. He was a good coach.

Back at the Morellino I told Tanisha about the weird aphrodisiac store.

"Yeah that's funny," she said with a completely expressionless face. "I'm going to put a thirty-minute timer on, okay?"

"Oh, okay."

I had never had sex with a timer before. Maybe this was how enlightened people did it.

She started a timer and put on a playlist. The first song was an RnB track called "Sure Thing" by Miguel. Tanisha didn't move her lips when we kissed. I wasn't sure what she was trying to do. I wasn't sure what I was doing. Everything felt dead downstairs. The drink wasn't working. Damn you herbal remedy man!

I asked if I could go down on her. That would give me time to think. I tried licking the alphabet as my dating coach taught me. After half a song she asked me to stop.

"I'm *not* going to get off from this," she said.

Oh. I thought climax was just an ember that shot off Orgasm, not the goal. Or maybe the ember was the goal. I was confused. I'd have to ask Sergio later.

She turned me over and went down on me. My lower belly was painful to touch and I spazzed when she grazed it. My parts were totally lifeless and wouldn't wake up.

"What would turn you on?" she asked.

"I don't know, this feels good, but..."

The timer went off. Phew.

She sighed and we got into a cuddle formation. We were cuddling as a formality. There was no warmth between us. She must've thought I was such a loser.

Every moment is a stroke.

Her breathing was tight and controlled, I noticed. A thought I never had before popped into my head.

"Hey, uh, does this happen to you a lot?" I asked.

"What?"

"Guys not getting hard with you."

She paused. "Yes, it does, actually."

"Yeah, I kind of knew it wasn't going to work before we started," I said. "I'm... I'm a little intimidated by you."

She let out a groan and there was new animation in her face. "Why are guys always intimidated by me? I don't want to be intimidating. What should I do differently?"

This was not the direction I expected us to go.

"Um. Well. Maybe seeming more friendly would help," I said. "Like when you said you saw me as a little brother I thought..."

"Yeah, but I still wanted to have sex with you."

Oh.

I didn't understand what was going on. But it did feel a lot better to say what I was feeling. We were cuddling for real now. My lower belly softened. She softened. Something was flowing now.

"It's not just you," I said. "I... have an issue with getting it up." I swallowed hard. "I usually take Viagra every time. I need to."

I had never shared that with anyone before. Lisa knew I took them, but never the real reason why. My lower belly was starting to hurt again.

"You don't need that stuff," Tanisha said.

She touched my chest in a different way. Her hand was warm, affectionate. I took a full breath.

"I know but, I mean, I do though. What should I do?"

"Live in community. Put your attention out. Open your heart."

We cuddled in silence for a few more minutes. We got up in silence and dressed up in silence. I asked her about the butterfly tattoo on her ribs. She said she got it after her divorce. We hugged goodbye. She seemed cold again.

I went home and told Brad and Roger I just hooked up with a hot doctor. Then I told them I was moving out.

Stage 2: Resolution

The Refractory Period. The subject reconciles with what was lost.

"After the moment of animal ecstasy, there follows invariably a sense of melancholy, a feeling of emptiness, which may be taken as the very basis of the devil's laughter."
~ Arthur Schopenhauer

ONETASTE HAD EXPANDED MASSIVELY.

A year ago, few people had heard of OneTaste outside of the Bay Area. But the recent endorsements from Mama Gena and Tim Ferriss, and Nicole's *Slow Sex* book, brought in a ton of interest.

Coaching Program 6 was in the Pennsylvania Hotel in Midtown. About one hundred laughing and flirting people filled the conference room. They represented the world OM Community, which was even more diverse and energetic than the New York OM Community. There were college students and retirees, hippies and tech bros. East Coast, West Coast, Southern, British, French, and Hispanic accents could be heard through the crowd. Only about fifteen of the students were local to New York. The rest would fly in for each monthly immersion.

"You're late!" Bonnie yelled with a smile and slapped a name tag on me. "Get in there!"

Everyone was buzzing at a level far beyond my range. OMers would say they were all "high on Orgasm."

There was one guy who also was standing alone, but not awkwardly. He was medium height with broad shoulders. His forehead was collecting perspiration. The rest of his face had an eager smile like he was about to find something funny.

"Hi I'm Daniel," he said.

Daniel was from Vancouver. He was a psychotherapist, but was on a sabbatical. He had just moved into the New York OM Residence last week.

"Oh so you live at the Morellino?" I asked. "I'm moving there too, next weekend."

"Cool."

I did some quick mental math. All the bedrooms were full now as far as I could tell. I wondered where I was going to sleep.

"Lots of hot girls here, huh?" Daniel said.

I nodded.

One caught my eye. A dark-complexioned woman in a satin red dress. She looked like Miss Scarlet from the board game *Clue*. She was smiling at someone from across the room. When I realized that it was me, I looked away.

Mingling already made me nervous. This particular mingling situation was basically a screening for Orgasm students to decide who they were going to get naked with this weekend. My body went numb.

The truth carries the most sensation, I recalled.

"Social situations like this give me bad anxiety," I said. "I usually latch on to the first person I can get into a conversation with. I just realized I'm doing that with you. So I figured I'd call it out."

"Thanks for sharing that," Daniel said. "Let's go meet some people."

We entered a conversation with a guy and gal standing very close together. They were Texans, here through OneTaste Austin.

"Bonnie is responsible for all of us," said the guy. He had very blue eyes and very pink lips.

"So y'all are New York, huh?" said the gal. She was tall and had powerful-looking traps. I guessed she was a swimmer.

Daniel introduced himself.

"Oh there's another Daniel here, from France," the Austin gal said. "He's France Daniel. So that makes you... Canada Daniel."

"Yeah Canada Dan!" chimed the Austin guy.

Daniel shrugged at his new nickname. He shared how he just left his job and moved to New York to do CP6 full time.

"Are you *Hyper-Volatile*?" said the Austin guy with the lips.

"I don't know what that is," said Canada Daniel.

"He looks *Fixed*," said the Austin gal with the traps.

"What about you?" the Austin guy said to me. "Are you *Fixed*?"

"Um, I'm not sure."

They explained that they were referring to the *Tumescent Types*. "Tumescence" literally meant "engorgement," but in OneTaste it meant "sensation beyond your ability to handle." Your Tumescent Type was how you tended to deal with overwhelming sensation.

"There are three types," the gal said. "*Fixed, Hyper-Volatile*, and *Dissipated.*"

The Austin guy explained that Fixed people try to control situations when they feel overwhelmed. Most Fixed people tend to be analytical males. They are called such because they try to fix the 'problem' of having feelings.

"Us Fixed people usually are disconnected from our sex," he said with his head down.

The gal explained that Hyper-Volatiles deal with overwhelm by creating chaos and drama. They tended to be emotional females. Hyper-Volatiles were the most persecuted in society because they led to disorder.

"The witch trials were basically an attack on Hyper-Volatiles," she said. "HV's worry the patriarchy because they make people feel things. They are hard to control and usually have a lot of raging Orgasm."

"They also have trouble following rules and keeping their word..." the guy said.

The gal glared at him. He cowered.

"But Fixed people and Hyper Volatiles usually get together because they balance each other out," he added.

Lisa must have been Hyper-Volatile, I thought. I wondered if she would think it was cool that I was at an Orgasm Coaching Program.

"What about Dissipated?" Canada Daniel asked.

"Dissipateds dissipate," the gal said. "When sensation is high, they usually check out and drift off into their heads."

She punched me in the shoulder with surprising force. "Like this one."

Nicole took the stage at seven sharp.

The chairs were perfectly aligned in ten rows of ten chairs each. I sat in the back.

She wore a burgundy dress with puffy shoulders and folds that looked like theater curtains. She sat on a barstool-height chair next to a barstool-height table with a tall glass of water and a clear vase holding a single white orchid.

"I don't know all of you yet, but I love you," Nicole said. "I will do everything in my power to stroke you so you will actualize. So sometimes I will stroke you very firmly. Sometimes I'll stroke you very lightly. Whatever is the resonant stroke is what I'll give."

Nicole gave us homework. We were to watch a movie called *The Game* with Michael Douglas. It was about a man whose life was seemingly destroyed but then finds out it was all a game created for him to grow as a person.

"That's basically what we're going to do to you," Nicole said.

Nicole looked to the back of the room. Sergio and Bonnie scrambled to either side of the audience, each holding a microphone.

"Okay," Nicole said. "What do you want me to know?"

For the next hour, Nicole 'stroked the room'. Students raised their hands to get the mic and shared what was going on for them— emotional concerns that ranged from serious traumas to general curiosities. Nicole responded with a mix of empathy, humor, and impressive one-liners.

Somehow it felt like time was flying and yet a lot was going on at the same time. Many students laughed and cried and laughed again.

"And just think, we're not even one day in..." Nicole said.

The class laughed. I forced a smile.

"Okay we're going to do an exercise, and we're going to record it," Nicole said. "Each of you will come on stage and take the mic. You will address all of us as if this is the last day of the Coaching Program, and you will share how you've changed."

The students shared on a wide range of topics. The Austin guy celebrated "All the great Makeouts we had." A woman from France told a long story about how using what she learned in the Coaching Program, she traveled around Europe spreading Orgasm. The Asian Cowboy said in almost the same words how he brought Orgasm to Hong Kong.

Lila, the silver-haired witch, said something about making magic. Canada Daniel said he was just grateful to have made so many good friends. After about forty people, it was my turn.

I understood that this was an exercise in creative visualization. Pretty much every type of self-help book suggested doing something like this. But I had no idea what to say. I wasn't sure what I wanted out of all of this except for my life to be different. I just wanted to be happy for a change.

"It's crazy to think how much life has changed in the last ten months..." I said. "I don't think any of us could have imagined how great life could have become. And... that's the best part isn't it? That none of us could have expected how much our realities could be transformed."

That was a pretty good answer, I thought.

THE NEXT MORNING, WE received a mass text.

The location of the immersion had been moved to somewhere in the West Village.

"This is your first RCR (Rapid Changing Reality)" read another text following.

The new immersion location was on the corner of Bank Street and the West Side Highway. It was a huge white loft with giant industrial windows overlooking the Hudson River. I was late for the morning OM practice so I sat next to the staff's production booth across from the teaching stage. I overheard Bonnie and Jane whispering.

"So what the hell happened with the venue?" Bonnie said.

"Hotel Pennsylvania didn't know there would be *actual* pussy stroking in their conference hall," said Jane. "They told us during opening night that we weren't going to be allowed back the next day. I was like, 'Okay, I'm just going to get off here' and I made some calls and found the new space before midnight. Some photographer owns it. He's cool. I told him what we're about and he was like, 'Cool me and my wife could get into that.'"

Nicole took the stage at nine sharp.

"Have you heard my unfunny joke?" she said. "So a man falls in a hole. And a priest comes by. The man yells 'Help! Help! I've fallen in a hole!' The priest tells him to do ten Hail Marys. The man does it then says, 'Okay, now how do I get out of the hole?' The priest shrugs and says, 'God works in mysterious ways' and walks away. Next a psychiatrist comes by. The man yells, 'Help! Help! I've fallen in a hole!' The psychiatrist says, 'And how does that make you feel?'"

The class laughed.

Nicole smirked and continued, "The man says, 'Not good. Listen, I just want to get out of the hole.' 'Well,' the psychologist says, 'the reason you're in a hole is your parents. Let's meet every week and talk about how they are to blame for everything.' 'Then will I get out of the hole?' 'Maybe after a few years', the psychiatrist says and walks away. But then, an Orgasm Coach walks by. 'Help! Help! I've fallen in a hole!' the man yells. And the Orgasm Coach jumps in the hole. The man says, 'Why did you do that? Now we're both in the hole!' 'Yes,' the Orgasm Coach says, 'but I've been here before, and I know the way out.'"

The class made sounds of recognition.

"I told you, it's not a funny joke," Nicole said. The class laughed. "But this is what we're doing here."

A few months ago, the idea of an 'Orgasm Coach' would have made me laugh. Even the idea of a 'life coach' was strange. (This was many years before everyone and their grandma became a coach of some sort.) But now it seemed like a normal-ish idea: A Orgasm Coach was someone that guided people to connect to their Orgasm. 'Orgasm' in this context meant one's feelings and instincts. In other contexts, it meant a state of high sensation. In other contexts, it was the sensation itself, or one's life force energy—like *qi* in Chinese medicine.

The longer one immersed in the OM Community, the fuzzier the definitions of certain words became. When meanings become fuzzy, they can seem like multiple things and ultimately be in a totally different shape when they come back into focus.

Nicole was a PhD candidate in general semantics, the study of how people create meaning and perception of reality from symbols, including language. Much of the OneTaste lingo, including the abstraction of common words, was built around general semantics principles.

But I didn't know that yet.

Next, Nicole taught about a core part of OneTaste's philosophy called the *8 Stages of Orgasm*. A slide on the projector screen showed a large figure eight with eight dots on it in different locations on the figure. Four of the stages borrowed the names of Masters and Johnson's *Sexual Response Cycle*. But like everything in OneTaste, the sexual imagery was used as an analogy for life.

In this context, 'Orgasm' meant something like the flow of the Universe, like the *Tao* in Taoism. According to Nicole, a person passed through these eight stages in order.

"But you know, it's the Feminine, so anything can happen," Nicole said.

The class laughed.

The first stage was *Climax*. As the imagery suggested, it was where one's life rapidly contracted forcing them to release something.

"Climax brought most of you here," Nicole said.

That was true, for me at least. If Lisa didn't dump me, if I hadn't been struggling to find what to do with my life, if I wasn't so inhibited socially, and dysfunctional sexually, I wouldn't have joined something as strange as an Orgasm Coaching Program. But I was beginning to see all those problems as symptoms of a deeper issue that I couldn't recognize before: That I was dissatisfied with the low sensation, disconnected norms of society. It was the world that was broken, not me. And maybe in OneTaste I had found a way to fix it.

Nicole told us that she wouldn't see us again till Sunday. So if we had any other questions, we should ask them now.

Hands shot up and Nicole stroked the room. She always responded with the perfect aphorism or one-liner. She said a great many things. I wrote it all down for future reference.

THE REST OF THE weekend was taught by the 'Exec Team'.

The *Exec Team* were seven individuals who ran different elements of the OneTaste corporation. They also were also referred to as "OneTaste Senior Faculty" as they were each in charge of teaching a certain subject. They also were the only people in OneTaste who directly interacted with Nicole.

OM skills were supposed to be taught by a man named Ken Blackman. His official title was OneTaste's Head of Education, but most referred to him as "The Master Stroker." But he was sick this weekend so other OneTaste staff guided us through OMs.

Coaching skills were taught by Rob Kandell, OneTaste's CFO and Nicole's co-founder.

As every Marine is a rifleman, and every Spartan man had to know how to wield a shield and sing cadence, every OneTaster was expected to be good at two things: OMing and coaching—in other words, stroking with your finger and stroking with your words. Rob taught us that they followed the same principles: You put your undivided attention on the other person and follow the sensation.

Business skills were taught by OneTaste's CEO, Priscilla. Prior to OneTaste, she had founded a major men's fashion startup. She taught us how to market ourselves as 'Orgasm Coaches' so that we could be well-received. She had a vision of a future "Industry of Orgasm" where corporate cultures would be shaped to be more "feminine" or feeling-driven.

Sales skills were taught by Rachel, OneTaste's Head of Sales, the Head of OneTaste New York, and Nicole's protégé. Just like everything in OneTaste, sales was a form of stroking too. I had worked sales jobs before, mainly to help get over my social anxiety. I had sat through many sales trainings. But this was totally different. There were no techniques. The only "technique" we learned was empathy.

"When people feel good, they buy," Rachel said.

All the information was interesting. Throughout the weekend I took many notes. But I couldn't help feeling that I didn't really get what I had come for.

Nicole returned on Sunday night to close us out.

"This is our last break," Nicole said. "If you've gone the entire weekend without speaking, make sure you sit in the front when we get back."

I spent a thousand dollars that I didn't have to be at this weekend. If I didn't make myself seen, then all of this was a waste. I sat in the first chair in the first row and nervously took the mic from Sergio.

"I've felt like a robot this whole weekend," I said. "I look around and everyone seems to be feeling so much. Like I see when everyone is laughing, I understand what makes it funny, but I don't feel like laughing. I don't feel anything at all."

Nicole smiled down at me. "I don't believe you that you don't feel. I think you've been conditioned for so long to bury your feelings that you don't recognize what you have in there. You need to start putting attention on what you do feel. When you do, you'll slowly peel back the layers of numbness that have been hiding you from yourself."

Nicole looked at Sergio. "Go get another mic."

She turned back to me. "I want you to hold onto that microphone. For the rest of the evening, I want you to say what you feel into the mic every time you recognize a feeling. Like 'happy', 'angry', 'sleepy', 'sad.' Okay?"

I nodded.

She raised her eyebrows and leaned in. "You can start now."

"Uh, okay... content."

"Thank you."

The next person to share was a fitness model wearing a CrossFit tank top.

"So like, I just got married," she said, "and like, I've been worried about people judging me for being conventional, but like, I'm not really conventional because we're totally polyamorous, and I've had some great Makeouts this weekend, but like, that also doesn't mean I'm like, open to all advances, because like..."

"Bored," I said into the mic.

A couple students chuckled and Nicole grinned. The young woman glared at me.

I felt embarrassed but didn't say it.

The next person was a guy named Arjun. I hadn't spoken to him, but multiple women had told me that he and I had similar "energy" and therefore should be friends. He was tall and thin and wore his hair in a ponytail. He always wore the same dirty hoodie, gym shorts, and sandals.

"I wanted to share something vulnerable," he said. "So I usually dress and act poor, so people don't know I'm rich. But I'm a self-made millionaire. My net worth is about three point five million and counting. I wanted to out myself here and stop hiding."

There was an odd silence that felt weird, but I wasn't sure how to name it. One day I'd realize that was the sound of OneTaste putting Arjun in their crosshairs.

Next was a professional poker player from Philadelphia.

"I feel like I didn't get what I wanted from this weekend," he said. "I was expecting something more."

"Oh, what were you expecting?" Nicole said.

"I dunno. Something more spiritual, or deeper or something."

Nicole craned her neck and smiled sideways. "Oh? You sure you weren't expecting more *sex* at an *Orgasm* Coaching Program?"

"Nah, I dunno." He looked sheepish.

She repositioned her hands on her microphone like she was holding male anatomy. "You sure you don't want something more... stimulating?"

"I dunno..."

Nicole moved her open mouth over the mic. "I think we can do something about that." She teased her mouth closer. And closer. She tilted her head and batted her eyes like a starlet on the casting couch. She wet her lips and hovered them right over the head.

"Happy," I boomed into my mic.

Everybody laughed. So did I.

"IF YOU'RE IN THIS House, then you're here to Wake Up!" Rachel said.

It was Sunday morning in Penthouse A. 'PHA' was a bit smaller than PHC but with much nicer furniture. Rachel and Jane sat on a pristine white leather couch while the rest of us sat in a semi-circle of white folding chairs on top of a white faux-fur rug. We were having a House Meeting. House Meetings, I'd learn, were a huge part of living in Orgasm.

I moved in on Friday. My first two days felt like a month. As soon as I put my stuff down in Penthouse C it seemed to disappear amongst everyone else's. Throughout the weekend I found half of my stuff on random shelves and drawers as if the apartment had absorbed them. But the other half and the suitcases they were in had vanished. As I searched the house, I kept finding little post-it notes with OneTaste adages such as, "Orgasm is the Map. Desire is the Compass."

I was one of seven CP6 students to move in to the New York residence. There was Tanya from Iowa, Lila from Austin, Wallace from Canada, Daniel from Canada, Elodie from France, and me from downtown. Apparently, we were just the first wave. Jane was working on acquiring a third penthouse in the building to pack in more students.

"This is not some roommate situation," Rachel continued. "If you're in this house, you're here to *Wake Up*."

Waking Up was OneTaste's verbiage for Enlightenment. OneTaste didn't claim to be spiritual on the surface. It was officially a Health and Wellness business. But the deeper you went the more the reality took on a different flavor.

"Your Wake Up comes from *Compression*," Rachel said.

Compression was a term borrowed from Bikram Yoga—the idea that one grows by consciously entering discomfort.

"We've been a little loose with everyone moving in. Starting tomorrow we're getting everyone in the rails!"

Rachel went over the Morning Practice schedule. It was mandatory Monday through Friday. It started at seven a.m. sharp and would go roughly till eight-thirty, but those with day jobs could leave early if they had to. Out of the seven of us, only Tanya had a real job. The rest had some other way of getting by.

Living in Orgasm wasn't cheap. To afford the luxury to work on "Waking Up" all day, one either had to have a lot of money, or operate outside of money. Therefore, OneTaste seemed to attract two kinds of people: wealthy individuals who wanted to buy an experience, and young bohemians who forsook financial security for the sake of adventure.

I was of the latter category. My income came from a freelance blog-writing gig that allowed me to work from home. Still, I was just barely making ends meet. The thousand dollar per month Coaching Program payments were already putting me in debt. But I was able to slow the bleed a little by letting OneTaste use my car in exchange for a five hundred dollar discount on rent.

Rent at the Morellino was only four-hundred and ninety, plus another three-fifty for shared groceries. So for eight hundred and forty per month we got to live in a Manhattan penthouse with our breakfasts and dinners covered. You couldn't beat that anywhere in New York.

But we weren't supposed to call it "rent." Jane insisted we write "game admission" on our rent checks to her. Living in an Orgasm residence was seen as another course. This one just happened to be twenty-four/seven and included a place to sleep.

They were able to keep rent low by putting us two to a bed. This was another opportunity for Compression. Sharing close quarters with a stranger would force the dormant parts of our personality to emerge.

"We're pairing each of you with your energetic opposite to balance out your limbic systems," Rachel said. "We always match fire with water."

Rachel read out our bed assignments. For the last few nights, everyone had been sleeping wherever they found a space.

"Ruwan, you'll be in the loft bed with Lila..."

"Yayy!" Lila said.

I groaned. Lila, the dyed silver-haired witch, believed in astrology and all sorts of nonsense. I had overheard her talking to someone about the reptilian overlords. I couldn't imagine how this could possibly be good for my limbic system.

"We expect you to be at OM Circle and TurnON every Monday and Wednesday. This is part of your training as space-holders. Every Thursday evening we'll have our weekly House Meeting. House Meetings are also mandatory."

"I can't make it this Thursday," I said. "There's an event I go to once a month." The ginger anarchist had invited me to a philosophy salon he facilitated.

Rachel pursed her lips and squinted as if scanning my mind. Then she smiled. I felt all warm inside. I hadn't thought of her as particularly pretty before. But in this moment, I found her incredibly beautiful.

"You can miss *this* one," Rachel said. She tilted her head forward and smiled up in a way that reminded me of Nicole. "But just know that I'm going to slowly take away your independence."

I didn't know how to respond.

"Okay we have a lot of open cycles to complete," Rachel said then put a warm hand on my knee. "And we need to finish getting *you* moved in."

I wasn't sure if I liked Rachel or not. But she seemed to like me and that seemed to be a good thing.

The meeting broke and we all returned to PHC to move our stuff to our assigned bedrooms. Some of my missing stuff had somehow reappeared. I sifted through my stuff with the Canadians, Daniel and Wallace.

"How did you feel when Rachel said she's going to take away your independence?" Wallace asked me.

"Um fine," I said. "I mean, it was a joke, right?"

I WOKE TO A blast of hot air.

My throat was parched, and my eyes were tearing. PHC's upstairs bedroom had exposed heat ducts, and the vent was right over the head of the bed. All night it had periodically been pummeling us with heat in accordance with the thermostat. Beside me, Lila was sleeping with a silk scarf protecting her face, her silver-dyed hair pointing out the top. Below us, Tanya and Wallace were snoring.

Croak, croak. Wheeze. Croak, croak. Wheeze.

I couldn't tell who was the croaker and who was the wheezer, but they seemed to have found a limbic resonance throughout the night.

The heat blast stopped. A cold draft bled through the floor to ceiling window. The sun was just rising over the Harlem skyline. Lila's butt was up against my thigh. It was warm. I didn't want her to think I was trying to feel her up in her sleep. I tried to inch away.

Her breathing changed. She was awake. If I moved away now, I'd look guilty. Maybe I should pretend to be asleep. How do I breathe when I'm asleep? I hoped she couldn't feel my heart racing. Below us, the snoring was speeding up.

Croak, croak, croak wheeze. Croak, croak, croak, wheeze.

A small square hand grabbed mine from under the sheet. Lila pulled my arm around her. Okay. Her body was surprisingly toned. I fit perfectly between her firm butt cheeks. I thought of ice cubes so I wouldn't offend her with an erection. I considered the irony of a guy with erectile dysfunction worried about having an offensive erection.

"Do you have any desires?" her sleepy voice said.

"No," I said as calmly as possible.

"Hmph."

The snorers slowed down to half speed.

Croaaak. Wheeze. Croaaaak. Wheeze.

"I mean, um. Cuddling feels really good."

Lila spun around and nuzzled her face into my neck. Her bare breasts pressed into me. Her nipples were warm. Her hand reached under my shirt and her fingertips grazed my chest. My skin tightened with goosebumps.

Croak croak, wheeze. Croak croak, wheeze.

Her small fingers danced down my sternum. I was afraid she could feel how hard my heart was pounding. I couldn't inhale. The snoring symphony began to crescendo.

Croak croak croak, wheeze. Croak Croak CROAK...

"Morning practice in five minutes!" Sergio yelled from downstairs.

The croaker and the wheezer snorted to an abrupt finale. Yawns were heard and doors began to open throughout the penthouse. Lila sat up and stretched like a cat. She arched her back and the blanket slipped off her revealing her form.

"That was nice," she said and climbed over me and down the ladder.

Despite being packed four to the bedroom, Lila was able to claim the top of an entire nightstand for what she called her 'altar'— a cloth with geometric designs where she laid out crystals, spiritual baubles, and a deck of circular tarot cards. She waved her hands, cut the deck, and pulled a card that showed a topless woman wading in the ocean with a reflection from the sky.

"Yes! The Moon! I'm so the Moon," she said, then noticed me watching. "Would you like me to draw a card for you?"

"I'm alright."

Sergio had the nests set up. We were in them by six fifty-nine. Sergio held time with a meditation app that made a gong sound.

"And begin," he said.

OMing was just the first part of Morning Practice. Serious OMers adhered to what was known as the *Threefold Practice*, an allusion to Buddhism's *Eightfold Path*. The Threefold Practice was OneTaste's prescription for how to cultivate energy to raise one's consciousness. The three parts were 'Flooding', 'Clearing', and 'Metabolization'.

Flooding meant filling the body with energy. This was primarily done through OM, but conscious sex, or anything physically stimulating without release counted as flooding.

We did two OMs back-to-back. As with any OM circle people switched partners in between.

Sergio's meditation app made its gong sound.

"And time," he said.

After OMing, two people were assigned to cook breakfast while the rest of us were supposed to clean the house. This was part of our *Metabolizing* practice. Metabolizing meant moving the cultivated energy through the body.

"Back in the early days of OneTaste," Jane said, "we were Flooding ourselves with Orgasm all day, then wondering why we all felt crazy. Then someone realized that maybe we should *do* something with all this energy. That's when Nicole decided we all needed to do Bikram."

Bikram Yoga was the primary Metabolizing practice for OneTasters. Nicole admired Bikram Choudury for how he was able to normalize yoga in America at a time that it was considered weird. But anything where you moved your body counted as Metabolizing.

Our cleaning assignments doubled as both metabolizing and keeping the space nice. Other spiritual traditions called this *seva*, or selfless service. The lady in *Eat Pray Love* did this by scrubbing tiles in an ashram.

Cooking and cleaning were supposed to take exactly fifteen minutes.

"Just like an OM," Sergio said.

We all ate breakfast together. Breakfast was always some version of organic scrambled eggs, kale, bacon, and sausage. Sergio made everyone lattes with heavy cream and agave syrup. I declined because it wasn't Paleo. I made my own butter coffee instead.

After fifteen minutes of social eating, Sergio handed out notepads so we could do our *Clearing* practice while finishing breakfast. Clearing meant purifying the thoughts that came with the increased energy.

"Clearing is the most important part because when the energy increases, the ego tries to find problems to attach to them," Sergio said.

"I thought OMing was the most important part," said Wallace.

"It's all the most important part."

The primary Clearing practice was something called *Fear Inventory*. Fear Inventory was a written meditation adapted from the Fourth Step of the Twelve Step Program of addiction recovery. We were supposed to write a letter to a higher power, then read it to someone, then rip it up.

"Dear Universe..." I read,

"...I'm resentful at the assholes who tried to push me off my rollerblades because... I have fear that I give off some low status vibe that makes alpha males want to dominate me. I have fear that that's why Lisa dumped me. I am resentful at women because I have fear I'll always feel inferior to them. I am resentful at myself because..."

"No no no, you can't direct a Fear Inventory at yourself," Sergio interrupted. "Resentment means you're re-sending an old thought in your mind. It's your fears creating separation between you and someone or something else. Fear Inventory is to release your fears and so you can reconnect to that which you've separated from."

"Okay... I am resentful at... my dick because I have fear I'll always have erectile dysfunction. I have fear that nature wants to weed me out of the gene pool. I am resentful at personal development because I have fear it's all a scam. I have fear that I made a huge mistake with signing up for the Coaching Program. I have fear that OMing is a trick Nicole made up to get men to service women as retribution for the patriarchy. I have fear that it was a mistake to move into the Morellino. I have fear that I am just being used for free labor... Um, how does it end again?"

"Dear God..."

"Uh, dear Universe..."

"I ask you to remove these fears and pray for the knowledge of your will and the power to carry them out. Amen."

"Cowabunga."

"Now tear it up," Sergio said.

I did. It did feel pretty good to have aired what was bothering me. And now I guess Sergio knew how I felt about being asked to do all these chores.

"Hey Ruwan, can you help me with something?" Sergio asked.

I tightened up. "Can't someone else help you?" I said.

"No one else is here."

He was right. The entire apartment cleared out. Somehow whenever Sergio needed help, no one was around but me.

He wanted me to help fold some OM towels. OM towels were white hand towels that OMers used to put under the strokee's butt to prevent lube or bodily fluids from getting on the nest. After the OM they were used to clean the strokee's labia. OneTaste had them laundered by a service down the block. It was only a small grocery bag full. I agreed. I figured it would only take a few minutes.

"I'm going to get the rest," he said.

Sergio reappeared with an industrial-sized contractor bag full of towels.

"How are there that many towels??" I said. "Only twelve people live here!"

"We need them for the community OM Circles too."

"But..."

"Ruwan, if we do it together it won't take that long. What else do you have to do right now?"

I didn't have an answer. I hadn't had the time to think about what to do with my time since I had moved in four days ago.

"Thank you, I appreciate it," he said. "I'll just get one more bag..."

Sergio disappeared down the hall on gentle footsteps before I could protest. The apartment door opened and closed. A bedroom door opened and heavier footsteps shuffled towards me. A broad-shouldered figure entered the living room.

"Oh hey Daniel."

"What time is it?" he grunted.

"Ten something."

Canada Daniel went to the fridge and poured himself a glass of coconut water.

"You skipped Morning Practice?" I said.

"Yeah," he said, then downed the glass in one gulp.

"I thought it was mandatory."

Daniel shrugged. "I like to wake up gently," he said and poured himself another glass. "Hey Wallace and I are going downtown to Moksha Yoga. Have you heard of it?"

"No."

Daniel's face lit up. "It's the best yoga studio in New York. It's originally from Canada. It was started by instructors of Bikram Yoga who branched off when Bikram became too culty. The one in New York is owned by the band Arcade Fire and lots of celebrities go there, like the cast of *Sons of Anarchy*."

"Oh cool. I used to watch that show."

"Want to come?"

"Uh, I can't. I need to fold these towels."

"You *need* to?"

"Well, I told Sergio I would."

Daniel glanced at the contractor bag and shrugged. He tossed the now-empty coconut water bottle in the recycling and started back to the hallway. Before disappearing, he turned back to me.

"You know, you're supposed to say 'No'."

"Huh?"

"To Sergio," he said. "You're supposed to say 'No'. There's no such thing as '*I need to*' or '*I have to*' when you're living by desire. Living by desire means you only do what you want. To own your 'Yes', you need to own your 'No'. That's why you're the only one here folding towels."

"Wait, so this is a test?"

"You could say that."

"Oh."

"Yeah."

"Okay, I WANT to come to yoga... oh but I need to get some work done for my job..."

Daniel raised an eyebrow.

"...but I guess I could do that later."

"Great," Daniel said. "But we need to get some coffee first."

I motioned to the moka pot half full of espresso on the stovetop. Daniel made a face like he was going to hurl.

"No real coffee," he said. "Come. I'll show you a few things."

I WAS A NEW Yorker being led around New York by a couple of Canadians.

Canada Daniel had only been in New York for three weeks, but he knew all the hidden gems of my city. On the way downtown, he took Wallace and I to the 'the best cafe for a flat white', 'the best bakery for a croissant', and finally the 'best hot yoga studio for hot yoga'.

"You did really well for your first time," Wallace said.

"Thanks. I'm usually not this flexible," I said.

"It's the heat," said Daniel. "It softens your tissue so it can be remolded."

I followed their hairy, sweat-soaked bodies to the locker room. There were only two free shower stalls.

"You go ahead," said Daniel. "I need to cool off."

When I got out of the shower, the Canadians were speaking in low voices.

"You ever notice how if you tell one staff member something, they all seem to know it immediately?" said Daniel.

"Yeah, someone is always asking where I am every second," Wallace said.

They got quieter when I approached.

"Yeah, Sergio keeps trying to fill my schedule," I chimed in. They relaxed.

"And the weirdest part has been..."

"Everyone acts like this is normal..." Daniel said slowly.

The three of us tensed and searched each other's eyes.

"So..." Wallace said. "OneTaste is a cult right?"

We burst out laughing.

"It's such a cult!"

"I'm so relieved. I didn't mind moving into a weird cult house, but what freaked me out was it seemed I was the only one who thought it was weird."

"Yeah, I thought you guys were Orgasm zombies too, so I was afraid to say anything."

"It's like *The Emperor's New Clothes*," Daniel said. "No one wants to be seen as 'unable to see' so we're all playing along."

Daniel wanted to take us to the 'best Asian fusion place in the city' for dinner. It was only a few blocks away, but it took a long time to get there because Daniel was constantly looking from side to side to make sure he didn't miss anything. He had puppy-like enthusiasm, desirous of everything at the same time.

"Hey so if we acknowledge that it's a cult, but we choose to be in it, what does that make us?" Wallace asked.

"I knew a lot of people called it a cult on the Internet," I said. "But I didn't mind because the benefits seemed to outweigh the risks."

"Most psychologists can't even agree on what a cult is," Daniel said. "What we need to be concerned about is the fact that we're putting ourselves in a very vulnerable state. Vulnerability softens the mind the way heat softens the body— It makes it easier to be reshaped. That's great if we're talking about healing. But we can also be reshaped in other ways. There's a reason tissue hardens in the first place... to protect itself from harm."

"Hum," said Wallace.

"So we know that if we go deeper into OneTaste, it will change our lives in *some* way," I said. "But we don't know, and we won't know till much later, whether it actually leads to Enlightenment or if it will mess us up."

"There's this Jewish parable," Daniel said. "A man goes out hunting, then comes back to his village to find all his friends and family are doing crazy things and speaking a crazy language. He tries to remind them of who they are, and to tell them to stop doing crazy things, but they can't understand him. He figures out that something poisoned their water supply that had totally changed everyone's mind. Days pass and he tries to get them to stop drinking the water, but he can't. He's just one person against the whole village. So after days of isolation, he realizes that there's only one way to stop them from seeming crazy. He drinks the water."

"Hum," said Wallace.

"So you're saying reality is arbitrary?"

"Reality is a set of agreements between people," Daniel said. "There are endless ways to make meaning from events. So we need to confirm what we perceive with other people, otherwise we feel insane. The more people confirm our perceptions, the more *real* reality feels. Every group has its own interpretations of reality, and they all can find evidence that theirs is right and everyone else's is wrong."

"So if that's the case, all that matters is that our chosen reality leads to being happy, right?" I said. "And that our group can keep it stable, of course. I guess the thing that would suck the most would be to live in bliss for twenty years, then 'wake up' one day and realize it was all bullshit."

Daniel made a sound that was neither confirming nor denying.

I whipped out my notebook and drew a two-by-two matrix. The vertical axis had the options, '*Go Deep into OneTaste*' and '*Don't Go Deep*'. The horizontal axis read, '*OneTaste leads to Enlightenment*' and '*OneTaste ruins life*'. I filled in the four possibilities with symbols. Go Deep x Enlightenment equaled a big smiley face. Go Deep x Ruins Life equaled a sad face. Don't Go Deep, in both instances, equaled a neutral face— life remains status quo. I showed the Canadians my chart.

"Well based on this, I wouldn't go deep," said Wallace. "That's kind of been my plan anyway. I'm trying to get everything I can from this, but I don't want to get sucked in."

"You must be an Anxious Attachment style," Daniel said. "I'm the same way. Most OneTaste students are Anxious types."

"I don't know, I think I would like to work for OneTaste," I said. "I mean, my life has become so much more interesting since I came across them. Just to be able to help others experience that sounds like a dream job."

"You're probably an Avoidant," Daniel said. "Most people who work for OneTaste are Avoidants."

The 'best Asian fusion place in the city' had many more dollar signs than I was used to. While Wallace and I recovered from sticker shock, Daniel ordered a bunch of appetizers and multiple courses, then proceeded to tell us the backstory of this place. Daniel lived in a different reality when it came to food. He believed everything needed to be tasted and never looked at prices, ever. On a later outing he'd reveal that he spent over two grand a month on dinner alone, and to our shock would say, "Why? Is that low?"

I was glad that Wallace confirmed my reality that this place was crazy expensive. He ordered a small wonton soup and so did I. Unlike Daniel, Wallace was not a free spender. He was living off savings and wanted to make it last as long as possible.

Wallace was supposed to get married last year, but it was called off because his fiancé cheated on him. In putting himself back together he found Brene Brown's work on vulnerability and decided that was his path to healing. He quit his programmer job and went down to San Francisco to take workshops in something called 'Authentic Relating,' a sort of vulnerability-focused group therapy practice. The Authentic Relating group shared an event space with the OneTaste San Francisco. Before and after TurnON events he'd see the OneTaste people in the lobby.

"The OneTaste people were so... intense," Wallace said. "I had never seen people so intense. I wanted to be intense like them. So I started going to TurnONs instead of AR. Rachel pitched CP6. I never spent that kind of money on myself, but I thought, why not? It's worth it if I become intense like them."

"Has it worked?"

"I'm definitely better at expressing my desires and holding boundaries. My whole life I had been too much of a nice guy. When I was a kid, my friends called me 'DW' for 'Doormat Wally'."

"But now you're IW for Intense Wallace?"

"Working on it."

Daniel had a different path from Canada to OneTaste. Daniel was almost forty but looked a good ten years younger. In graduate school he had a class on ideological communities. His professor assigned Nicole's book *Slow Sex*. Daniel tried OMing and received some coaching from OneTaste. He went on to become a state-employed psychotherapist that was on call twenty-four hours per day. He saved a lot of money but basically had no life. One day his OneTaste coach brought Rachel into their coaching session to sell him on CP6. He took it as a sign to take leave from his job.

In the last month he had been making up for lost time. He was a true epicurean, looking to see, taste, and feel everything. Daniel regaled us with fantastical seduction stories from around the city. I had heard plenty of braggadocio from pickup artist guys, but Daniel's didn't sound like egotistical social engineering. In his stories, *he* was always the one being seduced. *He* was the one taken out of control. It was as if his life was a romance novel and Cupid had put a bull's eye on his back.

Wallace and I had finished our soups a while ago, so we sat and watched Daniel finish his meal.

"Hey so even if OneTaste leads us to dark places," I said, "who's to say that it wasn't part of the path to Enlightenment anyway?"

Daniel chewed for a moment before speaking.

"Enlightenment leaves no scars."

IT SEEMS THE MORE feminine a woman is, the more unnecessary pillows she has on her bed.

Xena leaned back into the pile of pillows against her headboard. Her painted toes poked out through knit leg warmers. She pulled me on top of her.

Sister Goddess Xena and I had become more than just OM partners. Although OneTaste recommended against it, it was a natural occurrence in the OM community. People often progressed from OMing at Circles, to OMing privately at their homes, to having "Makeouts."

A *Makeout*, in OneTaste verbiage, was any sexual act besides OM. Like the colloquialism "hooking up," it could involve anything from kissing to penetration.

"Would you like to have a Makeout?" was the standard invitation. If accepted, it proceeded much like any sexual activity, but with OM's influence. OMers treated sex as a "goalless practice." We were trained to 'follow the sensation' rather than try to achieve a specific end. Think less. Feel more.

But for me there was always a point where the sensation disappeared. I had a sort of Pavlovian stress response to intercourse. The moment I thought of penetration I went dead inside.

Sergio said I needed to quit Viagra cold turkey and go through a period of re-sensitization. But I wasn't ready.

But I did tell Xena about my chemical dependency. As all vulnerable acts, first it was scary, then thrilling, then a relief. This was the first time I took Viagra in front of a woman who knew the real reason why. Being so vulnerable with her immediately made me feel more attached.

"So what happens now?" she asked.

"We carry on. It can take thirty minutes to kick in."

Once I felt the flushing in my cheeks, I reached for a condom. This was a different kind of "following the sensation," of course. The sensation I followed was no longer from connection with the woman in front of me, but from a chemical reaction provided by the Pfizer Corporation.

Xena could feel I wasn't really in my body. She looked up at me to bring me back to the moment. I could see she was really seeing me. I could feel she was really feeling me. And under that spotlight I began to shrink away. I tried to force it but soon I was just pushing a half empty condom.

"Ruwan, it's okay."

I grunted and flopped on my back.

"Tell me how you feel."

"Fine."

She sighed and slipped on a bathrobe.

"Can I do some somatic experiencing something with you?"

"Okay."

The room was dark, but I could faintly see her hand hovering over my midline. I closed my eyes. I wanted to disappear. Two plus months of this dumb clitoris-stroking practice and I still had the same problem. Even the pharmaceutical industry was failing me now.

"Ow!"

It felt like I was punched in the bladder, but from the inside. Xena's hand was floating twelve inches over my lower belly.

I had often felt pain there before. Every time I had an erection issue, that area was painfully sensitive. Xena put her hand gently on top. My lowest abs were knotted. She put her other hand under my sacrum, making a lower belly sandwich. She took a deep slow breath, encouraging me to do the same. After holding me for what felt like a long time, the pain seemed to fade away.

"Ruwan, were you ever molested?"

"What? No."

"Are you sure? You can tell me."

"Yes I'm sure!"

"Okay, okay. You just have trauma in your body. You are blocked up in your second chakra."

Chakras, she explained, were wheels of energy on the centerline of the body from the anus to the crown of the head. There were seven chakras. Each corresponded to a different emotional function.

In other words, some hippie shit.

But I didn't have a better explanation for how she made that spot spasm without touching me.

"It feels like you have a lot of anger trapped in there," she said.

"I don't do anger. Anger isn't a productive emotion..."

"Ruwan! All emotions are important! Your emotions are a landscape, a garden. Each flower is important."

"My garden is all roses."

"You think so, because you think roses are the only beautiful flower, but a garden that's only roses is... boring."

Xena switched on the bedside lamp. An unnecessary amount of pillows were scattered everywhere.

"Well, I'm glad you moved into the Morellino. It's probably good for you to be shaken up."

ONE MORNING I WOKE up with my lower belly spasming.

I texted Xena. She said my second chakra was opening from all the sexual energy in the Morellino.

Later that morning, Rachel called an impromptu House Meeting. Most residents and staff were out and about, so the only people who showed were Wallace, Lila, Elodie, Dr. Tanisha, and myself.

"Okay, let's check-in," Rachel said.

This was the first time I had something specific to check in with.

"So my second chakra has been opening..." I said.

"No Ruwan! No!" Rachel scolded with her index finger raised and a smile on her face. She had a way of being both cute and threatening at the same time, like a sock puppet on a knife handle.

"We don't speak hippie-dippie woo-woo in here," Rachel said. "We speak Orgasm! Right T?"

"Right! We speak Orgasm!" Tanisha said, also raising her index finger.

"You should listen to Tanisha. Tanisha's a doctor."

"I'm a doctor!"

"Okay..." I said. "My lower abs have been spasming and... I guess Orgasm is... opening a blockage in my body."

"Better." Rachel smiled. I didn't like that I liked her approval.

After check-ins Rachel went into a speech on how we need to "tighten the rails" in the Morellino. I wasn't sure what she was talking about. She said we all need to do more Fear Inventory. We needed to follow the structures more closely.

"Pardon, a question," said Elodie from France. "Why are the OM Circles so strict? Other OMers sometimes complain to me that they like OMing but the OneTaste OM Circle is so rigid."

Rachel's gaze zeroed on Elodie like a laser. Elodie shrank in her seat.

"The OneTaste OM Circle is the only OM Circle," Rachel said. "OneTaste is *the only game in town*. We keep a strict Container for the Orgasm to keep everyone safe. Anyone who doesn't hold the Container with reverence is doing the community a disservice..." Rachel's head snapped around. "Where's Daniel?"

"He's sleeping," Wallace said.

"It's eleven o'clock!"

"Hum, he might be getting up then."

"Who's his bedmate??"

Dr. Tanisha raised her hand, but only as high as her shoulder.

"T! What the hell! Why is Daniel waking up so late?"

Tanisha's hands went palm up.

"This is not okay." Rachel sighed and pinched the bridge of her nose. "This is what I was afraid of. We need more masculine in this house... No offense. I've decided we're moving Andrew here."

"Yay!" Tanisha said.

"Who's Andrew?" Daniel said as he walked in and opened the fridge. His hair was tousled and there were sleep lines across his face.

Rachel glared death at him and his posture straightened up. He closed the fridge and took a seat next to Wallace.

"Andrew is OneTaste's legal counsel," Rachel said.

"Andrew's a lawyer!" said Tanisha.

"We hired him out of CP5," Rachel said. "He's going to come to New York and help us ground these rails."

APPARENTLY ONETASTE WASN'T THE only game in town.

This wasn't their first time in New York either. Five years ago, they attempted to set up a New York community, but it quickly folded. Most of the staff members moved back to San Fran, but one decided to stay in New York. She ended up defecting and starting her own OM circles.

Her name was Theresa. Her circles, called 'O Nights,' were secret and invite-only. She was popular with the Sister Goddesses because she allowed theatrics that OneTaste didn't allow. Xena invited me. Other Sister Goddesses invited Daniel and Wallace.

Theresa gave all the newcomers an introductory talk before the event started. She was in her mid-thirties, slender with long hair. She wore librarian glasses and a flowing dress. Like Nicole, she sat with a perfectly straight spine.

"For those who are here for the first time, you may notice I do things a little differently," she said. Her version of the Container included three minutes before the normal grounding step where the strokee could ask for any kind of touch.

OneTaste preached 'nothing extra.' That meant one should not add music, mood lighting, romantic gestures, or any touch outside of their strict OM Container. This forced the practitioners to heighten sensation through their attention only.

O Night had everything extra. Theresa held her event at an upscale yoga studio illuminated with glowing sconces. The room was filled with tapestries and statues of Hindu goddesses. There was incense burning in the corner. Soft new age music was playing over the surround sound speakers. And unlike in an OM Circle, our nests were all in a circle, pointed at the middle like spokes on a wheel.

"I never understood why OneTaste called it an 'OM Circle' then set up everyone in a square," Theresa said.

As in OM Circle, O Night had two OMs. Xena was my first partner. For my second partner I had asked Theresa herself. After the first OM, I hugged Xena and went over to Theresa's nest.

"You can touch me however you like," Theresa said to me, during the Grounding step.

I played it safe and just stayed on her legs and feet. Wherever I touched her seemed to be orgasmic. If she was faking it, she was a damn good actress.

I had had a few high-sensation OMs so far, with women who really got off. But Theresa was next level. More than that though, her body transmitted a clear signal— it told me exactly how it wanted to be stroked. I stroked lighter and faster and she went higher and higher. Her vocalizations were like Rachel's in the OM demo, but more girlish and less guttural. Her toes also wiggled in rhythm. She kept going higher and higher, so I stroked faster and faster. My hand began to cramp so I paused. Theresa's body rattled and shook. After a few seconds I switched to slower heavier strokes, to bring us back down.

"And time!" Theresa said. In addition to being stroked, she was also the timekeeper. I helped her sit up to share frames.

"I like how you paused there," she said, "but you didn't need to go back down. I know OneTaste probably taught you to take women down on the peaks, but you don't have to do that with me... There's always more *up* to go."

Something moved in my pants. Maybe it was a chakra.

At the end, Theresa pitched her upcoming class. It was on combining OM with a type of hypnosis called Generative Trance. It was one evening a week for four weeks. It was only three hundred dollars. I was already in debt for a few grand. What's another couple hundred? I signed up. So did the Canadians. I wanted to see if Xena wanted to join too.

She was sitting in the lobby on a divan, laughing and radiating joy. There was a man standing over her cracking jokes. My belly knotted up. I sat down next to her. Neither of them acknowledged me so I introduced myself to him.

"I'm Andrew," he said. He had a firm handshake.

"Oh, you're OneTaste's lawyer."

"I am."

"I live in the Morellino too."

"Cool." He turned back to Xena. "We should OM sometime. I'll message you."

"Yes, I'd like that."

I felt nauseous, like I took a hard punch to the gut. I walked Xena down to the subway.

"Ruwan, what's wrong?" she said.

"Nothing."

"Ruwan..."

I sighed. "Okay, I'm jealous of that Andrew guy."

"I'm probably just going to OM with him," she said.

"Probably?"

"Well, I don't know yet. What? It's not like you and I are dating."

Another punch in the gut.

"Oh come on," Xena said. "I know you're doing more than just OMing in the Morellino..."

She had me there. But I still felt horrible and didn't know what to say.

Xena sighed.

"Ruwan, sometimes you're great. I feel your presence and I can really be in my feminine with you... But anytime things get uncomfortable you just go blank."

She mimed a catatonic face. I hoped I didn't really look like that. But I knew it was true. My whole life people had been asking me why I looked upset when I didn't think I was. She kept looking at me as if I was supposed to say something. But I didn't know what that should be. So I stuck with catatonia.

"Well, if you really want to be connected here," she said, "I can let you know what I end up doing with him."

I felt the punch in the solar plexus. That was my self-esteem chakra, I recalled.

ONE OF THE PERKS of living in an OM Residence was the *Stroker's Clinics.*

A Stroker's Clinic was a secret event to learn advanced OM skills.

Sergio had set up a nest in the living room of PHC. The rest of us sat in a semi-circle on the floor around it. Everyone was here. Tanya took a day off from work. Even Daniel was awake. No one wanted to miss our instructor, OneTaste's Head of Education, 'The Master Stroker,' Ken Blackman.

I had heard a lot about him. He and Nicole met at another conscious sexuality group called *The Welcomed Consensus.* He was Nicole's primary stroker there. A couple years after she created Orgasmic Meditation, she recruited him to teach at OneTaste.

Rachel often said that Ken had more Orgasm in his little finger than most men had in their entire bodies. Many women said that when he entered a room, all the pussies lit up.

He looked way different than I expected.

We heard two soft clicks of the apartment door opening and closing with minimal effort. Ken entered the room on silent footsteps. He was no more than five feet tall. He wore a baggy button-down shirt and slacks. He had a five o'clock shadow and a completely phlegmatic expression.

"Hi all," he said in a gentle voice.

He sat on the meditation cushion with a samurai's economy of movement.

"So," he said with no introduction, "how's everyone's OMs going?"

"I've been having *energetic* OMs," said Elodie from France . "I am having my strokers start five centimeters above my clit. And I feel every stroke."

I was pretty sure I misheard her. Ken didn't bat an eye.

"And is this with every stroker, or just certain ones?" he said.

"Every stroker."

"I would play with having your strokers stroking from further and further out. See how far out your field reaches," Ken said.

"Merci Ken."

"When I started OMing I was stroking from my cock," Andrew said. "Then I learned to stroke from my heart, and it felt a lot more connected. But lately even when I try to stroke from my heart, the energy still comes from my cock..."

"Great," Ken said.

Energy? Fields? No one spoke in this way in the intro class.

"Lately OMing has been hurting," Lila said, "like when your foot falls asleep, but it's my clit."

Ken nodded. "Yes, *shards of glass*," he said. "That's a pretty common experience for intermediate strokees."

Rachel walked in and unbuttoned her jeans. "Just so you all know, I felt *shards of glass* in every OM for like a year. I had to feel through every time I didn't ask for what I wanted, every time I didn't hold my boundaries, every time I lied, and every time I abandoned myself."

Rachel took off her pants and got in the nest next to Ken.

"I'm sure you all know Rachel," Ken said. "I'm going to show you different stroking styles for different types of strokees."

Ken put on latex gloves and fingered a dollop of lube onto the back of his right hand.

"Rachel's anatomy is very sensitive to pressure" Ken said, "so with someone like her, it's important to penetrate energetically."

All this 'energy' talk was making me feel weird. Or maybe it was the OM demos themselves. I was beginning to get a headache.

"So with my finger I'm making contact, but I'm putting almost no pressure. I want to give her clit space to come out," Ken said. "For all the strokers, I recommend you get a postal scale, one that can measure grams to two decimal places of precision. You want to be able to vary your pressure to one hundredth of a gram. That's the kind of sensitivity you need to be a good stroker."

Ken stroked Rachel till she made her signature glottal sound and wiggled her toes. Ken explained some nuances, then Rachel got up. Ken changed his gloves and Jane got in the nest.

"Jane has a training clit," Ken said, referring to her more visible anatomy. "With someone like Jane, you want to do heavier downstrokes from the start."

Ken stroked Jane with a totally different type of stroke. She made rhythmic vocalizations and her toes also wiggled. After a few minutes, Jane sat up, and Tanisha got in the nest.

"Hey Ken," Wallace asked. "How do you determine your stroking rhythm? Are you following her breathing or her moaning?"

"Neither," Ken said. "I'm going off of the sensations from her clit."

"Yeah, you can't trust a woman's moans," Jane said. "Sometimes the sounds we make are off our own rhythm— kind of to throw you off and test if you're really feeling us."

On Tanisha, Ken showed us how and when he varied strokes.

"Remember, a peak is when the next stroke will have less sensation than the last," he said. "A good stroker changes the stroke right before the sensation drops."

Tanisha was blushing through her dark skin when she got out of the nest. Ken went on to stroke Lila, Tanya, and Elodie, each time pointing out different OM skills. I had a headache and felt wobbly. I felt this way during Nicole's demo at the How to OM class.

"Okay, let's see the strokers now," Ken said.

Daniel, Andrew, and Wallace each stroked one of the women while Ken suggested adjustments. But his general instruction was the same: Pay attention, feel, stroke, feel the feedback, adjust accordingly.

This was summarized by OneTaste's aphorism, "Stroke for your Pleasure." To stroke for your pleasure was to do what felt right for you, not what would please the other person. The idea was that if a stroker was trying to figure out how to please his partner, he'd go into his head and miss her moment-to-moment cues. But by stroking in the way that felt best to the tip of his finger, he could connect to her feelings and therefore was more likely to intuit the resonant stroke.

"Don't try to create sensation," Ken said. "Focus on connection and the sensation will come."

On my turn he paired me with Jane. My headache was searing now but I tried my best.

"I can't feel any energy off of Ruwan," Andrew said. "I'm trying to feel him, but I can't."

"I can feel Ruwan, fine," Jane said between moans.

"Maybe he's not reaching out with his field?" Andrew said.

"Maybe he's blocking you," Ken said.

"Yeah, it wouldn't be the first time..."

Everyone laughed. Andrew had gone on a date with Xena recently. She had come back to the Morellino with him but didn't want to sleep with him, knowing I was upstairs. Everyone knew I was one of those poor souls who still struggled with jealousy.

We closed the clinic with more discussion on "penetrating with energy" and "stroking one's field" and other things that made no sense to me.

"Wow this feels like a Mystery School!" Lila said.

My headache kept raging through the afternoon. I stuffed my face with chocolate chip cookies that I found in the pantry. This was called "Coming down pleasurably." The idea was that sensation, like water or air pressure, tends to move from high to low. If you don't consciously bring your energy down after a peak experience, it will find a way to do so unconsciously. Nicole said sugar feels good because it brings your energy down. Sergio often consumed huge bowls of Frosted Flakes at night for this reason.

The pain in my head reduced, which reminded me of the pain in my solar plexus. Jealousy. I had become hopelessly attached to Xena, and a part of me wanted to just drop this whole OM thing and be in relationship with her. Anything to get that gnawing feeling to go away.

I had only theorized about polyamory before. As with everything, I read some books on it such as Chris Ryan's *Sex At Dawn*. It made sense on paper. But I also couldn't imagine anything feeling that intense being a good thing. How could I "stroke for my pleasure" here when every cell in my body was screaming?

I heard two soft clicks and felt a tingle up my spine. Ken walked in with no sound. He looked at me. He smiled. He took a cookie off my plate, holding just the edge with the tips of his index finger and thumb. He dipped the cookie in my milk, gently, with the precision of two decimal points of a gram, turning the cookie so that the maximum amount of cookie was submerged, without his fingers getting wet. His action created a sine wave across the surface of the milk.

This was known as *Skillful Violation*—the ability to feel someone's false boundaries and step past them, while stopping at the real ones.

"Thanks," he said, then disappeared down the hall.

I heard two clicks. Then I remembered to exhale.

THE NEXT DAY I told Xena I loved her.

As with all vulnerable moves, it felt thrilling and courageous, like jumping out of a plane.

But by the second word I knew the parachute wasn't going to open.

"Uhh," she said, "thank you."

Goddamnit.

We were on our way to Theresa's Orgasm-Hypnosis class. I imagined we'd spend the class blissed out and in love from my bold proclamation. This was not how I expected the evening to go.

Theresa's class was in a smaller room inside the same yoga studio. There were eight students in all. Both Daniel and Wallace were cuddling with Sister Goddesses in different corners. Xena and I sat near but not directly next to each other.

"This is more of a research group than a class," Theresa said. "Together we're going to discover the next form of stroking."

Orgasmic Meditation was just one iteration in a lineage of stroking, Theresa explained. Before OMing was something called '*DOing*' which stood for '*Deliberate Orgasm.*' It was created in the sixties by a guy named Vic Baranco and his wife Suzanne who ran a commune called *Lafayette Morehouse*. Legend had it that Vic's appendage was too large for them to make love, so they sought the help of a witch doctor, trained in western occultism and 'sex magick.' This witch doctor taught Vic how to "open Suzanne up" by stroking her clitoris. Vic and Suzanne practiced this while on LSD and Suzanne channeled instruction to Vic that eventually became DOing.

An experienced OMer told me that Vic Baranco was friends with other commune leaders from the sixties such as L. Ron Hubbard, founder of Scientology, and Werner Erhard, founder of est (Erhard Seminars Training), which eventually became the self-help conglomerate, Landmark Education. The three of them traded secrets on covert communication. L. Ron Hubbard taught them how to mold perception of reality using language— much of the terminology used by all groups came from Hubbard. Werner Erhard taught them about sales and how to change people's minds using the environment. Vic taught them about intuition through feeling the body.

Morehouse's physical stroking practice went on to be developed by others. A couple of Vic's students, Steve and Vera Bodansky, created an iteration called *Extended Massive Orgasm* or 'EMO'. Regena, the founder of The School of Womanly Arts, trained extensively with the Bodanskys and Morehouse. Another group called 'The Welcomed Consensus' split off from Morehouse and made their own version of DOing called *The Welcomed Method*. Ken Blackman was a top student at the Welcomed Consensus back when a young woman named Nicole Daedone came to visit.

The week that Nicole came to visit The Welcomed Consensus, it so happened that many of the women in the commune didn't feel like getting stroked. Part of what made the women resistant was that they never knew how long a stroking session would go. DOing, EMO, and the Welcomed Method had no time limit and could literally go on for hours. The Stroker had total control.

The consensus that Welcomed came to was that everyone had to practice stroking for at least fifteen minutes a day, then could stop after that. Nicole realized that a more restricted container would make women more willing to try stroking. And she was right. In just a few years, OM had far surpassed its predecessors in popularity.

Nicole also reframed the practice from the patriarchal DOing to a more egalitarian, pro-feminist one. We were taught that the "strokees' clit was stroking our finger back" as much as a the other way around.

Theresa's goal was to create the next iteration in the stroking lineage.

"I decided to call our practice, 'GO' or 'Gateway Orgasm'," Theresa said.

"So if you're talking about it in the past tense, do you say, 'We went'?" Daniel said.

Everyone laughed.

After the GO class Xena said it's better that we stop seeing each other. She did her best to let me down gently, but it still felt like a punch to the solar plexus. I knew my face was catatonic, but I couldn't help it.

BETWEEN PENTHOUSE A AND Penthouse C was Penthouse B.

Jane heard that it would be vacant soon. One afternoon in PHC, she announced her plan to take it over.

"Then we can knock the walls down and turn it into one huge apartment!" Lila said.

"Who the hell is going to knock the walls down?" Tanya said.

"I don't know, somebody."

"Well I'll tell you one thing, that sure ain't gonna be me," Tanya said then made a trumpet sound. It was a thing she did.

OneTaste was rapidly expanding. Nicole was being featured in more mainstream media and had had a few celebrity endorsements. Graduates of Coaching Program 5, which was held in San Francisco, were returning to their hometowns and starting OM communities around the world. OneTaste New York, London, and Los Angeles would each triple in size in the next month.

"No one is knocking down any walls!" Jane said while scribbling numbers in her notebook.

Jane was the official 'House Mom', the manager of the residence. The Morellino penthouses were leased in Jane's name, not OneTaste's. They even tasked Jane to personally come up with the deposit for the new place on her own. I wondered why an enormous corporation would put that on the shoulders of an employee.

Jane had a plan.

"Next immersion I'm going to rent out PHC to the incoming CP6 students," Jane said.

"So everyone will sleep on the floor?" asked Wallace.

"Yay slumber party!" Lila said.

"Well, no," said Jane. "They will rent your beds. I'm going to put the four of you in a hotel for the weekend."

"Oooh fun!" said Lila.

"That's only in four days," said Wallace. "I would have appreciated more notice."

"Four days?? Four days is a hella long time in Orgasm time, Wal-lace!" Jane snapped. "Rapid Changing Reality! Get with the program!"

We all decided to give Jane some space.

Before I could leave, she asked me if I could stay somewhere else for the weekend. She noticed I sometimes stayed at Xena's.

"Are you and Xena dating?" Jane asked.

"No. I mean, I thought we were. We kind of went through an entire relationship cycle in a month."

Jane smirked. "Yeah, OM relationships can be like that," she said. "Sometimes when the sensation is hella high, it feels like you've known someone forever. Then the sensation drops, and you wonder what you saw in them a few days ago."

"Oh."

"Be careful with that, Ruwan. Guys like you often get into trouble with this stuff."

I didn't know what she meant. I decided not to ask.

THE CP STUDENTS WERE given an assignment to complete before the next immersion.

We were supposed to help create an "Orgasm Is..." party. This was the latest marketing slogan of Priscilla, OneTaste's CEO. The idea was to host a party where we helped people redefine what *Orgasm Is*.

This could mean anything. Except the normal definition, of course.

I had been OMing four months. Already my perceptions had changed so much that if someone were to refer to having "an orgasm" around me, I'd roll my eyes at them. Already I was seeing non-OMers as a different, inferior kind of people.

Every major OM city was supposed to do their own "Orgasm Is..." party. Many of the CP6 students lived in random parts of the country, so the New York students decided to do ours the night before the next CP immersion weekend, so students from other cities could participate. Wallace found a sangria bar in the Lower East Side that would let us hold the party there for free.

A couple hours before the party I got a call.

My phone screen lit up with a picture of me attempting to dip a girl holding a cigarette. It was Lisa. She said she was home from the detox center. She had been for a few months. But she was going away for a long time and wanted to give me back my stuff. She was flying out in two hours. If I wanted to see her, I had to go right now.

"You okay dude?" Wallace said without looking up from his book.

I explained I couldn't drive everyone downtown and I headed for Jersey. Rain began to pour as I went over the George Washington Bridge. I tried to remember what of my stuff she could have possibly had. I didn't care. I wanted to see her. I wanted to tell her so many things.

Lisa asked me to meet her in the parking lot of a shopping mall. She was driving her mom's Escalade. I parked next to her and got in her passenger seat. She exhaled a long puff of smoke that formed a cloud around us. My stuff was in the cardboard box in the back seat, she said. She flicked her cigarette butt out the window and lit another one.

"I fucked up," she said. "They are sending me away."

"You just were away..."

She explained that after the detox center, she had been clean for a while. While I had been going to OM Circles and TurnONs, she had been going to daily Narcotics Anonymous meetings. After one meeting, the speaker asked her for a ride home. She agreed. He asked her to stop in Patterson, a small city in Jersey known for drugs. He ran out of the car and returned with a crack pipe. He hit it, then offered it to her.

"So you kicked him out right?" I said.

"I didn't know what to do. I froze up."

"Then you kicked him out!?"

"I was scared. Froze up. Fucked up."

"Why didn't you kick him out?!?"

"Because I AM AN AD-DICT!"

She snapped her body to face me. Her blue eyes were faded. The whites were webbed with red capillaries. She looked like she was about to cry but stuffed it and took another drag instead.

I took a cigarette from her pack too.

When we first started dating, I would always have a cigarette when she did. It was partly so I wouldn't mind her tobacco breath, and partly because I'm impressionable. She didn't want me to smoke. "You need to be the good one. You're my guardian angel," she would say. She wanted me to help her quit. But towards the end of our relationship, she would chain smoke in front of me like she was taunting me. Then she would get furious when I tried to stop her.

"You know I only smoked in front of you back then to make you mad."

"Why?"

"I don't know. I just felt like it."

Hyper-volatile, I thought.

We smoked in silence for a moment. The menthol light was making me nauseous. I hung my arm out the window and let it fall to the ground. The rain slowed down.

"After ten weeks I go to a halfway house with all girls. That will be good for me. I'm probably addicted to men too."

My third chakra hardened.

"I told my mom to PayPal you," she said. "I told her I owed you money."

"For what?"

"Probably a lot of things. But I need you to take out a hundred in cash and give it to me. For methadone. I need it before my dad drives me out tonight."

"A hundred bucks of methadone?"

"And a gram of coke."

"I dunno…"

"Please. I just need it to keep me awake till I can get on the plane."

I knew I was getting played. But it hurt too much to see her in pain.

She drove me to the ATM and I gave her the bills. She dropped me off back at my car. I took the cardboard box from the backseat. It began to rain again.

"Send me your address so I can write you," I said.

"Yeah."

I opened the box in my car. There were many clothes. Most weren't mine. There were many books. Most were, except a small one titled *Tao Te Ching*.

A fist knocked on my window through the rain. I rolled it down. Lisa handed me my phone. I had left it on her seat.

"You're such an idiot," she said with a quiver in her voice.

She had always been afraid of vulnerability, I realized. She was afraid to feel emotions and used sex and drugs as a substitute. In that moment, I took her off the pedestal. My longing for her disappeared. I just wanted her to get better.

I reached the party around seven. Throughout the bar was your typical Thursday evening crowd—late happy hourers and early partiers. They bustled with the entropic movement of numbed inhibitions.

Over by the couches was a very different group. They sat with the economy of movement of people who fully felt their feelings. Every so often a person from the first group would get pulled into the gravitational field of the second.

I sat down next to a young woman whom I had met at Theresa'a GO group named Sally. She was a Sister Goddess and ballerina at a prominent dance company. She was explaining something to Bonnie called 'The Alexander Technique'.

"It makes your nervous system sparkle!" she said.

"Okay...," said Bonnie.

"It's like OMing, but for your posture!"

"Ohhhh I get it now," Bonnie said.

I noticed Sally was sitting on the edge of the couch with a perfectly straight back and long neck. I straightened up my back to imitate. Sally noticed me and giggled.

"Is that you trying to have good posture?" she said.

I nodded with a stiff neck. Sally burst out an uninhibited feminine laugh. I knew I couldn't take any credit, but making a beautiful woman laugh always feels rewarding.

"No, no, don't do that," she said. "In Alexander they call that *end-gaining*, losing connection to the present moment just to get a result. When people end-gain, they are trying to force control and that puts them out of alignment."

"So what's good posture then?"

"Well, anything can be good posture as long as it's a conscious choice," she said.

"This can be good posture..." She put her elbow on her knee and her chin in her palm.

"This can be good posture..." She turned and leaned her side against the couch.

"Or *this* can be good posture..." Her body collapsed and slid down the couch till her feet hit the floor. Everything she did seemed to be graceful.

"There is no one perfect alignment," she said. "Any action can be the right one so long as you're consciously choosing it."

Hot air blasted my feet.

It felt good. Lila had the bright idea for us to turn our bodies around so we slept with our feet under the heating vent instead of our heads. We laughed that it took so long to think of that. A lot of things I used to do seemed backwards.

"Do you have any desires?" she asked.

I did. Her favorite question no longer made me freeze.

Stroke for your pleasure applied to everything, I realized. Most of life is far beyond one's control. The best you could do is focus on the moment and let it tell you how to stroke next.

"Morning practice in ten minutes!" Sergio called from downstairs.

Lila popped out from under the covers. The blankets fell off her toned body which glowed orange-purple in light of the first sun. She climbed over me and down the loft bed's ladder. She had named our bed the *Birdy Nest*. I thought it was cute. In OneTaste, even the beds had nicknames.

"That was fun," she said. "I can feel you a lot more now."

After practice, Lila was at her altar shuffling her round tarot deck. She noticed me noticing her.

"Would you like me to draw a card for you?" she asked.

"How does that work?"

"Well, you can ask *Motherpeace* a question, or have an intention..."

"Uh, I don't know..."

"How about... *this card will represent the next chapter of your life.*"

"Okay."

Lila closed her eyes and shuffled the deck while chanting an angelic sound.

"Pick."

I drew a card from the middle. It showed an androgynous-looking naked youth doing a handstand next to a river. He or she had long curly hair and brown skin. Around it were mushrooms, a crocodile, and a condor.

"You drew the Fool!" Lila said.

"Aw, man."

"No, Ruwan! The Fool is like the best card. She represents innocence. She's your Inner Child. She hasn't learned fear or shame, so she can go anywhere and do anything."

"But doesn't that mean she's naïve? Just because she's not afraid of the crocodile, doesn't mean it won't eat her."

"No..." Lila frowned. "The Fool is still connected to the umbilical cord of the Great Mother. She hasn't separated yet, so nothing can hurt her."

"But what happens when that cord is cut? Eventually she'll learn that there are things in the world that you should fear. She'll learn the hard way not to hang out with crocodiles."

Lila thought for a moment. "I guess that's part of the Fool's Journey."

"The what?"

"The major arcana in tarot shows the stages a soul goes through. The Fool is the zero card. It's where we all start. As innocent wittle babies."

Lila had the most adorable cat-like eyes. Somehow I hadn't noticed that before.

"So what does the Fool become when he's not a fool anymore?" I asked.

"The Magician."

STAGE 3: RESTORATION

Healing through pleasure. The subject is reformed.

"And those who were seen dancing were thought to be insane by those who could not hear the music."
~ Friedrich Nietzsche

NICOLE WARNED US ABOUT attachments at the next immersion.

"I can see the lights turning on in many of you, so I'm saying this as a kind of warning. When someone first experiences Orgasm, we usually see them spend it in one of two places: Romance or Finance. Romantic love and money are the two most dangerous temptations because they feel so immediately gratifying... How many of you fell in love with your first OM partner?"

Many CP students laughed and raised their hands.

"We see this a lot," Nicole continued. "A woman OMs for the first time and her lights turn on. Naturally she thinks it's coming from her stroker. By now you should all know that no one gives you Orgasm. Your Orgasm belongs to you."

Nicole paused for effect. It was the last weekend of March. There was gray slush on the New York streets. But Nicole still wore a miniskirt and open-toed heels. She stood on stage with a bare knee pointed at the audience.

"Finance and romance are barbarians," Nicole said. "They create attachment, and they will take you off your path. You can have as much of them as you want… after you Wake Up. And once you wake up, you may find that you don't even care about these things anymore."

The second CP immersion, and every following one, was at the artist loft at the corner of Bank Street and the West Side Highway. In the worldwide OM community, the space became known simply as 'Bank Street.' Every OM location had a nickname. Bank Street's huge windows overlooked the Hudson River. The bright mornings sun backlit Nicole's figure.

"I know it's tempting," she continued, "it feels so good to spend your Orgasm on money or romantic attachment. Sugar feels good because it drops your sensation from high to low. But the cost of spending your Orgasm is giving up *raw, unlimited, power.*"

A middle-aged woman raised her hand. Sergio ran over to give her the microphone.

"I understand the money part," she said, "but love? Isn't love the most important thing? Why shouldn't we fall in love?"

Nicole smiled down at her. "I didn't say don't love. Yes, love is the most important fundamental human need. But romantic love and true love are two very different things. We've been conditioned to confuse them. Women especially have been conditioned to think this way… waiting around for Prince Charming to complete them instead of becoming whole themselves. Until you're whole, you cannot really love anyway. Romance from an incomplete place is a *toxic mimic* of what love really is…"

Nicole gazed into the audience in such a way that it seemed like she was looking at each of us at once.

"The problem with romance and finance is that they are conditional. They create obligations. Commerce. The masculine world runs on commerce. Most of us have learned sex through commerce, 'I'll do you, then you'll do me…' but even if you balance the books, you're still not connected. Commerce is one hundred and eighty degrees opposite from Connection. What we really want is Connection. In Connection there's nothing to balance. Because you aren't two separate entities. You're one… So when you get lost, return to your commitments."

She scanned the room for effect, then took a sip from her tall glass of water.

"We tend to blow out on the good, not the bad," Nicole continued. "We sabotage ourselves when we hit up on our Havingness Level."

Havingness was how much you allowed yourself to have. It was another idea coined by L. Ron Hubbard. In OneTaste, it correlated to how much sensation you could hold in your body. Sensation beyond your capacity is what led to Tumescence.

"You can move from inspiration or desperation," she said. "We all would like to move from inspiration, it's more pleasurable, but most of us wait for desperation to hit."

Nicole explained that we always subconsciously reverted to our Havingness Level. Any time we fell below our Havingness, we went into emergency mode to bring ourselves back up. Whereas when we exceed our Havingness, we subconsciously find a way to bring ourselves down.

"In biology this is known as *homeostasis*. It's the process of bringing us back to status quo."

The way to break free from the status quo was to increase your Havingness. In One-Taste that meant increasing the amount of sensation you could hold in your body.

"So this immersion," she said, "we're going to teach you to *get off*..."

To "GET OFF" ON something is to derive pleasure from it.

OneTaste taught that while some things were easier to get off on than others, a sufficiently well-trained person could get off on anything. It was similar to an Enlightened person being able to find peace in all circumstances, except more focused on the body, and more sexual.

Ken taught the weekend's guided OM training. If the masculine aspect of OM could be summarized as *Stroke for your pleasure*, then the feminine counterpart was *Get off on every stroke.*

"The stro*ker* may determine the physical stroke," Ken said. "But it's the stro*kee* that determines how the stroke feels. If you've ever gotten a spontaneous erection during an OM, it probably means your strokee was thinking about sex. Mind you, that doesn't necessarily mean she was thinking of sex *with YOU*. But she is thinking of sex, and your body is responding accordingly."

"So our body is supposed to always respond to her body?" Wallace asked.

"There's no *supposed* to. We are wired how we are," Ken said. "Our limbic system was designed to feel another person's feelings."

"Wait, so what do I do if I get hard in an OM?"

"Keep stroking."

The class laughed. Ken maintained his deadpan.

"There's a reason why when it comes to masturbation, men use porn and women use vibrators. Men are wired to crave sympathetic arousal— to feel another's pleasure. So they'll watch a woman coming on a screen because that's the nutrient they are missing."

Ken explained that most guys felt empty after masturbating because porn delivered dopamine without the oxytocin of a real intimate experience. Porn was empty calories.

"How many of you lost interest in porn when you started OMing?" Ken asked.

Almost every guy raised his hand, including me. Before my How To OM class, I probably watched porn three to five times per week, regardless of how much actual sex I was having. I had only watched porn once in the four months since, and only because I thought it was weird that I had gone so long without it. Even then, I couldn't really get into it. It felt weird to sit in front of a screen watching other people have sex.

Ken said that once a guy fills in his oxytocin deficit, porn doesn't do much for him anymore. He referenced a study done on rats where isolated rats would choose cocaine over food or water, effectively killing themselves in pursuit of pleasure. But when the same rats were placed in happy communal environments, they lost interest in the cocaine. That's why addiction recovery programs emphasized community— connection was the antidote to self-destructive pleasure-seeking.

"Women, on the other hand, often experience too much sympathetic arousal," Ken said. "Sex becomes all about what the man desires because the woman can't feel her own."

Every woman nodded her head.

"Women use vibrators because they need more direct stimulation," Ken said. "One great thing about OM is that it gives both parties the nutrients they are usually lacking—women get direct stimulation and men get sympathetic arousal."

Both men and women made affirmative sounds.

If a good stroker was like a precision sharpshooter, a good strokee was like a huge target. A highly skilled strokee could essentially paint the bullseye around the arrow making any stroke an orgasmic one.

This put the power back in the strokee's hands. A woman who mastered getting off never had to feel victim to a bad stroker. Her experience was independent of her partner's skill, or even intention. She was in full control of her own Orgasm.

But "getting off" wasn't about enduring an unskilled stroker, Ken explained. By getting off, a strokee could influence what the stroker did. Getting off made it clearer to the stroker what would feel good versus not. You got the stroker to stroke you the way you wanted, because you made it feel so good for him to do so.

In this way, an advanced strokee could control an entire OM from her back. By getting off on what you want *before* getting it, you influence the other person to give it to you.

"Like the Law of Attraction!" Lila exclaimed.

"Sure," said Ken.

Ken had us pair up for a guided OM. He let us OM as normal for a few minutes. Then he instructed all the women to "stop getting off."

"Don't think too hard about what that means, just do it," Ken said.

The moaning that was filling the room stopped. The clit I was stroking suddenly had almost no sensation. There was no feedback. And nothing I tried seemed to bring it back.

The first step to getting off is acceptance, Ken explained. Sensations themselves are neutral. Whether we experience them as pleasure or pain depends on how we react to them. Most pain is a result of resisting or contracting against an experience. Pain that persists long enough causes us to numb out.

Couples often hired Ken to help save their sex lives. Ken said that when a couple's sex life tanked the problem wasn't usually technique, it was resentment. Resentment means you're stuck in past emotions, re-experiencing an old sentiment. It makes one unwilling to accept the present moment and any sensation that comes with it.

"That's why when a woman is shut down, nothing you can do is right," he said.

Affirmative male groans filled the room.

Ken then instructed the strokees to turn the lights back on.

"Whatever stroke you're getting, get off on it," he said. "Even if your stroker is off the mark, see if you can *make him right*."

All the sensation returned to my finger and my body. My strokee joined the moans in the room and I felt flushed. Her heightened sensation gave me clear feedback on how exactly she wanted to be touched, which made me more confident, which made her get off more, which made it even easier to read her body. It was a positive feedback loop.

There really was something to this.

"So what did we learn?" Ken said after the OM closed.

All students shared the huge effect that the strokee's openness had on the OM. A lot of the guys had their egos shattered realizing their "ecstatic OMs" had a lot less to do with their skills and more to do with the woman's ability to be open. Many women were gloating at the realization of the power they had.

"Good," said Ken.

We had a ten minute break between class sections.

I went to the snack table and filled a glass of water as something to do. I still felt shy around the intense CP students, but I wasn't as shut down as before.

I looked up and saw Bonnie was staring at me as if waiting for me to look at her. Jane was next to her preparing a snack tray.

"How are you RU-wan?" Bonnie said.

"Good," I said.

Bonnie giggled.

"Ruwan," Jane said, "you remind me a lot of how Ken Blackman was when he came to OneTaste."

"Cool."

"She's saying you're awkward," Bonnie said.

"Oh."

I tried to stop being awkward by joining a conversation. Daniel was chatting with a granola hippie chick from Boulder.

"So when you say 'Fourth Dimension'," he said, "what exactly are you referring to?"

"The Third Dimension is the one our bodies live in," she said. "The Fourth Dimension is one higher than this one. We can't see it, but we can feel it. And when we make changes over there, it makes changes over here."

"So it's like the ant on a piece of paper," he said. "He lives in a two-dimensional world, so it all looks flat to him. He can't tell if the paper itself is bent or twisted. But *we* can see it from the third dimension. We can fold the paper and poke a hole through it. But to the ant it looks like magic."

"Yes, now you get it! Magic is when you do stuff in the Fourth Dimension that you can see in the Third Dimension. It doesn't make sense if you're only in your cortex. But it makes perfect sense if you can feel it with your limbic system."

"Are you guys talking about the 'getting off' stuff?" I interjected. "I figured it could be explained by mirror neurons or something. I wouldn't call it 'magic'."

"Magic..." Daniel chuckled. "Clarke's Third: *Any sufficiently advanced technology is indistinguishable from magic,*" he said.

"What's that?" I asked.

"Arthur C. Clarke was a science fiction writer. He wrote these three laws about futurism. For instance, the First Law is: *Any time a distinguished scientist says something is possible he's most certainly right. Any time a distinguished scientist says something is impossible, he's almost certainly wrong.*"

"So 'magic' is anything that can't yet be explained?" I said.

"Yes, Ruwan," said the hippie chick. She seemed annoyed.

"It's like the thing between Power and Force," Daniel said. "Two six-hundred-pound silverback gorillas will travel miles through the jungle to find each other and fight, ripping each other to shreds and tearing down everything in their path, just for a chance to mate with a female. That's a huge amount of Force. But the female, she just sits there. She will just emit an invisible pheromone that makes those two male gorillas do all that work for her. That's Power."

The hippie chick smiled and nodded.

"Wait, is this how you get women?" I asked. "It seems like you do nothing... and then women just run to you."

"I suppose the only thing I *do* to women is drink them in. I drink in their beauty, their essence. I don't think about what I can get from them. I'm just appreciative to be able to witness them in their beauty..."

The two of them were holding eye contact and smiling. I realized I was interrupting their flirtation. I started walking back to the classroom area.

OneTaste attracted a lot of magical thinkers. Many reported seemingly paranormal occurrences such as randomly thinking of someone, then receiving a text from them moments later. I wrote most of it off as confirmation bias. Same with the "energetic fields" people claimed to have felt. I figured that was something like a hypnotic suggestion—you could convince someone to feel anything under the right conditions.

But my brain was getting tired trying to find rational explanations for everything. I was starting to envy people like Lila who would just explain everything as "magic" and leave it at that. Even if false, "magic" was a more workable mental model.

Just a few months ago, the idea that a stroker could intuit the exact stroke a strokee desired would have seemed supernatural. But now it was totally normal to me—it was all just sensory feedback. A man getting an erection from a woman thinking of sex, or a woman controlling the stroke by getting off, also would have seemed crazy before. But I had just experienced it. Maybe none of this was supernatural. Rather, conventional assumptions were *sub*natural.

It would be easier if I stopped questioning everything. Life would be more fun. But on the other hand, magical thinking was a slippery slope. Without some skepticism, I might detach from reality.

Something stopped me mid-step. I felt a tingly sensation on the back left side of my head. I turned in that direction and saw a woman staring at me from across the room.

It was the Miss Scarlett-looking woman who was wearing the red dress on opening night. She was wearing a pastel hoodie with the zipper halfway down. I walked towards her.

"I felt that..." I said. "How... what did you do?"

"Thank you for noticing," she said in a resonating contralto voice.

"But how did you do that??"

"I have my ways, habibi."

"Can you teach me how to do that?"

She batted eyelashes so long I felt a breeze. "You don't need to know how to do that, habibi. You can do other things."

"No, I definitely want to learn how to do that..."

"Seats in one minute!" called Sergio.

She walked to her seat without saying another word. I closed my jaw.

Daniel sat next to me in the classroom. I wanted to ask him so many things. But the next class section was starting.

"Hey, what's the second law?" I whispered.

"Hm?"

"You said this Clarke guy had three laws. You said the first and third. What's second?"

"Oh Clarke's Second Law," he said. "*The only way to discover the limits of the possible is to venture past them into the impossible.*"

I WANTED TO VENTURE into the impossible.

I had already spent money I didn't have. I already uprooted my life and moved into the Morellino. *Sunk-Cost Fallacy* or not, I had less to lose and more to gain by applying faith from this point on. After all, if I kept questioning everything, I would never know what I was missing.

Many OMers repeated Brene Brown's line, "You can't selectively numb." It was the perfect slogan for a community based on emotional vulnerability, connection, and heightened sexual states. OneTaste practices even proved the quote beyond Dr. Brown's intention— that by being emotionally open to everything, you could feel more sexual pleasure.

Truth carries the most sensation.

OneTaste made it seem safe to be open to everything. From the first TurnON event, you were shown that it was safe to be emotionally vulnerable. Deeper in the OM Community, you were shown that it was safe to believe in unprovable things. Over time and in stages, you continuously keep letting down your filters, your protection mechanisms. And you were rewarded for doing so.

"Our approval determines our experience," Rob said. "Sensation is neither good nor bad. It just is."

No one stuck around after class that day. We were three months into the Coaching Program. Most students were rushing to pre-planned extracurriculars: threesomes, foursomes, moresomes. Some students had planned an excursion to a BDSM dungeon.

Somehow, Lila and I were the only ones left standing on the sidewalk. We had gotten much closer the last few months. She had recently expressed her desire to have intercourse. I kept brushing her off.

"So what do you want to do tonight?" she asked.

"I don't know. Do you know who's going to the BDSM thing?"

"Ruwan, what is *your* desire?"

"Well honestly, any group activity feels overwhelming. But I feel I need to be pushing my edge. I'm not going to be in OneTaste forever. I need to be taking advantage of these opportunities."

Lila nodded. "You have serious *FOMO*."

"What's FOMO?"

"Fear Of Missing Out."

"Oh."

"Well I have the antidote to FOMO," she said and grabbed my shoulders. "It's this: *The party is where you are.*"

We were down the block at the corner of Hudson Street. A taxi drove by honking. The sun was setting. The smell of warm garbage bags was being replaced with the smell of cold ones.

"But it's not," I said. "We're just standing here."

Lila pushed me over a few feet then pointed down. On the sidewalk under me there was some spray-painted street art that read, *'STAND HERE TO ACTIVATE MAGICAL POWERS'.*

Lila released me and pirouetted into a ballet position. Her perspective was contagious.

In OneTaste, there was a concept known as "going on someone's ride." It usually happened when someone was getting off so well that you couldn't help but adopt their emotional reality.

I was powerless.

We ended up doing cartwheels down the street. We climbed up scaffolding and hung down from our legs. We hopped up on fire hydrants and practiced one-legged yoga poses. Another taxi honked while it drove by and the driver smiled and yelled something at us.

Lila was someone who could have fun anywhere doing anything. I wondered why, of all people, she'd choose to spend her Saturday night with me.

It was eventually too cold for hijinks, so we walked arm in arm down to the hotel. She nuzzled into me. These moments of affection with her felt the most uncomfortable. Sometimes sex is the least vulnerable thing you can do with someone.

At the hotel room, Lila lit a Santeria candle that she pulled from her giant black purse and started running a bath. She asked me to check the temperature. I guessed that meant she wanted me to join her. She undressed and began doing something in the mirror. I laid down in the tub.

The warm water just covered my ears. All I could hear was the droning of liquid hitting liquid. I closed my eyes. I couldn't tell where my body ended and the water began. It felt very womb-like. I heard a voice.

You don't have to attract every woman.

I opened my eyes. No one was there. My ears were still submerged. This was my first clear auditory hallucination. It wouldn't be the last.

I realized so much of my life was driven by the feeling of inadequacy. I always felt I needed to accomplish more, experience more, be more. Something in me relaxed. The bliss of being. Of just existing Now without trying to be anywhere else. This was what magic was about. This was what Orgasm was about. Perpetual Orgasm. The unending bliss of being. Immersing me. Consuming me. Perhaps Enlightenment was nothing more than getting off on every moment.

I sat up and coughed water out of my nose.

Lila had been sitting between my legs and stroking me. I didn't notice her enter the tub. She turned around and leaned into me.

After the bath we went to bed. It was romantic. Hypnotic. A melting kind of foreplay where the boundaries were blurred. But the moment I realized she wanted intercourse and I felt my anxiety return.

I could get off on this too, I thought. I could follow the stroke, stroke for my pleasure. I slid on a condom and entered her. Immediately I began to lose sensation.

Lila took my hand and put it on her heart.

"Penetrate me here," she said, "with your *energy*."

Energetic Penetration was a common concept in OM. It was the idea that felt sensation is created by attention more than physical stimulus. I tried applying everything I had learned so far. I got off. I stroked for my pleasure. And as in an OM, we were visited by *the* Orgasm.

I was cured.

I fell into a deep sleep. I dreamt that I was kidnapped, hogtied, and thrown in a van with a bag over my head. I was brought to a warehouse, strapped to a chair, and forced to receive fellatio. My head was uncovered and I saw my ropes were being held by the Exec Team. Nicole was kneeling in front of me and laughing.

I laughed too.

JANE HAD SOME BAD news.

"We weren't able to get Penthouse B," she said at the next House Meeting. "Some man and his son moved in."

"I met him in the elevator," Bonnie said. "He's nice. I told him about OM."

"Isn't he like a rapper or something?" Tanisha said.

"Yeah, Fatman Scoop!" said Wallace.

"You know him?"

"Yeah Fatman Scoop," added Daniel. "The undisputed voice of the club."

Wallace started singing, "You got a twenty dollar bill, get your hands up! You got a ten dollar bill, get your hands up!"

Daniel joined in. "Single ladies, I can't hear ya, single ladies, make noise!"

"Ugh, of course the Canadians know who this guy is," said Tanisha.

"All the chickenheads be quiet! All the chickenheads..."

"ENOUGH!" snapped Rachel. "Jane, continue."

"Well anyway," Jane said. "I did get us another apartment. It's on the second floor, apartment 2E. Ruwan and Lila, I'm going to put you two down there. Bonnie, you're also going downstairs with... Rach, did you tell her already?"

"We're moving Liz to New York to run production," Rachel said.

"Oh my god!" Bonnie squealed with joy. Lila and Tanisha celebrated too.

Liz was Bonnie's longtime girlfriend. For reasons unknown, OneTaste had split up the couple. It seemed that they were being put back together as a reward for Bonnie's recent good work.

"We're entering a new peak," Rachel said. "I will be spending more time on the West Coast to help them expand. We expect you all to take more responsibility holding the Orgasm in New York."

Jane delegated certain house responsibilities to us. Wallace was put in charge of setting up morning practice. Lila was in charge of organizing the kitchen. I volunteered to become the grocery-orderer.

"At OneTaste, we fill what's empty and empty what's full," Rachel said. "All of you came here as *Party-Goers*. That was great for awhile. But if you want to keep growing you need to become *Party-Throwers*. We're a third of the way through the Coaching Program now. You're going to see over the next couple months, some of you will step up, empty out, and receive more. Others will keep consuming and grow fat, stagnant and resentful. Service is the best way to increase your Havingness."

On that note, there was a great opportunity for all of us to increase our Havingness. We were invited to serve as 'Back of House' staff for the next How to OM class.

"It's good training for all of you to become space-holders," Jane said.

"It's time for you to transition from Children to Adults," Rachel said. "There are three types of people in the world: Children, Adults, and Parents. You all have come here as Children. Children get to play and don't have to take responsibility because someone takes care of them. Adults take responsibility for themselves. Parents take care of the Children."

Like much of the lingo at OneTaste, this was a bastardization of another's terminology, in this case Dr. Eric Berne's Transactional Analysis—a mode of therapy that influenced many early self-help teachers. Though Rachel was using the terms inaccurately, she was pointing to the crux of how consensual cult brainwashing worked:

OneTaste had all its members gradually return to a state of childlike innocence. This began the moment we chose to be vulnerable at a TurnON event. Each time we chose to be more vulnerable, to trust in spite of rational "adult" fears, the more childlike we became.

This was part of the high. Once you came to believe that the Orgasm would take care of you, you could think less and feel more. It was like being on a cruise ship where you could do whatever you wanted because you knew someone else was making sure it reached the destination. You no longer had to worry about the outside world. You could play. You could be the Fool. You could experience "magic."

This was how so many were able to have profound healing experiences so quickly in OneTaste. By dropping your guard, you became hyper-receptive to change. You can let go of protection mechanisms. As Daniel said of hot yoga, you become moldable.

But there's a reason most adults aren't so emotionally vulnerable. There's a reason most hold on to their worries and close off to new ideas. Being receptive to healing means being receptive to change in other ways.

You can't selectively numb.

"Every time you evolve from one stage to the next, parts of your identity come into question," Rachel continued. "Over the next few months, you all are going to have to transition to Adults. Some of you won't be willing to because it's too hard, and you'll get stuck. But trust me, it's way worse to get stuck."

THE NEXT HOW TO OM class was held at the new OneTaste event space in Soho.

From now on there would be a How To OM class every month, with fifty or more students. I had been OMing now for four months. I watched the new students walk in and remembered how awkward I felt back in December.

Rachel taught the class. Nicole was phasing out of teaching intro-level classes. Rachel and other Exec Team members were going to replace her. This meant there was a lot of growth opportunity for others.

Despite being much smaller, darker, and feistier than Nicole, Rachel basically became Nicole as she stroked the room. She spoke in Nicole's stop-and-start cadence. She had the same quality of piercing insight and spontaneous one-liners.

"Women want sex just as much as men," Rachel said, "they just don't want what's on the menu."

Affirmative female sounds came from the audience.

I started writing down the line when Sergio slapped my arm.

"You're not here to take the class!" he said.

I didn't see what the big deal was. There were over twenty staffers for about fifty students. There was nothing left to set up. The staff simply sat in the back with their legs spread.

Like a restaurant, OneTaste split its event staff into 'Front of House' (FOH) and 'Back of House' (BOH). Front of House were those that directly interfaced with students—teachers and salespeople. Back of House were those in charge of production.

"The purpose of Back of House is to ground the room," Sergio said during the first break. "It teaches you how to hold people's nervous systems."

"When the sensation gets hella high, people are going to look for ways to check out," Jane added. "You'll see that people will start getting up to use the bathroom around the same time. They don't really need to go. They are just trying to dissipate the energy."

"So as BOH, we ground the room by keeping our attention on the students. If we check out, they will check out," Sergio said. "This is especially important during the demo."

As Rachel was promoted into Nicole's place, Bonnie was promoted to Rachel's place. That meant that for the demo, Rachel would be stroking Bonnie.

At the deepest level, OneTaste hierarchy resembled something of a series of mother-daughter relationships. Nicole stroked Rachel— both physically in demos, and verbally through special training. Rachel stroked Bonnie in the same way. It was a chain of succession where each master groomed, and stroked, her replacement.

As Bonnie removed her bathrobe and got on the table, we could see many of the students begin to fidget and look around.

"GROUND THE ROOM!" read a text to our BOH group message thread.

To 'ground' meant to give space for your sensations to settle down, as in grounding an electrical circuit. The more deeply you feel your feelings, the less you feel the need to fidget. That part I understood. But I didn't get how us being grounded would affect the experience of the students.

The OneTaste staffers slid to the fronts of their chairs, planted their feet on the ground, spread their legs, and breathed slowly. Us CP6 students tried to imitate.

Oddly enough, the class seemed to settle down. The BOH staff looked at each other and smiled and nodded.

"I'm taking her up now..." Rachel said.

"Tingling in my chest!"

"Flushing in my cheeks!"

"Buzzing in my genitals!" called out BOH members.

As in my first demo, Rachel had encouraged the class to call our Frames of what they were feeling. The first frames all came from the BOH. But soon most of the class followed the lead.

This was the deeper reason why there were so many BOH staffers: *Social Proof*. The How to OM class was an indoctrination event. Three or four people calling out frames could easily be written off as crazy by a group of fifty. But twenty confident staffers made their reality the dominant one. Even a bold skeptic would have to question himself against such a group.

"I'm going to bring her down now," Rachel said.

Bonnie made the same kind of guttural moans that Rachel did when she was the model. The OneTaste lineage was more than a passing of knowledge and skills. It was the replication of the same character in a different body.

"Look at her glowing face," Rachel said after Bonnie sat up. "That's the Orgasm mask. It's like the pregnancy mask, but sexier. Makeup was designed to replicate a woman in orgasm: flushed cheeks, red lips, darkened eyelids."

Affirmative sounds came from the audience.

I SNUCK OUT DURING the lunch break.

I got another headache during the demo. I didn't know why that kept happening.

The OneTaste event space in Soho was walking distance from my old apartment, so I decided to visit Roger and Brad. It had been awhile.

They were happy to see me. We hadn't spoken much since I moved out. They passed me a joint and I took it. I had been abstaining from substances the last couple months, but it was nice to feel like one of the boys again.

There was a small tattoo I had wanted to get from a shop down the block. I put it off before because I didn't have much cash, but now that I was a couple thousand dollars in debt, it seemed silly to worry about another hundred fifty bucks. Roger came with me. Afterward we went to a Mexican place for lunch.

I was relieved he didn't ask me about my life. The things I had been experiencing would be unrelatable to him. Besides, he had something else on his mind.

"So I've been seeing these two girls," he said. "They both started out casual, but then you know, the timebombs went off. The thing is they are each great in their own ways. I really like them both. I don't know how to choose, and I don't want to lie either."

"That's easy Rog, you just need to express your true desire."

"Explain."

"You like them both right? Tell them the truth about the situation. Then get off, I mean, accept and appreciate whatever their response is. You might be surprised that their desires match with yours."

"Dude." Roger sighed and put his burrito down. "You're the only one of my friends who I can talk about this stuff with... but the problem is you're fucking crazy."

"No I'm not. You're crazy."

"C'mon bro. If we went around and asked all the people in this restaurant what they thought of this, they would say that what you just said is batshit. Normal people don't do this weird free love stuff. Therefore, you're crazy."

"There's this Jewish parable," I said. "A man lives in a village where the water was poisoned. Everyone drinks the water but him. They all start speaking in this weird language and doing things that don't make sense to him. He tries to snap them out of it, but they can't understand him. They think he's the crazy one. After many days of being frustrated and lonely, he realizes there's one solution to the problem... so he drinks the water."

"Right."

"So drink my water, Rog."

"What? No you're the crazy one."

"Drink it."

"No, the rest of the world and I are the town. You're the one whose…"

"Drink my water!"

"We're the town! How did you turn that around?"

"DRINK IT!"

I slammed the table a little too hard. The cashier and all the other patrons looked at us then looked away when they saw my manic grin. Maybe I did need to tone it down.

After lunch I realized Roger and I were in different realities. Mine was evolving. His was staying the same. Even though he was still a good friend with good intentions, he just couldn't understand the context of my experiences. How do you explain ultra-high definition to a blind man?

"Wanna play ping pong tomorrow?" he asked.

"No, I have some OMs scheduled."

"Okay. Want to go to the gym on Monday?"

"No, I have OM Circle then TurnON."

"Has your whole life become a walking clitoris?"

I shrugged. We did our special handshake. It felt juvenile. I had a feeling I wasn't going to see him again for a long while.

"One day you're going to look back at this time and see how crazy your life was," he said.

"I don't think so. This is what I do now."

I RETURNED TO THE class just as they were finishing the lab portion.

The class shared Frames, then Rachel did a sales pitch for the next Coaching Program, CP7, which would be in San Francisco.

"And that's an OM class!" Rachel said. "Okay so we're going to put on a little music, mingle a little, and then we can all go home."

The students stood up and floated around the room. A couple men looked confused, but most everyone else was wearing a bright orgasmic expression.

"What did you do to your arm?" Jane said when she saw me.

"I got a tattoo."

She smirked. Jane had a different kind of smirk for every occasion.

After about twenty minutes Rachel signaled the end to the socializing. The staff began to usher the students out.

"You don't have to go home, but you can't stay here!" Sergio said.

Some people laughed.

The team gathered around for the debrief. Rachel motioned for me to sit next to her on the couch. She slouched into the couch and put her legs straight up in the air. She peeled off her white jeans and threw them. She wasn't wearing underwear.

"Das betta. Those things are tight!"

Someone handed her a pair of sweatpants and she put them on. Then she looked at me as if she forgot I was there.

"What happened to your arm?"

"I got a tattoo."

Rachel squinted and scanned me like a metal detector. Then she burst out laughing.

"Ruwan is stoned! Look at him, he's so stoned!"

I smiled uncomfortably. Substance use was highly frowned upon in OneTaste. I expected her to scold me. Instead she patted me on the leg then turned back to the rest of the staff.

"So that was a huge success," Rachel said. "How much money we make?"

"Twenty-two thousand in revenue," Jane said.

"And we planted a few more CP seeds," Bonnie added.

"Wonderful," Rachel said. "For those of you who are new to Back of House, something that you will learn is that sales is the best marker for how well we held the room. When people feel good, they buy."

Every event was a sales event, Rachel explained. Whether it was an intro event, class, or even community hangout, any gathering was a chance to bring people deeper into Orgasm. Money was a measure for how much Orgasm we gave them.

"Okay, I want to give out some strokes," Rachel said. "Wallace, I want to tell you that I noticed how you really showed up today. Many new BOH have trouble staying grounded, but you were solid the whole day."

Wallace glowed. I felt bad that I didn't stay. I'd later learn this was a technique known as a *Bankshot*. Rachel gave out a few more strokes and said something about the Orgasm entering a new peak.

"And that's a debrief!" Rachel said, then switched into a baby voice. It was a thing that she did when she was in a good mood and no students were around. "Janey, whaz for dinna? I hungwy!"

"I ordewed you sushi Rach-O"

"Thank you Janey. You my friend!"

We packed up the space. With all the hands we were done in a few minutes. I sat on the couch and tried to stop being stoned. Lila curled up next to me.

"What's your tattoo of?" she asked.

"It's a game theory notation."

"What's game theory?"

"It's mathematical decision making. This game is called Prisoner's Dilemma."

"How do you play?"

"It's not that kind of game... A game is any situation where the outcomes for the players are affected by each other's decisions."

I explained Prisoner's Dilemma. Lila's cat eyes were glazed over like that of a porcelain doll.

"Therefore," I concluded, "Prisoner's Dilemma represents morality in society. It's not that people are inherently good or evil, it's that we're in a game that makes us so."

"I wouldn't rat on you," Lila said.

"Well, you need to look at the incentives because..."

"Would you rat on me?"

"That's not the point. The point is..."

"I don't think you would rat on me either. You're a lot sweeter than you try to come off."

"But..."

Lila meowed and snuggled her face into my armpit. I put my arm around her. Okay, I guess game theory really isn't that interesting.

Abby appeared on the other side of the couch.

"Hey Ru," Abby said, "I'll be at the Morellino for Morning Practice on Monday. Would you like to be my Two?"

"Sure."

"Can I be your One?" Lila asked.

"I already have a One."

"What about later?"

"Um, I don't know. I have some OMs scheduled for the afternoon downtown."

Lila frowned. Abby smiled. Lila made an annoyed sound and stormed off. A moment later, Abby also left without acknowledging me further.

I had no idea what just happened.

Jane had been listening from the sales table. She kept typing on her laptop but directed her smirk at me.

"Something you'll notice, Ruwan," Jane said, "is that the women in the OM community sometimes act like men."

"What do you mean?"

"Women who OM compete over who has the biggest TurnON the way boys compete over who has the biggest muscles. Every strokee wants to prove that she has the most lit up pussy."

"So..."

"So if you don't want to stroke a woman, she feels... the female version of emasculated."

"I didn't say I wouldn't, I'm just fully booked tomorrow."

"Doesn't matter."

"And there's way more strokees than strokers so obviously some women won't get stroked."

"Doesn't matter."

"So what am I supposed to do?"

"Nothing. It's not about you. You're not even a player in this game. You're just the soccer ball," Jane said. "Even though you're new to OMing, you're already one of the more experienced strokers in New York. So that puts you in high demand."

Rachel came out of the back office with her nose in her phone and a big smile on her face.

"Ruwan," she said without looking up. "There's someone special I want you to OM with tomorrow."

"Oh, I already have some OMs scheduled."

"Reschedule them. This is important. I'd really appreciate it."

"Okay."

RACHEL BROUGHT THE SPECIAL someone to PHC the next day.

"This is Cheryl," Rachel said. "Cheryl, meet Ruwan."

"Hi," she said.

Cheryl was about five three with toned arms and shoulders. She wore yoga attire and a timid expression.

"After you OM with Ruwan, come see me in PHA," Rachel said to her. Rachel squeezed my biceps and whispered, "Use heavy pressure with this one."

This was the first time Rachel arranged for me to stroke 'a special someone.' This would not be the last. Later I'd realize this was sort of a tryout.

Rachel smiled and looked around PHC. It had been raining all day and the apartment was full of grey light.

"It feels sleepy in here," Rachel said.

No one disagreed. The house was empty except for Wallace and me. He was sitting in a lotus position on the couch, reading a book called *The Way of the Superior Man*.

I had the nest set up upstairs. She got in fully clothed. I waited.

"Oh yes, I need to take these off, don't I?" Cheryl said. She put her hands over her face and sighed. "I can-NOT believe I'm doing this. This is so, SO crazy." She slowly rolled off her tights.

Her thighs were firm. They trembled as I applied grounding to them. I seemed to be trembling too.

I did the lube stroke. Her clitoris inflated against my finger. And just as quickly, my anatomy inflated against her thigh.

"If you get an erection during an OM it means your partner is thinking about sex," Ken had said.

I was technically stroking her, but I was not the one choosing the stroke. My finger moved on its own and I felt every stroke in my body. Cheryl's body stiffened. So did I. She held her breath for what seemed like a long time, then around the two-minute mark rattled out a cry that shook the windows and made my taint spasm. She caught her breath and proceeded to weep. It was a quiet, slow sob like air escaping from a tire.

When the timer rang I remembered to exhale.

"Well, I haven't done *that* in a while," she said.

As she dressed, I flipped my erection under my waistband. I was both surprised and relieved to see no fluids had escaped.

I walked her over to Rachel in PHA. Cheryl was a totally different woman. Her posture was relaxed and her face colorful.

"Oh you look *much* better," Rachel said.

She motioned for Cheryl to come in. Rachel winked at me with both eyes as she closed the door.

Back in PHC, Wallace wasn't reading anymore. His eyes and grin were wide.

"That sounded like a helluva OM."

"It was a lot of sensation," I said.

"Yeah, I could feel it."

His book was still open, but face down on his lap at an odd angle.

IF THERE WAS ANYONE who had mastered "getting off" it was Wallace.

Every day Wallace would do what he called "vulnerability challenges." This usually took the form of doing something socially taboo. He'd approach people on the street and talk to them about intimate things. He'd go into stores and ask for free stuff.

Sometimes it resembled the 'Cold Approaching' that pickup guys did, but with a very different intention. The goal wasn't to get phone numbers, or even to get anyone to like him. It was simply to raise the sensation.

You could always tell when he was getting off because his ears would turn bright red. And he was so committed to feeling his feelings that the other party would eventually open up too.

Often a woman would drop her jaw at the outlandish thing he said. But a moment later she'd relax and laugh when she felt how open he was. Many bodega owners gave him free coffee while shaking their heads. It was impossible to get mad at a guy who got off that hard.

Wallace had discovered and mastered a piece of OneTaste's hidden curriculum. One-Taste had its official curriculum that was taught in their classes. But there were also hidden skills that could only be learned indirectly. If you were in the OM community long enough, you would hear experienced OMers mention these terms from time to time. And like a baby learning its first language, you eventually figured out what they meant via context.

One of these skills was *Bottoming*.

The term originally came from the gay community, meaning to be on the "receiving end." But in OneTaste, *to Bottom* was to get off so well from the passive position that the other party can't help doing what you wanted because you've made it feel so good.

Most people only understood power dynamics from the active position, *Topping*. To Top someone was to dominate them, to override their will. Topping was the masculine way to influence people. It required action, like stroking. Topping was Force. But Bottoming was Power.

Going out with the Canadians had become a daily routine. Right after morning practice I'd squeeze my entire workday into about an hour. Around eleven Daniel would be ready, and we'd hit the town.

Daniel always decided our general itinerary, though I insisted he keep where we ate under two dollar signs.

Wallace on the other hand, started getting off on his frugality. When we entered a restaurant, he'd eat directly off the plates of people who had just left. The serving staff never knew what to do but stare at him. His ears would be bright red.

After lunch we'd usually claim a back table at Daniel's favorite coffee shop, *La Colombe*. We'd practice generative trance as Theresa taught us, sometimes going so deep into hypnotic bliss that we'd each begin to cry. Often a crowd of curious coffee-drinkers would gather and watch us from a safe distance.

"What do you think they're doing?"

"Maybe that's like a meditation thing."

"Maybe they're on drugs."

At some point we'd snap out of it and talk to them. Some people would be thrown off guard and share random vulnerable details back at us. Wallace got a few people to attend TurnON events that way. When we weren't trancing, we'd philosophize.

Periodically throughout the day, each of us would peel off for a scheduled OM. As compared with other major OneTaste cities, New York had a reputation of having generally bad strokers. Many women, especially Sister Goddesses, complained about New York men being too "in their heads." Combined with the physical shortage of men in the New York OM Community, any halfway-decent stroker became super high in demand.

On top of this, the Sister Goddesses had a message board where they rated and reviewed different strokers. If you got a good review, your number was passed around and you consistently got new requests to OM.

Orgasmic Meditation attracted all kinds of women. Just as interesting as discovering what was inside different women's pants, was seeing inside all the different homes. My weekly OM schedule took me to every part of New York City. I would go from a Columbia professor's university housing to bartender's subsidized apartment in Spanish Harlem. I would stroke a trust fund heiress in a West Village mansion, then hop on the crosstown bus to an actress's shared room in Alphabet City.

Every woman's Orgasm was different as every woman's home was different. Both seemed to reflect a unique energetic signature. Every woman had her specific "flavor" or "style" of get off. Like a sommelier or a coffee snob, I was pretty sure I could recognize these subtle notes. To others, it was even more clear.

"Do you spend time with Sister Goddess Xena?" a woman asked me after an OM.

"We used to hang out a bit, yes."

"I knew it. I can feel her energy on you."

Naturally, many of these OMs developed into Makeouts.

This of course, could mean anything. For me, that usually meant stopping before intercourse. I decided to only move to penetration when I really felt it. I finally realized what was a ridiculous thing it was to take Viagra in order to "perform." For if my body didn't want to have sex, why was I doing it?

Most men live in sexual scarcity. They pursue sex not for pleasure, but as proof that they are worthy individuals. To "stroke for my pleasure" then, meant maximizing sensation, not conforming to expectation. I began sharing about my ED issues.

Every woman received it well. Many said they were happy to know not to take it personally. Each time I shared, it was as if a layer of numbness was removed. The shame slowly was replaced by more feeling. Vulnerability is the opposite of shame. *Truth carries the most sensation.* And taking intercourse off the table, made the experiences more present and less pressured for both of us.

So I spent a lot of time on my back.

Getting off is a lot easier when you physically do nothing. One only has so much attention. Less attention spent on doing meant more attention for feeling. Oral sex, both giving and receiving, became another meditative practice.

When I reciprocated, it no longer felt transactional. In the giving position, I stroked for my pleasure. In the receiving position, focused on getting off— which made it easier for the woman to stroke for her pleasure.

OneTaste presented a different kind of sexual economics where everyone behaved in their own interests and somehow was a net benefit to all. It was a solution to the Prisoner's Dilemma.

Nicole always said, "Desire co-creates." The idea was that when people are limbically connected, they tend to desire the same things in the same moments. But through getting off, one party could also direct the co-creation.

I began experimenting with this in my Makeouts. I'd try to get off on a specific desire before she touched me, then see if it influenced her behavior. A great thing about the OM community was that you could try covert things on each other and talk about it at the same time.

"Hey so what made you want to knead my thigh right now?" I'd ask.

"I don't know, it felt good," she'd say. "Like if I touch your belly, I don't feel much sensation. But if I touch your thigh, there's a lot of sensation."

This was the essence of Bottoming. Unlike Topping, you weren't imposing your will. Instead, you made it feel good for the other person to align their will with yours.

But that raised an ethical question: If you get someone to desire something that they previously didn't, are they still acting on free will?

I posed this question one afternoon to the Canadians at *La Colombe*. We all had to think about it. I knew Wallace was thinking hard because his ears lost all their redness.

"Well, if the two people are really connected, then both would genuinely want what was best for the other," Wallace said.

"Hmm so then if we could just get *everyone* connected, then there would be no conflict in the world, because everyone would want the same thing," I said. "I guess that's what OneTaste is doing, right? We keep recruiting people into this reality where everyone's desires get met."

"*Isn't it nice that we can all be in the same reality,*" Daniel said hypnotically. He was using an NLP technique from Theresa's class known as 'loaded presuppositions.'

"Hey stop trancing me!"

"*Yes, isn't it nice that we can all be connected,*" joined Wallace. His ears had regained their color.

We laughed. Their pupils were dilated. Mine were too. I forgot what we were talking about.

OMing changed men.

If you took a time lapse of a guy from when he began OMing, you'd see a similar progression month by month. He'd stand straighter. He'd make better eye contact. He'd speak more slowly. He'd greet you with a hug instead of a handshake.

His outward appearance would change as well. His wardrobe would improve. He'd pay more attention to grooming. He'd get a more stylish haircut.

Even Wallace, who refused to spend money on anything, did look a lot sharper. He had shaved his balding horseshoe and grew out a well-trimmed goatee. He looked less like a stingy programmer and more like a stingy night club owner.

As far as I knew, no one was getting explicit fashion instruction. All these changes seemed to happen organically. Perhaps learning to feel more made one naturally more sensitive to aesthetics— the way women tend to be.

My appearance had also changed. I replaced my everyday sweatpants with fitted clothes in matching neutral colors. I grew my hair long for the first time ever. No weightlifting and lots of yoga had made me skinny and lithe. I looked like the youth in the Fool card that Lila drew months ago. All these decisions were made independently, but somehow all carried the same quality.

Both inwardly and outwardly, I had become more feminine.

I wasn't sure if that was a net positive, but it had its benefits. The last month of feeling my feelings and "getting off" had been healing. I felt less anxious and more alive. I stopped worrying about my future and instead trusted the moment.

Nicole called this *bending the paper backwards*. She said that attempting to change yourself was like flattening out a folded piece of paper. It wasn't enough to just unfold it because the crease would still be there. To make it flat again, you must fold the crease in the opposite direction.

But just to be sure, I got my testosterone checked.

Last year I had it checked due to my erection issues. My levels were average. This time I was hoping that with all the recent sexual activity, my T levels would have increased.

It was the opposite: My testosterone levels had plummeted to the very bottom of the normal range.

I brought this up with the Canadians at our next hangout.

"Maybe it's too much time in the Feminine," Wallace said. "I've been wondering that too. At first, following desire all the time was energizing. But lately I've been getting lazy."

"That makes sense," Daniel said. "Testosterone goes up when men compete for sexual selection. If you get sex without working for it, then you don't really need to be competitive."

In many ways, OneTaste was exactly the social utopia I had dreamed of— a community where connection and resources were abundant, competition was obsolete, and the Prisoner's Dilemma had been overcome. But something seemed to be missing.

"Hey I have an idea," Daniel said. "We should start a Men's Group!"

"Yeah! A Men's Group!"

"It can be an alternative to all these pickup groups in New York," Daniel said. "We can show them how to connect with women through empathy instead of tricks."

"Yes! And we can do vulnerability challenges."

"Yeah!"

"And focus on the deeper purpose!"

"Yeah!"

"Let's put our dicks together!" said Wallace.

"What??"

"It's a vulnerability challenge."

Daniel and I shook our heads. Wallace grinned. His ears were bright red.

We planned out our structure for the Men's Group. We'd have weekly meetings. It would be open to both OMers and non-OMers alike. We could introduce the non-OMers to OM and earn commission from OneTaste. Maybe we could hold the events in the Morellino.

"This feels good," Wallace said. "I have to leave in a minute. I have a Makeout."

"With who? The Morrocan girl in Washington Heights?" Daniel asked.

"No."

"The French Sister Goddess in Soho?" I asked.

"No, it's with... a man. From CP," Wallace said with red ears.

He had always been bi-curious, he explained. But before he was afraid of "being gay," or that choosing to be with men meant he couldn't attract women. But now that he had an abundance of women, he didn't have that shame anymore. Being with women was no longer an edge. Being with a man felt way more vulnerable, way more... intense.

Daniel and I shrugged.

Wallace was part of a growing trend. After months of being surrounded by pussy, many guys in CP6 were beginning to explore with other men. Few were actually bisexual. It was more a way to show what a man you were.

Dr. Robert Sapolsky said that testosterone makes men want to compete for highest status. But what is considered "high status" depends on the given culture. In the real world, sex with lots of women is rare and therefore a status marker amongst men. But in OneTaste, that was commonplace.

Instead, the highest virtues was a willingness to enter discomfort. So straight males did so by exploring homosexuality. Like drunk girls on spring break, guys would makeout during class breaks with others cheering.

But ironically, the women ended up feeling left out.

"I'm all for men exploring with each other," Dr. Tanisha said one CP6 weekend. "But seriously, why are all these guys making out when there are all these unfucked women around??"

In a way, "playing gay" was the Collective Masculine in CP6 resisting the Devouring Feminine. They were creating a space where women couldn't go.

Later that evening I emailed Rachel about the Men's Group idea. I wasn't sure why I reported this to her, but it felt right.

She responded right away. "That's a great idea! But you need training to run a OneTaste Men's Group. I will talk to the Exec Team about it and get back to you."

I told her it wasn't a 'OneTaste' Men's Group. It was just a Men's Group, so we didn't need training. I was just letting her know.

She responded with, "You are ABSOLUTELY NOT AUTHORIZED to run a Men's Group yet! I said I will get back to you!"

That seemed like an excessive reaction.

We moved into the third apartment just before the next CP Immersion.

And by "we," I mean me and Sergio. The women weren't expected to move heavy objects, and the Canadians and Andrew somehow found a way to not be there.

Sergio and I were assembling the bed that I had brought when I moved in. It had been in the basement storage. I told Sergio about the idea to make a Men's Group and Rachel's weird response.

"Rachel has her reasons," Sergio said. "If she told you to wait, then you should wait."

"Isn't it better to ask for forgiveness than permission?" I said. I read that in a self-help book once.

Sergio frowned.

"The Masculine's role is to set the rails for the Feminine to send the energy through," he said.

Sergio was probably the most feminine straight guy I had ever met. He sang Alanis Morrissette in the shower. He spent his free time painting watercolors. One time I found him weeping because he read something about a baby elephant being separated from its mother. Jane often called him "a lesbian in a man's body." Sergio embraced that description. And in violation of everything my dating coach ever taught me about women only liking "masculine" men, Sergio got a ton of pussy.

He didn't Bottom in the sense of influencing others, but he had an extreme gentleness that put everyone around him at ease. This made him a good coach. He got me to cry for the first time in ten years in one of our sessions. I wouldn't have felt comfortable doing that with a manlier man.

But he was always burnt out. As the only man on the official New York staff, he did all the literal heavy lifting— setting up TurnONs, laundering towels, moving supplies to and from the storage unit. In addition to working for OneTaste, Sergio had a part time job as a morning janitor at Columbia University. I heard that OneTaste staff only got paid two grand a month— an unlivable wage in Manhattan, even with shared bedrooms. I wondered why he didn't ask for a raise.

I helped him hang up a painting. It made the tiny bedroom beautiful and bright. He painted it himself.

"Wow this is really good," I said.

Sergio was once a child prodigy in visual arts, he shared. His family had immigrated to New York from Colombia when he was little. He grew up poor. His father was an Episcopalian priest.

"My Dad always said, 'No matter what you do, don't become a priest. They make no money.'" Sergio chuckled.

Somehow his family was able to save enough to send their son to the top art academy in Florence.

"My specialty was frescoes," he said. "That's the one where you put plaster directly on the wall."

But Sergio proved to be too sensitive for the world of fine art. He got married and divorced before his final year. He fell into a period of depression. While back in New York, he attended a swinger's party in a BDSM dungeon. There were some women there who kept their clothes on and kept telling everyone about Orgasm. One of those women was Rachel.

"OneTaste saved me," he said.

He showed me a picture of himself from back then. He was probably forty pounds overweight, had a weird mullet haircut, and looked way older. Despite his fatigue, he did look a lot happier now.

"Have you ever thought of going back to art?" I asked.

"No. I serve the Orgasm now."

"But can't you serve the Orgasm by making frescoes?"

"You don't understand," he said. "If you knew what they've done for me... OneTaste took me in. That's why I'm grateful to be able to volunteer my time..."

"Wait, what?"

Sergio turned away and leveled the painting.

"You're telling me OneTaste doesn't pay you?? You work like a hundred hours a week for them."

"I'm doing service. It's *seva*. This is my path to God."

"But they could at least pay you something... You work this janitor job all morning, just so you can volunteer all night??"

"You don't understand," he said. His voice cracked with emotion.

He was right. I didn't understand. And there was no way I was going to get completely absorbed by the Feminine like him.

In many ways, OneTaste embodied what Jung called the *Devouring Mother*, the archetype of feminine authority that consumed its children's identities. Like flies to a carnivorous plant, men were allured by sex, got attached through healing, only to realize the same nectars were preventing their escape. It would be years before I realized this consciously. But already I was feeling my feet slipping out from under me.

I emailed Rachel that we were going to proceed with the Men's Group. She didn't respond. I figured that was a good sign.

ONE EVENING, WALLACE AND I were looking over the pantry.

I had embraced my role as the residence's grocery-orderer. All of us who had been given roles were taking them more seriously now.

"You should order much more granola," Wallace said.

"We have two boxes already."

"Yes, and I eat a lot of granola. It would be great if we had more." His ears were bright red.

"Uh, okay. I'll order more."

Rachel stormed in from the hallway.

"No! Wallace, no!" she said. "We're *NOT* doing this anymore in this house. Wallace, this stops now!"

Wallace looked down and didn't say anything.

"And Ruwan, you need to stop getting pushed around."

"I don't know what you're talking about," I said.

"I refuse to believe you're that dumb."

"Uhh..."

"You can play dumb with other people, but I don't buy it."

"Rachel, I really have no idea what you're talking about."

Rachel scanned me with piercing eyes. Then she softened her expression.

"You play at a very literal level of abstraction," she said. "This is why you don't get sarcasm. This is why you go along with other people's realities. What just happened is an example."

"What just happened? Is this about granola?"

"The fact that you asked that question shows how deeply you have been dominated."

"Uhh, I'm getting a little foggy here."

"When you feel foggy, it means we've hit a truth you don't want to see. Come see me in my room," Rachel said. She glared a dagger at Wallace then walked off.

Rachel shared the first bedroom in PHA with Bonnie. When I walked in, Bonnie was in her pajamas brushing her teeth. Rachel was standing in the middle of the room with her nose in her phone as if waiting for me.

"Hi Ruwan," she said without looking up.

"Hey."

Rachel continued texting for an uncomfortably long time. Bonnie smiled at me through a mouth full of toothpaste.

"Um, so you wanted to talk?" I said.

"Ruwan, I genuinely believe you have good intentions," Rachel said. "But you're naïve. We need to fix that before we send you out into the world. A leader needs awareness. Otherwise you will keep getting dominated by other men."

"You mean with the grocery order?"

"I told you to wait. Then you went ahead without me. I have a feeling that didn't come from you."

"The Men's Group? That did come from me," I said. "I wasn't trying to undermine you or anything. I just figured it couldn't hurt to get started…"

"You got excited," Bonnie said, still brushing her teeth. Rachel glared at her and she returned to the bathroom.

"I'm going to have Ken Blackman and the other men from the West Coast train you. And then you can do it right. You will lead the New York Men's Group with Sergio."

"But Wallace and Daniel…"

"Wallace and Daniel have a lot more work to do before they can lead men. They are jealous of you, so they are trying to control you and your Orgasm. And you're too innocent to see it."

I didn't think that was true. But I did seem to go along with other people's ideas. Maybe she was right.

"We're going to teach you to feel beneath the surface of things, Ruwan. You let your brain get in the way of your heart. You like game theory because it gives you a false sense of control. But it's an illusion. You're only looking at the finite games and not the infinite one."

Rachel pulled a book from her shelf. It was titled *Finite and Infinite Games* by James Carse.

"This is the copy that Nicole gave me. I want you to have it."

"Okay I'll read it."

"Good. Next time we're going to have to have a conversation about all the *women* who are trying to steal your Orgasm."

"Why would they do that?"

"That's for another night. "Come, I want to give you a hug."

Rachel opened her arms and I stepped in. Her tiny body completely enveloped mine. She put a small hand on the back of my heart. I suddenly felt emotional, as if she pressed a button back there. I didn't like that she could do that to me. But I loved it at the same time.

Later that night, I received a text from Bonnie.

"Hey I have an idea," she wrote.

"Yes?"

"We should totally have a Makeout."

Bonnie was attractive. But I had never gotten the vibe that she was at all into me. Also it seemed that she was more into women.

"Okay," I said.

"Great. But you need to get approval from the Ethics Board."

OneTaste permitted staff to sleep with students. But to ensure that there was no coercion or improper use of power, any non-OM sexual encounter between a staff member and a student had to be formally approved by the OneTaste Ethics Board.

The Ethics Board was Jane. Once upon a time it had as many as seven people on it, but it took too long to get approval, and the answer was always 'Yes' anyway. But I still had to write a formal email to Jane@onetaste.us, declaring 'my' intention with Bonnie.

This all seemed like a lot of work for something I didn't even ask for. Jane approved 'my' request, but we'd never actually get around to our Makeout.

One day, I'd learn that was never the point.

A THIRD APARTMENT MEANT many more residents.

Liz, our new production lead, was coming in a few days. We also had a bunch of part-time residents. These were people who had a home somewhere else, but just wanted the experience of staying in an OM House a few nights a week. They usually slept on one of the stored mattresses in one of the living rooms.

One more full-time resident moved in too, Abby Shakti, the bright smiling young woman who sold me my How To OM class. She had previously been in Coaching Program 5 over in San Francisco, and was hired onto the staff, along with Andrew and Tanisha. But for reasons unknown she dropped out of CP5 and disappeared for a while, only to reappear when CP6 started in New York.

I offered to help her move. She previously lived in a shared apartment on the Upper East Side. She didn't have much stuff— Just a bed and a few suitcases. Her roommate gave us a funny look in the way out that reminded me of Roger.

I drove the U-Haul and Abby rode shotgun. She took out a glass jar full of green mush and began eating it with a spoon.

"What is that?"

"*Kitcheree*. I made it myself. Want some?"

"No thanks. Are you a vegan or something?"

"I used to be. I mean, I love animals. But part of what I love about animals is that they do some of the work for us. Like, they say that bell peppers have vitamin A, but that's not true. They have beta carotene, which your body can use to synthesize vitamin A, but it takes extra energy. When you eat an egg, the chicken has already done that for you. The egg has vitamin A that you can immediately absorb. So I respect the chicken and love it for what it does for us."

I liked Abby. She was spiritual and graceful, but also very New York.

"I thought there would be a lot more vegans in the OM community," I said. "Every other conscious group I've ever come across had a lot of vegans."

Abby nodded. "Do you know why OMers eat meat?"

"Why?"

"Because we deal with the dark stuff... OneTaste is a *Left Hand Path*."

Spiritual paths were either *Right Hand* or *Left Hand*, Abby explained.

Right Hand Paths were those which sought order and control as a means to Enlightenment. They abstained from anything that could stir up the emotions— sex, psychotic substances, and aggression, which included eating meat. The idea was that these base desires could enslave people. So to be free, one must avoid them.

Left Hand Paths embraced chaos and disorder. They used sex, darker emotions, and altered states of consciousness as vehicles for enlightenment. They believed that base instincts were a natural part of existence. So to be free, one must integrate them.

Right Hand Paths were slow and safe. Left Hand Paths were fast and dangerous.

"You know, I was afraid to move into the Morellino before," she said. "Because I knew if I moved in then I'm really in."

"What do you mean?"

OneTaste wasn't Abby's first alternative community, she said. After college, she went to California to live in a yoga ashram of a famous Indian guru. That's where she got her yoga name, *Shakti*, after the creative/destructive feminine energy. It was very much a Right Hand Path. They woke up at four a.m. each morning to meditate and do yoga. They shaved everyone's heads, including the women. They ate vegan and everyone was supposed to be celibate.

"But I got kicked out," she said.

"Why?"

"I had sex with my swami."

"He wasn't celibate?"

"He was... until he met me."

Apparently, Abby Shakti's shakti was too much for the celibate yogis to handle. She was condemned for poisoning her poor swami's chastity and the imaginations of all the other venerable men. They kicked her out.

"So they projected their shame onto you."

"Yeah. But it still really hurt to get kicked out. I was there for months and had learned to really open my heart. Like, really open. When you're that connected to people, they become your family. They become a part of you. You love them and are attached to them even if you don't agree with everything they say. Even if they hurt you... The only thing that really feels bad is disconnection."

After being put out of the ashram, Abby found OneTaste. She enrolled in CP5 and moved into the San Francisco OM Residence. The exact traits that were condemned in the yoga ashram were celebrated in OneTaste. OneTaste was a sanctuary for sexual, emotional, outspoken women who would otherwise be shamed in conventional society. Nicole took a special liking to Abby and put her to good use. She was the first student hired out of CP5. They made her OneTaste's poster child. Rachel took her on as her personal protégé.

But at some point, her training became too fast and too dangerous. Abby freaked out and ran back to the East Coast to become a normal yoga teacher. But when they announced Coaching Program 6, she couldn't help but re-enroll.

"Nicole always says, 'The Left Hand Path is best not started, but once started it must be completed'," Abby said.

She returned her spoon to her jar. We drove the rest of the way in silence. It was late in the afternoon, and we hit the beginning of evening rush.

I found a spot right outside the Morellino. Lately I had been finding great parking spots. Lila said it was because I was "in tune with the Universe."

"Hey about that chicken Vitamin A thing," I said. "I get the 'appreciating it for the egg' thing, but what about when you eat the chicken itself? The chicken has to die in the process."

Abby turned to look at me with her emerald green, celibacy-ruining, tractor beam eyes. "Yes," she said. "That's the problem."

WE HEARD LIZ LONG before we saw her.

The door of apartment 2E slammed open followed by the distinct sound of lesbians ripping each other's clothes off.

Abby was visiting Lila and me in our new room. The three of us giggled as the music of sapphic foreplay drifted into the apartment, then into the master bedroom followed by doors swinging closed behind them.

Apartment 2E was a similar layout as PHC except with all three bedrooms on one level. Bonnie and Liz had the master bedroom in the front. Lila and I took the middle room. It had one small window that opened to an alleyway. Lila named it the *Womb*, since it was warm and dark. The third bedroom was to be filled by more student-residents who would move in later.

Lila dressed up our new Womb room with tapestry-like silks that she had in her bottomless suitcase. It felt nice to have our own space after sharing a room and bathroom with four adults the past months.

Abby and Andrew had taken our place in the Birdy Nest. Abby had come down to visit us this evening because she missed us upstairs. She also had big news.

"OneTaste just hired me as a salesperson," she said

"Oooh that's so exciting!" Lila said.

Abby was ambivalent, though. She had been in this role before. And last time she couldn't handle it.

Despite the egalitarian appearances, at the core OneTaste was a power pyramid, Abby explained. While there was no explicit chain of command, it was clear who sought approval from whom.

At the top of the pyramid was Nicole. Directly beneath her was the first tier— The Exec Team. These were people that had been with Nicole from the beginning. They were also the only people who directly interacted with Nicole.

Beneath them was the second tier— people like Bonnie and Jane who had taken Coaching Programs 1 and 2 four and five years ago. OneTaste had run out of money shortly after CP2. Nicole temporarily stopped doing classes to instead focus on a special experience for an 'investor' that I'd learn about later.

Coaching Programs 3 and 4 were done online and were loosely held so few people from that era stuck around. Sergio was one of those exceptions. OneTaste was now building out tier three by hiring students from CP 5 and 6.

OneTaste needed to fill out the lower tiers in order to promote the higher ones, Abby said. Nicole was phasing out of teaching so she could focus on writing books. Rachel was expected to replace Nicole as the face of OneTaste. Bonnie was getting trained to replace Rachel. OneTaste had hired a handful of people out of CP5 such as Andrew and Tanisha and previously Abby. Abby was now getting a second chance to be the next lead saleswoman under Bonnie. There would be more hires out of CP6 soon. The Coaching Program was basically a tryout for employment.

"Wow, imagine we're all on the Exec Team one day!" Lila said.

We rolled around in our pajamas and daydreamed of the silly things we'd do if we were running OneTaste. But there was a reason Abby dropped out of CP5 after getting hired the first time.

"When you're in, you're REALLY in," Abby said.

Lila and I didn't really get what the big deal was about. Abby already spent almost all her time doing OneTaste things. Might as well get paid for it.

"It's like, when I see how Rachel treats Bonnie, I feel double bad," Abby said. "I feel bad for Bonnie because I know how stressful it is to get stroked by Rachel twenty-four/seven. But then I also feel jealous." She sighed. "Now I have the same chance again. And I don't know how to feel about it."

"I know, I'll draw you a card!" Lila said.

Abby and I rolled our eyes at each other. Lila didn't care or didn't notice. She undid the knot in a silk scarf holding the circular *Motherpeace* tarot cards. She cut the deck and made some angelic sounds. Abby frowned but drew a card anyway. It showed four women sitting on the ground, weaving what looked like tapestries.

"The Eight of Discs!" Lila said. "It's the apprenticeship card. It's about feminine lineage. The younger women learn the ways of the older ones. That must be about you stepping into your path with OneTaste!"

"Whoaa," Abby said. "Motherpeace don't lie."

I drew a card next. It showed a warrior dude that looked like a Greek soldier. He had a broadsword, red cape, and helmet with feathers in it.

"The Son of Swords," said Lila.

"Badass."

"No, Ruwan! That's like the worst card. The Son of Swords is the arrogance of Masculine. He's afraid of the Great Mother so he tries to control it. He tries to fight with the Feminine instead of penetrating it."

I looked closer at the card. In the background was an open treasure chest. At his feet were dead roses.

"That's weird, I've been having this conflict with Rachel lately about the Men's Group," I said.

"Motherpeace don't lie. Motherpeace don't lie," Abby sang.

Bed springs crunched in the master bedroom. The wall between our rooms shook. Dual moans reverberated through the entire building as Bonnie and Liz unleashed their mass of stored energy.

"That's some advanced level OMing," Abby said.

We laughed. Good times were ahead.

STAGE 4: TurnOn

Sensation rises. The subject moves from desire.

"The spark of desire is life's cheeky wager: bet everything, win nothing, and grin anyway."
~ George Santayana

THERE'S THE OVERT GAME and then there's the Covert Game.

The weekend following the April CP6 Immersion was a special course called TurnON Training. The explicit purpose of TurnON Training was to teach us how to run TurnON events. The implicit purpose was to turn us into *Players*—those who could read the "game beneath the game," the covert social dynamics.

Rob and Rachel taught most of TurnON Training. Together they were OneTaste's all-time most profitable duo in leading events, other than Nicole of course.

"TurnON is first and foremost a sales event," Rachel said. "You can measure how well it went, by the number of sales. If people don't buy, then you didn't turn them on."

"Many students say they want to teach for OneTaste, but we always start them in sales," Rob added. "You need to learn how to deal with sales charge if you're going to teach."

"Five years ago, Nicole asked me to become the Head of Sales for OneTaste," Rachel said. "I was like, 'What? I've never sold anything in my life.' But then I realized sales is just like an OM."

Rachel was single-handedly responsible for over four million dollars of sales revenue each year. But she didn't do it for commission. She took the same base salary as all other employees. She did it out of devotion.

"Sales is a goalless practice. Do NOT stroke for climax or you will turn people off. Stroke them in the direction they are going. Your goal is to leave them more turned on than you found them. When they feel good, they will buy."

First, we learned how to set up the game.

Every detail in a Turn On event was intentionally designed to heighten sensation. If there was one chair misaligned, it would dissipate people's attention, taking away the urge to buy the next course. A lot of this was inspired by Werner Erhard's sales techniques in *est*, later Landmark Education.

"Everything is a communication," Rob said.

Next, we learned how to type the different kinds of people in the room. Every person, whether they knew it or not, had an effect on the group reality.

There were *Leaders, Supporters, Non-Confronters, Control Problems,* and *Saboteurs.* Leaders were people overtly leading the game. Supporters supported the leader, usually covertly. You wanted to "plant" one every five seats or so in the audience. Most people were Non-Confronters—people who just wanted to go along with the prevailing dynamic. Whoever controlled the them, controlled the room. Control Problems were people who tended to resist and complain.

"Be grateful for your Control Problems," Rob said. "They will annoy you, but they will be the ones who give you the best feedback on how to change the stroke."

The final type were the *Saboteurs.* Saboteurs may or may not openly challenge the Leaders like the Control Problems. But unlike the Control Problems, they would actively try to shift the reality of the group and assume leadership. They would make jokes during serious moments or try to interrupt the sales pitch. They might even be coaches trying to enroll people into their own programs.

"You need to put Saboteurs in their place immediately," Rachel said.

Next, we learned how to play the game beneath the game.

Like an OM, each phase of a TurnON event was designed to increase sensation. But unlike an OM, there was a goal to have the attendees at peak emotional arousal by the ending sales pitch.

The first game, *Inside-Outs*, was where a facilitator called out prompts and each person had to respond with an answer. The purpose was to get everyone comfortable and on the same page.

"Inside-Outs is like Grounding the thighs," Rachel said. "Most of these people will have spent their whole day in work mode. Maybe they've gone their whole week or whole lives without speaking the truth. Inside-Outs gets them to take their filters off."

The second game, *Hot Seats*, was where one person went up, and anyone could ask them any question about anything. Contrary to how it looked, HotSeats were not for the benefit of the person on the HotSeat. The purpose was to increase the sensation in the room. A vulnerable, emotionally intense HotSeat had a hypnotic effect on the audience.

There was a design to how people were chosen for the HotSeat. You almost always had an experienced OMer come up first to set the tone of vulnerability. Then you selected newcomers who you guessed would follow suit. Like in an OM, you kept going so long as the sensation was increasing, then stopped once it peaked. That's why some HotSeats could last ten questions while others were only one. Then you wanted to end with someone with a lot of Orgasm, usually a young beautiful woman. This excited people to buy so they could "have what she's having."

"Hot Seats is like the stroking of the OM," Rachel said. "It's what everyone will remember and will have them come back. But it's not the most important part..."

The last game, *Intimacies*, was where each person could share a hidden thought they had of another person. For the attendees, it just looked like a simple way to close an event. But for the players, it was what the whole event was all about.

"Hot Seats will turn them on. But Intimacies is where you change their lives," Rachel said. "It's like Sharing Frames after an OM."

We learned different techniques for getting into people's heads.

A *Timebomb* was a cryptically worded sentence that the receiver would have to think about to understand. Since they had to unpack the meaning themselves, they would feel like it was their own idea.

A *Bankshot* was a communication explicitly directed at one person but meant to trigger a response in other people in the room. It was a way to deliver a harsh truth without being confrontational.

Timebombs and Bankshots could be combined with a *Hex*, a confirmation of someone's fear or insecurity. A good Hex shattered a person's perceptions about themselves and reality, which made them open to new perspectives, and sometimes desperate to find a solution.

"Skillful communication is not bashing someone over the head with the truth," Rachel said. "It's to penetrate someone with a surgeon's precision. To see exactly where their wound is, then stick in the knife slowly, and look them in the eyes as it goes in."

There was a collective shudder.

"Everything is a communication," Rob said. "Everything."

The entire TurnON event aimed to get the audience hot and ready to take the next step in their personal growth—which meant buying a OneTaste course. After the official event was a "mingling period" where the selling was done.

There were two types of salespeople in the OneTaste process: *Fluffers* and *Closers*.

Closers closed the sales. These were the more skilled staff members who could navigate the tension of asking for people's money. But to make the process seamless, they were set up by Fluffers.

On a pornographic film set, a "Fluffer" is someone who keeps the male talent aroused between scenes through oral sex. In OneTaste, a Fluffer kept people turned on about buying a OneTaste class without actually "taking them over the edge." A good fluffer would identify people likely to buy, flirt with them, make them laugh, keep them excited, and would bring them over to a Closer once one was available.

You only needed one or two Closers depending on the class size. But you needed a Fluffer for every demographic.

A young cute woman was best fluffed by another young cute woman. An older overweight woman might get triggered by a young woman, so she needed to be fluffed by a woman like her.

Rachel has us identify our own demographic. That was who each of us should target during mingling events. That was a relief. If there was one kind of person I felt comfortable talking to, it was awkward nerds.

Only when someone was sufficiently turned on, would they be brought to the Closer. The Closer then gave them the final strokes to "put them over the edge" and relieve them of their tension.

"Sales charge is sex charge," Rachel said. "When someone is tumesced, the kindest thing you can do is help them get off."

THE NEXT PEAK HAD officially arrived.

And as in an OM, that meant the stroke had to change.

At the next House Meeting, Rachel announced that she and Jane would be spending awhile in LA to get their community going.

"Bonnie's in charge of New York till I'm back," Rachel said. "Liz will run production. Remember what I said about Children, Adults, and Parents? Bonnie is now a Parent. For the rest of you, it's time to transition to Adults."

But Bonnie wasn't so interested in being a Parent. She wasn't really interested in anything but Liz. This was why OneTaste split them up. This was why OneTaste broke up almost all pre-existing relationships. Romance was a liability. It created a shared reality that felt more real than that of a group or the outside world. So Liz became the defacto leader of the Morellino.

Life under Liz was different.

As soon as Rachel and Jane left, everyone but Sergio stopped waking up for Morning Practice. We all liked Bonnie. We all respected Liz. But we saw them as peers, or maybe big sisters at most. No one was willing to inconvenience themselves over their authority.

Unable to exercise an iron fist, Liz decided to surrender and "stroke us in the direction we were going." She moved Morning Practice to ten am to accommodate. Daniel still didn't wake up in time.

The freedom felt great at first. Without Rachel's "rails" to limit us, the student-residents of the Morellino came up with all sorts of ideas. It was as if these months of *compression* were acting on a spring within us, and now all the energy was uncoiling.

Lila had the idea to create a book club for the CP6 recommended reading list—mostly books on philosophy and occultism. Andrew began organizing student-run OM circles. The Canadians and I began teaching other OMers Theresa's alternative GO-hypnosis technique. All of us began spending more time outside of the Morellino, having more Makeouts with more people.

These were things we could have done at any time. But when Rachel was keeping tabs on us, we just didn't.

Lila and I became a lot closer in this time. After each day of gallivanting with the Canadians and having Makeouts around the city, I'd come back to the Morellino and take a long bath with Lila. She was always in the tub when I came home. Each night we'd read from her poetry books.

She and I looked for ways to increase sensation with each other. We dressed up in costumes and woke up Daniel with an improvised play. We invited Abby to watch us have sex one day. We tried to hold eye contact while one of us pooped. At a certain point, it began to feel like we were just being weird for the sake of being weird. Raising the sensation didn't seem like it was helping us grow. It was indulgence.

I began to miss the compression. I felt I was wasting my hard-earned Orgasm on pleasure. I didn't want to cash out so soon. I wanted to keep learning and growing.

I needed a new teacher.

I MADE AN OFFER to Theresa that she could say yes to.

"When you asked to be my apprentice, I didn't know what to think," Theresa said.

It was a Thursday afternoon. She and I were in one of the small rooms in her Midtown yoga studio.

"I've never had an apprentice before. But then I thought well, *GO* is still in development. I could use someone to teach and practice with."

She sat perfectly still on a yoga cushion. In her presence, I found it unusually easy to do the same.

She taught me different generative trance inductions which we did on each other. One was simply eye-gazing and willing ourselves into lower brain wave frequencies. By doing this in connection with each other, it was easier to go deeper faster than we could on our own.

The idea behind GO, was that you started stroking from a hypnotic state. After we were sufficiently tranced out, we got into an OM nest. The movement made us lose our trance state, so we did another induction exercise while in stroking position.

"Wow, this is way more vulnerable in this position," Theresa said.

She no longer felt like my teacher. Slightly hypnotized, naked from the waist down, I realized she was surrendering to me to guide the rest of the experience.

Once again, it was a different kind of OM. She got off hard on every stroke. And she had no limit. There was always more *up* to go.

Afterward we discussed. I felt very strange, like I had taken acid. I found it hard to speak.

"Come to my house tomorrow morning," she said.

I nodded.

Back at the Morellino, the residents were hosting a pool party on the roof. It was one of the first warm nights of May, and many OM community members came to hang out. Lila had bought a kiddie pool. Some of the women were splashing around topless in it.

I silently entered the courtyard, but Andrew noticed me right away.

"You're glowing!" he said. "What were you just doing?"

"I had a hypnosis lesson."

Abby grabbed my shoulders and looked into my eyes. Her pupils visibly dilated on contact.

"Wow your energy is CRAZY right now," Abby said.

THERESA LIVED IN A Victorian home on a tree-lined block deep in Brooklyn.

It was an intentional community house, but not the Orgasm kind. Her roommates were stereotypical hipsters— artists, filmmakers, canvassers, baristas. Her room was on the third of four floors. It smelled of incense. Translucent curtains gave the room an orange glow.

As I entered her bedroom doorway, an erection inflated in my pants. It was immediate, almost like a comical Viagra erection or one of those embarrassing surprises of early puberty.

If you spontaneously get an erection, it means your strokee is thinking about sex, Ken Blackman had said.

"I'm going to smudge you," said Theresa.

I didn't know what that meant, but when Theresa turned away I flipped it under my waistband. She turned back to me holding an eagle feather and burning a bundle of white leaves. She fanned the smoke around my body. It was to cleanse my energy, she said.

We tranced.

We GO'ed.

We came.

Before I knew what was happening, I was deep inside her. I handled her with a confidence and skill I didn't know I had. As in our OMs, every stroke was orgasmic. I had the virility of a teenager with the control of a sage.

I knew I couldn't take credit for any of it. It was all because of *her* ability to get off. In OneTaste-speak, she had 'cultivated a lot of Orgasm.' She was bringing me along on her ride.

Before I left, Theresa asked if I would like to teach the inaugural GO class with her.

It was getting dark when I left her place. When I got home, 2E was empty except for Abby.

"Where everybody?" I said.

"Everybody gone," Abby said in muppet-like baby voice.

It was the night before the next CP immersion. Many of the staff and students had arrived earlier in the day. Now they were all presumably having Makeouts.

"Can I tell you a secret?" she said.

"Yes. Can I tell *you* a secret?"

"Yes. I just had sex with Rob."

"Wow... I just had sex with Theresa."

"Woahhh," she said like the little green men from *Toy Story*.

"What's sex with Rob like?"

"It felt like... being plugged into the Sun."

"Wow."

"What's sex with Theresa like?"

"I felt like... I was the best fucker in the world."

"That's hot."

"We're quite lucky to get such a hands-on education."

"Mm, yes. Quite," she said half-mocking.

We laughed. Since no one was home, we decided to sleep together in Bonnie and Liz's bed. They had the fluffiest blankets.

"Okay I have another secret," I said. "Can I run something by you?"

"Of course."

I shared that Theresa invited me to teach with her. It was my dream opportunity. Real purpose in life. But if OneTaste found out, they wouldn't like it. Abby agreed it was a tough choice.

"Yeah, OneTaste can be really culty," she said.

We half-gasped, then laughed.

"But it's not a *bad* cult..." Abby added.

"Of course. It's quite good as cults come."

"Yes, quite."

We laughed and cuddled some more. Then the dam broke. We went back and forth listing all the weird things that we had noticed but were too afraid to say; the way Rachel constantly contradicted herself, the way Jane clearly had beef with Bonnie but played nice, the way that Sergio was basically an indentured servant, the way that OneTaste rewrote the rules to justify whatever they felt like doing.

All of it seemed harmless, however. Yes, they got some people to buy things that they didn't need. But so did every advertiser. As long as we were aware, then it was all okay right?

"Hey, how will you know when it's the right time to leave?" I asked. "I mean, we can't stay in this bubble forever."

"Mmm, I'm waiting for OneTaste to jump the shark."

"Quoi?"

"Jumping the shark means things have gotten too crazy. It's from the TV show, *Happy Days*. The writers had run out of ideas, so they made a ridiculous episode where Fonzie had to jump over a shark. They say that's when the show lost its way."

"Ah. So like if they start talking about god and stuff?"

Abby suddenly felt cold. She took a long moment to respond.

"Hey, Ruwan," she said. "I just realized that we're *colluding*. We should stop."

One of the greatest sins in the OneTaste was 'Collusion.' *Collusion* meant you were justifying your resentments with another person.

"I mean, they warn against it because they don't want people to think differently than them, right?"

"Yes, and it also breeds resentment. We shouldn't be spending our energy like this."

It felt like the wrong stroke to argue with her. We broke our embrace and went to sleep.

The next morning, Abby was already dressed and out of bed when I awoke.

"Hey," I said.

Her tractor beam eyes avoided mine.

"I have a headache," she said. "I think I'm hungover from our colluding yesterday. I don't want to talk like that anymore."

"Okay."

I didn't feel so good either. Many spiritual texts warn against gossip. You can't be grateful and resentful at the same time.

"I don't know if you should teach with Theresa or not," Abby said. "You know OneTaste really won't like it. OneTaste is my path. So if you decide to do stuff with Theresa, please don't tell me about it."

RACHEL RETURNED WITH A fury.

She wasn't due back for a few more weeks. But when she got word that OneTaste New York's numbers were dwindling, she hopped on a plane and was back at the Morellino the next morning. She called an emergency meeting and motioned me to sit next to her.

"Have you all been asleep since I left?" she yelled with her index finger in front of her face.

No one said a word.

"Well, it's time to WAKE UP!" she said. "No mo' climax!"

We all nodded. In OneTaste, 'Climax' was what normal people called 'an orgasm.' But it also meant any kind of release of emotion. Crying was considered "climaxing out of your eyes." Indulging in pleasure was also considered Climax since it released the energy you were holding.

Rachel reiterated the practice schedule. From now on a full hour of Fear Inventory was mandatory. So was meditation. And everyone had to go together to Bikram Yoga.

She was yelling at all of us. But it was clear the message was really aimed at the "Parents." Bonnie and Liz slouched in their seats on the far end of our circle. Rachel asked me to sit next to her on the couch. I wondered why.

"And another thing, you all should be OMing more with each other," she continued. "Andrew, Wallace, Daniel, Ruwan... if the women in this house are tumesced, that's on you."

Every few sentences, Rachel would consult her phone. I saw she was texting with Ken Blackman. The last text from him read, "Remind them that the best ass is within this house."

"Remember, the best ass is within this house!" she said.

I wondered why she was holding her phone in a way that I could read it.

Everything is a communication, I recalled.

THAT MONDAY RACHEL CANCELED TurnON.

Instead she called for a "Town Hall Meeting." Like that of a politician, she answered the questions and concerns of the New York OM Community. It seemed like a way for the community to connect. But as with all OneTaste events, there was a deeper motive.

Most OMers in the community attended. Many were eager to air their complaints about OneTaste. Others were just interested to see what this new event was about.

"I love the practice," a man in the audience said. He was a physician who had learned to OM years ago when OneTaste first tried to set up in New York. "But I really don't like the high-pressure sales. The OneTaste OM Circle has become so..."

"The OneTaste OM Circle is the only OM Circle!" Rachel said.

"When Theresa OM trained me, she said..."

"Theresa is not a OneTaste-certified trainer! I don't know what she's teaching, but it's not OM!"

"But she was literally the Head of OneTaste New York when she did my OM Training," the man said.

"Well she's gone off the rails!" Rachel said. "She doesn't hold the container. The way she does things is *dangerous*."

More OMers shared concerns about OneTaste sales practices. Rachel had a masterful way of turning things around. She made people feel apologetic for criticizing her. And she had a way of making everyone feel good.

Many people bought programs after. Every event was a sales event.

"New York is back in the rails!" Rachel declared after the money was totaled.

Rachel decided to treat the staff to takeout in PHA. She invited Abby and me as well. Jane ordered a banquet from a nice uptown restaurant and laid it out on the kitchen island. Everyone crowded around and ate directly out of the takeout trays.

"We eat lion-style," Rachel explained while tearing a bite off a chicken leg.

"Okay," she said, stripping the leg to the bone, "someone give me a lay of the land."

The staff listed each student-resident of the Morellino, everyone who wasn't in the room with us, and gave Rachel an intel report— their participation level in OneTaste events, their general attitude, details about their personal lives, even who they were sleeping with.

Abby and I gave each other a look saying "wow." Rachel had a whole spy network.

"Wallace... he's a *Control Problem*, but he's been helping a lot at TurnON."

"Tanya is still attached to her job... she'll probably phase out."

"Lila... she's good. She's in love with Ruwan, so she'll do whatever he does."

Rachel winked at me with both eyes. Abby gave me a shrugging look. She and I were not mentioned on the list.

Rachel seemed pleased about the reports until it came to Daniel.

"Daniel... He's a *Saboteur*. He's been leading people away from TurnONs..."

Rachel slammed her half-eaten falafel onto the platter. "This stops now. Who's going to take on Daniel?" All the staff stared at her. "Well, who's his bedmate? T?"

"Um no, I have doctor things to do," Tanisha said.

"I'm close with Daniel," I said. "I can take him on."

Rachel laughed. "That's cute, Ruwan."

"I'll take him on," volunteered Liz.

"Liz, no..." said Bonnie.

Rachel grinned and craned her neck over to Liz.

"When was the last time you were with a *man*, Liz?" Rachel said.

"What does that have to do with anything?" Liz said.

Rachel squinted and pursed her lips in comical fashion.

"You know what *take him on means*, right?" she said. She arched her lower back, lifted a bent leg, and mimed holding something in front of her hips. "It means you... take... him... on..."

"Oh... no," said Liz.

"It's easy," Rachel said. "Just send him a text saying, 'Hey, I have an idea'. When he responds say, 'We should have a Makeout', then you use your pussy to put him back in the rails!" Rachel wagged her finger in front of her chest. She said all of this with a bright smile that was both cute and disturbing.

"Um, I'll pass," Liz said.

"Well, someone better take him on or we're going to have to push him out. They were all invited through the portal. If they don't want to come through, they leave. The next peak is coming. And we do NOT have room for dead weight."

IT FELT GOOD TO be "within the rails" again.

Once again, it was easy to wake up for the 7am OMs. We all had little resistance to cleaning the house and Fear Inventory. It was as if Rachel's presence gave meaning to the tedious practice once again. It became more fun and interesting to hang out at the house.

Morning Practice now continued past noon. This was partly because the closest official Bikram Yoga school was on the Upper West Side, adding forty minutes of total commute time. So Jane found an unofficial Bikram Yoga school in Harlem. It wasn't advertised well because it was run as a side business by its owner. She was a ballerina in a New York ballet company and didn't have time to work on her yoga studio.

Very often we were her entire class. She opened up to Jane and Rachel that she was considering going out of business until we started showing up.

"We're going to save her business," Rachel said after class one day. "We will infuse it with Orgasm. It's always good to have witches on your side."

After class we'd all get smoothies at one of the fancy super food stores that had been popping up with Harlem's recent gentrification. I had never spent ten dollars on a smoothie before. I thought it was crazy.

"You don't have ten dollars?" Lila said.

"No, that's not the point."

"Don't let Ruwan infect you with a scarcity mindset," Rachel said, laughing.

OneTasters had a very different view of money. They all worked on bare subsistence salaries. And since work life and personal life were blended, one could argue they worked for far less than minimum wage. This is on top of buying expensive courses and paying rent at the Orgasm Residences.

And yet, when you "live by desire" you don't have room to consider negative consequences. All the OneTaste staff bought lattes and green juices and thirty-dollar yoga classes daily. Even staffers like Liz, who would mutter about how she never had money, would still follow suit. To deny your desire was to act out of fear.

I eventually gave in. I was already in debt, I figured. And I could use the antioxidants.

Thankfully, I still had my day job as a content writer, though I was now putting in less than three hours per week. I considered that the more honest thing would be to quit my job and trust in following my desire. But I couldn't give up the security.

"I work very hard to make sure there is no scarcity in this house!" Rachel said.

The fact was, her reality was more solid and more fun. In ways that seemed magical, her attention could infuse you with joy, courage, and even increase your sex drive. She put everyone in the Morellino in great spirits.

Everyone except Daniel.

He had been isolating. He continued gallivanting on his own even after Wallace and I turned our attention back to OneTaste. I wanted to bring him in to the fold. I wanted him to understand what I had recently understood: Doing whatever you want is pleasurable, but it's much more fulfilling to be a part of a greater whole.

We met up for coffee and I tried to explain.

"I just don't trust OneTaste," he responded. "Sure things seem great now, but what's the cost? The deeper you go, the harder it is to get out."

"Oh come on, I can leave whenever I want."

"That's what addicts say."

"Yes, I'm doing a lot of OneTaste stuff. But I'm still doing GO and O Night. I'm Orgasmically agnostic..."

"You know OneTaste isn't going to tolerate that much longer..."

I knew he was right. I had been doing my best to ignore it. I told him Theresa asked me to teach a GO class with her and I wasn't sure what to do. Theresa and OneTaste were in direct competition. And even more than that, they represented alternate philosophies.

"You know in the Star Wars universe there's the Jedi who harness the light side of the force, and the Sith who harness the dark side," Daniel said. "OneTaste claims to be the Jedi, but we don't really know."

Many OMers, mainly males, made this semi-facetious Star Wars analogy: Orgasm was like the Force— it gave you an unseen ability and power to read and affect people.

"The Sith have this thing called the 'Rule of Two'," Daniel said. "That there can only be two Sith Lords at a time, a master and an apprentice. The master represents the concentrated power of the dark side. The apprentice represents the craving for this power. Once the apprentice can overpower the master, he kills his master and takes on his own apprentice. That's why the Sith never could get ahead of the Jedi... until Anakin Skywalker came along and destroyed the Jedi from the inside."

"Why would one follow the Rule of Two knowing that he'll eventually be killed by his own apprentice?"

"Power is addicting. Once you're hooked, you can't help wanting more even if it kills you."

THE NEXT HOUSE MEETING looked different.

Instead of joining us, Rachel was behind us in the kitchen making herself a cup of tea.

"I have to make some calls so Bonnie's running the meeting," Rachel said. "Bonnie, run the meeting!"

Bonnie looked nervous. Liz looked deflated. Jane looked annoyed. Tanya was glowing. She and Wallace had finally started sleeping together after many months of sleeping next to each other. We began check-ins.

"I'm feeling kind of tumesced," I said on my turn. "But it's probably nothing."

"Ruwan!" Rachel said from the kitchen. "Why don't you tell us what's really on your mind?"

"Um, well okay. So... Working for OneTaste seems like my dream job, but all I ever hear about OneTaste staff is that they're broke."

Rachel glared at Bonnie and Liz. She turned to me and smiled.

"Okay how's this," she said, "how about I personally mentor you to sell so well that you'll never have to worry about money ever again?"

"That sounds great," I said.

"Great. We'll schedule one on one time," Rachel said. "Ruwan is the new head of Lead Gen for New York. Bonnie! Take control of the meeting!"

Bonnie got flustered. Jane rolled her eyes.

Rachel left the apartment and let the door slam behind her.

"I want to share that I've had a great week," Wallace said. "I've uncovered new layers of vulnerability."

Tanya trumpeted. We all laughed.

STAGE 5: PEAKING

Bardo, the in-between phase. The subject must choose between falling back into Climax or retaining energy for a higher purpose.

"Music is much like fucking, but some composers can't climax and others climax too often, leaving themselves and the listener jaded and spent."
~ Charles Bukowski

I WAS AN ORGASMIC double agent.

My week was split between 'doing research' with Theresa and shadowing Rachel. Meanwhile, the tension between OneTaste and Theresa was increasing. I knew I would have to make a decision soon.

In many ways they were similar. Both women were my teachers. Both women were confident, sexy, and had empathic abilities nearly indistinguishable from magic. But they represented two very different realities, the Dionysian and Apollonian, chaos and order. This was apparent in how they related with me.

Theresa gratified all my desires beyond what I even asked for. She taught me esoteric skills, shared with me the secrets and 'game' behind OneTaste. She invited me into her body and into other realms of consciousness. Now she was offering me a break into my dream career— to teach with her. But she had fallen in love with me. It was hard to feel like a magician's apprentice when I had seen the magician naked and felt her surrender.

Don't fuck your gurus, some have said.

Rachel on the other hand, didn't gratify any of my desires. She never quite explained anything fully. Her advice was encoded in such a way that I'd sometimes spend the rest of the day pondering its deeper meaning. The sexual tension, if there was any, was so subtle, I was never sure if it was in my head. If we did touch, it was by her initiation. Her hand on my knee felt scandalous. When she hugged me, chakra or no chakra, I felt something expand in my chest. Rachel always kept me wanting more.

"Wanting is more compelling than Having," Nicole often said.

It began to bother me that I was hiding something from Rachel. I brought it up with Theresa one morning after I stayed at her place.

"Doesn't the secret make it kind of fun?" she said.

"But doesn't truth carry the most sensation... and lying cause numbness?"

I was confused about all these philosophies.

Theresa told me that she had been married before. She had come to OneTaste with her husband to learn how to deepen their intimacy. But OneTaste never let any pre-existing relationship continue. Nicole, usually through someone like Rachel, would find a way to break them up. Theresa's marriage was broken up through "jealousy research," which basically meant sleeping with other people in front of each other so they could learn to "get off" on the pain.

Nicole would also put relationships together, somehow making them fall in love and lust. Since we confirm our reality through our intimate relationships, this ensured that no two people could form a reality independent or stronger than Nicole's reality. Nicole's game was always the biggest game. Every other game was inside of it.

Theresa told me that in the early days of OneTaste, many of Nicole's lessons came from her time as a high-end escort. She presented prostitution as a practice of spiritual growth. She referenced the "Sacred Whore" concept via the Myth of Ephesus where after battles, the priestesses would "fuck the war out of men." Many of Nicole's early students tried escorting, not to just make money, but for their spiritual development—to be able to love like Nicole.

As OneTaste grew, Nicole cleaned up her image and stopped speaking about escorting. She eventually forbid OneTaste staff from doing sex work. But the culture remained. OneTaste attracted many sex workers as students. One escort in CP6 told me that OMing taught her how to open her heart so fully that she could genuinely love and climax with even the grossest client.

Escorting still informed a part of the hidden curriculum called *Hooking*, as what a hooker does. To "hook" was to create attachment under false pretenses. Hooking often involved gratifying or validating the mark's secret fantasies. This put them into an enchanted state where they suspended their better judgement. We were explicitly taught that Hooking was unethical, and something we should never do. But a version of this was still common.

In the OM Community, one would often see pairings of young hot volatile women with nebbish awkward tech guys. It was like the *Manic Pixie Dream Girl/Brooding Male Protagonist* trope pairing seen in the movies, except real. She would take him on an Orgasmic adventure, which involved paying for high ticket OneTaste courses.

OneTaste eventually came up with an idea for Coaching Program 1 at a time when high priced yoga teacher trainings and coaching certification programs were becoming popular. CPs 1 and 2 were their first big windfalls from courses. But CPs 3 and 4 were busts. So they decided to return to their roots.

Nicole had been involved with a man named Reese Jones, who invented the twisted pair cable used in ethernet networks. Nicole decided to have OneTaste focus on a twenty-four/seven "immersive experience" for Reese. Rituals were created on his behalf. The entire company existed to delight him. Turned On Women were sent to stroke him. Even when Nicole went to New York to be with her other lover, she'd assigned OneTaste staffers to give Reese "the girlfriend experience." Some of these women would testify in court years later.

"Her New York lover was a guy named *Om*, funny enough," Theresa said. "Om Rupani. He's the only man Nicole ever let Top her. I don't know if he still teaches. He's kind of a recluse. But if you want to learn power dynamics, you should seek him out.

Hooking was, in a sense, OneTaste's underlying business model. Like a pimp, Nicole had a stable of followers trained in the arts of sex and love, and she profited when that sex and love was given to others. Power dynamics in OneTaste always came down to emotional attachment. Like a pimp to a whore, or a whore to a john, or a parent to child, the former captivated the heart of the latter. And when you control someone's heart, you can control their behavior without force—for they *want* to do as you say.

I heard what Theresa said. I thought I understood it. But I left her place that day with two thoughts: One, Theresa was a love addict so I shouldn't trust her. And two, learning about a game is never as interesting as being in it.

Even if you're the one being played.

THERE HAD BEEN AN incident in the OM Community.

Few people knew exactly what it was, but we all knew it was serious. Everyone had heard a different story, but one thing was clear: A man who was OM-trained by Theresa had in some way violated a Sister Goddess who was recently OM-trained by OneTaste.

"I heard that during the OM he came on her," Wallace said.

"In his pants, or he took it out?" asked Elodie.

"I heard he basically raped her," said Tanya.

"How do you BASICALLY rape someone?" said Jane.

"No, he just whipped it out after the OM, because he thought she was coming on to him," Daniel said.

"Then he was waaay off the stroke."

"I wasn't there, but I've met that woman. She's super watery with her boundaries," Tanya said. "I bet she led him on."

"Tanya!" Jane yelled. "Don't spread memes like that."

"What? Maybe she co-created the experience."

Regardless of what really happened, I knew the fallout was going to be bad for Theresa.

Andrew, acting as OneTaste's legal counsel, released an official statement to the worldwide OM Community. He reported on what had happened and that OneTaste officials had smoothed it over. He requested that no one share details of the incident to "prevent spreading mistruths" but also avoid "slander or libel on the part of the company."

Rachel made a less official statement to the Wednesday OM Circle.

"This is what happens when people get OM-trained by people who aren't OM trainers. Theresa is not a OneTaste-certified instructor. She doesn't hold the Container. I know a lot of you think OneTaste is too rigid and too strict. But there's a reason why. We're dealing with Orgasm and Orgasm is volatile. Theresa wasn't willing or able to hold the container and now look what happened. I've worked too hard to make the OM

Community a clean, safe, well-lit place for Orgasm, and I'm not going to let someone ruin it."

Like a great propagandist, Rachel was able to take advantage of a scandal to crush her opponent. And it worked.

The following week, no one signed up for Theresa's O Night.

The Sister Goddesses and their strokers decided to go to OneTaste's Monday circle instead. I didn't hear from Theresa for a few days. I thought of checking up on her, but I couldn't bring myself to message her.

That Wednesday, I ran into her coming out of the OneTaste center on Broadway. I almost didn't recognize her. Her face was pale and her pupils constricted to pinholes.

"Theresa? What are you doing here?"

Her eyes were darting back and forth. She mumbled something inaudible then said, "I've got to go."

I was early, so no one was in the event space except Rachel. She sat in the middle of the couch, texting. She looked like a little queen on an oversized throne. When she looked up at me her eyes were sparkling.

"Oh hi, Ruwan! Good to see you here."

Sergio and Jane arrived after me. I helped Sergio set up the nests. Jane sat with Rachel.

"So I just met with Theresa," Rachel loudly whispered to Jane. "I killed her good. She had no words." Rachel mimicked a small trembling animal then laughed. "She won't be a problem anymore."

"You a killer, Rach-O," Jane said.

Killing was another part of the hidden curriculum. It meant to shatter someone's ego beyond their ability to respond.

"I'm a mama lion!" Rachel said. "I keep my cubs safe!"

They were across the room and looking at each other, but I couldn't help feeling she was talking to me.

That Saturday was both the next How To OM class and Theresa's scheduled GO class. I chose to do BOH for OneTaste instead of teaching with Theresa. Given the recent scandal around Theresa, it was no longer a hard decision. I called her to let her know.

"You don't believe what they are saying about me, do you?" Theresa said on the phone.

I didn't. I knew Theresa 'held the Container,' just a different one. This incident actually had nothing to do with her. But I couldn't put that into words.

"Eh, I don't really want to comment," was all I said.

Theresa sighed. She knew better than me where my head was at.

I often thought of what would have happened had I chosen the path with Theresa. Of my two mentors, she was the more honest and kind-hearted. At times I regretted my decision, particularly with some of the negative consequences that were to follow. But as time passed, I could see that I did what every social animal does— I sided with the winner.

When we first became intimate, Theresa told me how OneTaste was the best kind of education, but as with any Left Hand Path, I had to be careful I didn't become one of the many casualties.

She had emailed me a screenshot of an OM Hub post by a OneTaste LA staff member. It was about how pain is a sign you're about to grow— "real practitioners" don't shy away from discomfort but continuously seek *compression.*

The rest of Theresa's email read:

Promise me you won't think like this.

It's not true, and it's dangerous.

OneTaste will convince you that pain is growth. But it's really just you working your ass off for them. There is no room for joy.

It will not teach you about love, and relationships, and how to live a happy life.

Suffering is not a virtue. Joy is not a sin. Boredom is not an option.

Warmly,

Theresa

RACHEL DID EVENTUALLY GET me that "official Men's Group training".

She arranged a group phone call with Ken Blackman and the leaders of the Los Angeles and San Francisco Men's Groups.

"So what are we here to talk about?" Ken asked.

"Men's Group Training?" I said.

The other guys on the call murmured. No one had a clue about it. There was no such thing as "Men's Group Training".

As many things in OneTaste, it was something made up on the fly and spoken of as if real. The purpose wasn't to train skills, as much to ensure compliance. It was an arbitrary hoop for me to jump through before being given authority.

Being the facilitator of the One Taste New York Men's Group elevated my status within the community. So OneTaste had to be sure that I was "within the rails" by submitting to this task.

Sergio co-facilitated with me. Even though he was my coach, he mostly deferred to me. As a man very deep in his Feminine, he was well suited to empathizing and creating a space safe for emotions, but not so good at keeping track of conversational threads or time.

The first meetings were awkward, but after a few sessions we felt our stride. We had a core group of twelve guys with occasional stragglers. It became everyone's favorite time of the week.

"The thing about men in the OM community," Sergio said, "is that we're always so focused on the women that we rarely connect as men."

More than any experience, these group sessions honed my confidence as a coach. After months of handling women's bodies, the Men's Group showed me I could do the same for men's minds. Guys in the OM Community began reaching out to me for one-on-one coaching. I didn't join CP6 to become a coach. But somehow it became the next obvious step.

One afternoon, I received a text from Bonnie:

"Hey I have an idea!"

"I submitted the request to the Ethics Board months ago!"

"No not that! You should take Ignited Man. You need it to lead the men!"

Ignited Man was OneTaste's men's weekend, held in San Francisco. I had decided not to spend any more money on OneTaste courses. I was already about six grand in debt and counting. But she had a point. And it was only another four hundred bucks.

I FLEW TO SAN Francisco for the Ignited Man weekend.

I was able to rent a room at the San Francisco OM Residence, 1080 Folsom. It was both bigger and smaller than I expected.

One of the west coast staffers from CP5 gave me a tour. The first floor was a small common area with a long dinner table that could seat about a third of the sixty residents. There was a restaurant-style kitchen where three or four residents cooked for everyone in exchange for discounted rent. Many of the residents I knew from CP6. I was surprised at how many non-CP6 residents knew me.

"We've all seen your 'TurnON Bryant Park video'," someone said. I had been making videos for the OneTaste New York social media where I walked the streets and asked people vulnerable questions. Nicole apparently loved it and yelled at the corporate staff for not coming up with something like that earlier.

The second floor was where the more casual OMers lived. The public was allowed there, so you had to keep your clothes on. The third floor was only open to serious OMers. Clothes were optional. The only shower was a communal one that could fit twelve people.

Ignited Man was taught by Rob and Ken.

Rob told us his origin story. He was a newly married computer programmer. His wife dragged him to a course on sex, taught by a man named Erwan Davon. Erwan happened to be the man who introduced Nicole to stroking, whom she mentioned in her TEDx talk. After Rob introduced himself to the class, the teacher pointed and Rob saw that his wife was weeping.

"It was at that moment, I realized something was wrong," Rob said.

Rob and his wife went on to participate in what would eventually become OneTaste. I heard from others that Rob and Nicole were involved briefly while his wife went off with another man. He eventually got divorced and quit his job to co-found OneTaste. He seeded the first three hundred and fifty thousand to get OneTaste off the ground.

Ken had a different story.

"I was the most highly trained individual in a practice that was a precursor to OM," Ken said.

Ken had long been training at The Welcomed Consensus. Three years after starting OneTaste, she recruited Ken to teach and develop the curriculum.

"I learned how to talk to women by stroking them," Ken said. "In other words, I learned how to stroke them verbally using the skills I developed in stroking them physically. For some of you that might seem like a wild idea. But by the end of this weekend, you'll see that when you can feel, you no longer need formulas."

"How many of you are here because you want to learn about women?" Rob said.

Most of the hands went up.

"That's not a bad reason," Rob said. "I thought I was doing all this work so that I could get some nookie. There's nothing wrong with nookie. I want all of you to get nookie. But you'll find that it's not really about nookie?"

"Ehm, yes, hello?" a man with a Quebecois accent said. "What is *noo-kie*?"

"It means sex," said Ken.

The class laughed.

"I thought what I wanted was sex, women's validation," Rob continued. "Till a few months in and I had all these women chasing after me. I would run to my room and lock the door and they would all be pounding. I'd cry to myself, *please just leave me alone*," he said, fake crying.

Some of the class laughed.

"Because it never was really about getting women," Rob said. "It was about getting myself."

"We call this course Ignited Man, because our aim is to turn your lights on, to become the men you are meant to be," Ken said. "We've chosen women as something to relate over, but it doesn't have to be that. It could be anything."

Like the Men's Groups, *Ignited Man* felt like the one safe space where men who OMed could really think and speak freely.

"Men use language to exchange content. Women use language to exchange packets of emotion," Ken said.

Ignited Man wasn't that different than any OneTaste course.

It was low on content but high on improvisation, stories, drama, emotions. Somehow it all related back to OM. The final day involved a panel of women led by Rachel, who stroked the room.

I was beginning to be less impressed by OneTaste teachings, and more by their marketing methods. They had a whole menu of seemingly unique courses that all taught the same exact thing: *Feel and follow the stroke*.

The real growth happened in the community. When you immersed yourself amongst other magical-thinking, emotionally vulnerable, hypersexual people, you couldn't help but change. The courses were just a way to get you in the door. And make money, of course.

AFTER IGNITED MAN, I ended up hanging out with Arjun.

He was the self-made millionaire who outed himself at the first CP6 immersion. As many guys in OneTaste, he previously had trouble connecting with women. He had a girlfriend back in Boulder. She was wary of OneTaste but he recently convinced her to try OMing and open their relationship for their growth. He asked me if my time doing pickup was useful.

"Kind of, but at a cost," I said. "It got me to approach tons of women that I never would have talked to otherwise. Pickup is all about external results. But it numbed me out internally."

"I was at this tantra healing workshop last week in Ojai. I saw Neil Strauss there, the guy who wrote the pickup book."

"Yeah *The Game*. Cool, what's he like?"

"Pretty chill. I almost didn't recognize him at first. I asked him if he was Neil Strauss he hushed me to keep quiet. He was there undercover researching his next book on infidelity."

Arjun had tried many kinds of workshops— to learn how to be good with women, and otherwise. OneTaste clearly had something that others didn't. But without saying it explicitly, he seemed concerned about the cult aspects. He asked me what living at the Morellino was like.

I told him the hardest thing to get used to was the *compression*. We spent almost half the day doing practices. But it gets easier. He was concerned about having to do Bikram Yoga every day. He had fibromyalgia, so anything physical was a challenge.

"Well I've never been so flexible in my life," I said. "But I also have joint pains I've never had before. Bikram kind of forces visible results at the expense of what feels good."

"So Bikram is the pickup of yoga?"

We laughed. I liked Arjun. He and I hooked up with many of the same women. Rachel always said that when you really want to have a Makeout with someone, it isn't about about them. It's that you wanted to connect with their partner.

We both agreed OneTaste had the magic sauce when it came to human relating. By opening our perception, we could read and affect people to near psychic levels. Who needs pickup skills when you could feel what a woman wants in your own body?

"True," Arjun said, "But there's a tradeoff between clairvoyance and the ability to protect yourself."

Before I left San Fran, Rachel called a Men's Meeting.

OneTaste wanted to get more men to OM. They were specifically trying to hit the 'pickup' market. These were men who were already willing to spend a lot of time and money learning how to attract women. But OneTaste had been failing to bring them in. Rachel knew I dabbled in that community, so she invited me to join a brainstorming meeting with Ken Blackman, and John, the leader of the OneTaste San Francisco Men's Group.

John showed me some of their marketing materials. I told him it was a bit condescending to lonely men, and it was full of foreign lingo.

"Why wouldn't a man want to learn how to put *pristine attention* on a woman?" he asked.

"No one knows what that means!" I said.

John was a graduate of CP1, and was a leader in the OM community. He was often praised as the type of man other strokers should try to emulate—sensitive but strong, both empathic and manly.

Many women in CP5 credited John for "bringing them in." He was a true *messenger of Orgasm*. He'd go out and date normal women, presumably rock their world, then introduce them to OM.

The meeting with Rachel was short. She said I was the only one who understood how to talk to normal guys, so she put me in charge of OneTaste New York's social media.

After the meeting, John had more questions for me.

"How's your Tinder game?" he asked.

"Oh I don't have Tinder," I said.

This was 2013. I had just heard of Tinder through Brad and Roger a few months ago, but was so full on in OM land that it had no appeal. I couldn't imagine wanting to be with "regular" women after experiencing Turned ON ones.

"So how do you get Makeouts?" John said.

"Um, the OM Community?"

He frowned. He didn't speak further, but his disapproval seemed to say, "Shame on you for only fishing locally. You should be out growing our pond."

I was expected to be a Messenger of Orgasm, too.

A true messenger of Orgasm did not selfishly consume. He used his magnetism to bring more players into the game.

I hadn't tested if my new sexual confidence "worked" with non-OMers. And since Orgasm had given me so much, it made sense that I give back by spreading it.

I BOOKED A SPEAKING event for Bonnie at *Babeland,* the sex toy shop.

It was through an acquaintance of mine, a lesbian dating coach who taught women seduction skills. Rachel had put me in charge of "LeadGen," lead generation. I thought it would be a great opportunity.

Bonnie bombed. Like the OneTaste messaging to men, she spoke in terms no one could understand. Even worse, lesbian pickup artists could not relate to "surrendering" to the stroke.

The crowd was murmuring about how weird the clit-stroking thing was. So I decided not to pitch people on OM. But I could still be a messenger of Orgasm.

I settled into my body. I felt my desire. I noticed a pretty young woman next to me and verbally stroked for my pleasure.

Before I knew it, we had exchanged contact info and she was leaning on me. Her friend pulled her away, but minutes later I had a text from her with many emojis. "Stroking" really did work with non-OMers.

OneTaste referred to such people as "muggles," borrowing the term from *Harry Potter* for non-magical people. As almost all OneTaste lingo, it was said in a half-joking manner. But as all labeling, it helped draw a line between the Us and the Them.

If you were being ridiculed by someone for speaking about Orgasm, it was okay, they were just a *muggle.*

If you were bending someone's will with your charm, it was okay, they were just a *muggle.*

If you were smashing someone's ego, distorting their sense of reality, and making them desirous of things they wouldn't have otherwise, it's okay. *Muggle.*

I continued texting my "muggle girl" afterwards. She said she had never gotten so turned on by a guy by text. She half-jokingly asked me if I was psychic. I told her I wasn't psychic. I could just feel what she was feeling better than she could.

We went on a date near her place in Greenpoint. She was cute and bubbly. But she was also numb. I could see that she was totally unaware of her feelings.

Rachel often said, "Men have a teleprompter on their foreheads. Women have the same teleprompter in their bodies." Months of OMing had trained me to feel exactly how she wanted to be stroked. I could feel where her real boundaries were and raise the sensation as I stepped past the false ones.

We went back to her place after dinner. She lived in a shared apartment by a G train stop. Here I realized the drawbacks of sensitivity.

Her place was a mess. The kitchen trash was overfilled. The living room was full of random objects. She said her roommates were all Craiglist "randos" who never spoke to each other. I could feel the disconnection and resentment. It grossed me out.

Roger's date once asked me if feeling more pleasure meant feeling more pain. I would have never noticed a woman's dirty apartment before. But now I couldn't help being affected by it. I felt nauseous.

I went to her bathroom to splash water on my face. The toilet bowl was caked with brown film. There was no way I could get aroused knowing her toilet looked like this. I scrubbed it clean with a toilet brush that looked like it had never been used.

When I returned to her, she was already naked under the covers. The sex was unenjoyable. She pulled for climax. I wanted it to be over as soon as possible.

"You want to see me play with my toy?" she said. Then she pulled out a large head vibrator from under her pillow. She went to town and forced her way to another climax.

A previous version of me would have found this incredibly hot. A previous version would have felt lucky to have a woman want to expose herself like this.

But now it just felt strange.

Everything outside of OneTaste felt strange.

I DECIDED I WAS going to bring her to the doorway.

As many women, she found the idea of a female-focused orgasm practice intriguing. But she was afraid to try it. I told her our next date should be at TurnON. She just wanted me to come over instead.

After a lot of back and forth she wrote, "I'm starting to worry that you're dating me just to sign me up for this TurnON class."

I responded, "Wait, you thought I've been texting you this whole time, went on a date with you, and slept with you, just to get $10 out of you?"

"You're right. I'm sorry :(I'm just a little paranoid."

I wasn't technically lying. I didn't do this for ten dollars. I was hoping she'd spend way more than that at OneTaste.

My conscience did ring a warning bell. But it was a quiet one, easily ignored. I rationalized that I was doing something good. This numbed out woman would clearly enjoy life more if she was Turned On. And of course, I'd be serving the Orgasm (and the OneTaste community) by bringing in another attractive woman.

Brainwashing doesn't happen overnight. It occurs in small moments, tiny modifications to what's "right" and "wrong". Only over time can you look back and see you're following a totally different moral compass.

My muggle gal had to have carpal tunnel surgery that week anyway, so we decided to revisit the subject the following week.

One afternoon, Abby and I were tasked with moving around some production supplies with my car— now referred to as the *OMmobile*.

Abby was officially a OneTaste staff member. I had recently been brought on as a "probationary" staff member, which meant I was working part time for no pay.

Abby and I had been OMing a lot together lately. She had been under a lot of stress, and my left index finger was the most readily available stress reliever.

She had a long-term boyfriend whom she had been with on and off since childhood. They were in an open relationship because that was the only way to be with Abby Shakti. But he didn't feel comfortable with her adventurousness, and he was especially wary of OneTaste. With her recent re-hiring, their relationship was extra strained.

As we drove in the car, Abby was on the phone with him in a serious conversation. It sounded like she had broken one of their relationship agreements. Meanwhile, I was thinking about how to proceed with my muggle girl. I was trying to remember what day she had surgery so I could check on her.

"I'm sorry," Abby said. "I wish I could just *surgery* that all away."

When she got off the phone, I asked why she used the word *surgery*.

"I don't know. That word just popped into my head. That's a weird way to put it, huh?"

"I was just thinking about my muggle girl having surgery in that moment."

"Woahhhh."

A previous me would have written this off as a coincidence. Or at least labeled it as confirmation bias. But at this point, I had come to see nothing as coincidence. All of this was explainable— This is what happens when people live at higher levels of connection than the norm.

"You think you heard my thoughts because we've been OMing a lot lately?"

"Yeah maybe. We've been feeling each other deeply. Maybe feeling each other's thoughts is the next level."

"Wow. So maybe intuition really is a kind of magic."

At first, I was open to spiritual metaphors. Then I was willing to suspend disbelief. But now my entire lens on reality was different. And I only wanted to spend time with people who confirmed it.

My choice to entertain magical thinking, had now become contempt for those that didn't. If my muggle gal didn't want to experience Orgasm, I should take my finger off, so to speak.

I tried letting her down gently with a long text message.

She wrote back, "Well you're not the first selfish man in New York who just wanted to sleep with me, and you're not going to be the last."

I was deeply offended.

I wasn't being selfish, nor did I want to sleep with her. I wanted to make her feel things she had never felt before, totally change her sense of reality, uproot her life, convert her to my sex cult, and be a Messenger of Orgasm so that my cult mentors would approve of me.

What was selfish about that?

Amongst the bonobos, the free-loving matriarchal cousins of chimpanzees, there is only one sexual taboo:

Sons don't sleep with their mothers.

In another matriarchal society, the Morellino, there was only one woman whose pussy I hadn't stroked:

Rachel.

In six months of living here I had stroked every other residing clitoris, some more than fifty times. I had OMed with hundreds of women including OneTaste staff from different cities. It was a practice, and we were all practitioners. But it never crossed my mind to ask Rachel. And unlike every other woman in the house, she never asked me.

When I realized this, I asked her. She said yes, of course. But then she canceled and rescheduled three times. Only then did I realize she probably felt the resistance that I did.

When we finally did OM one Morning Practice, she didn't get off at all, nor did she ask for any adjustments. Her frame was monotonous and short. We both were incredibly awkward, as if we had violated an unspoken taboo. Though I had begun to find her incredibly beautiful, I didn't want to sleep with her. I didn't want to feel her surrender. I simply wanted her approval.

Rachel had in fact become my mother.

Rachel referred to all her mentees as her "kids." It was meant facetiously, the way an office employee might have a "work mom" or "work husband." But the more time we spent together, the more literal it felt.

Maternal lineage is extremely important amongst bonobos. Sons assume the status of their mothers. If you're a young male bonobo, the best thing that can ever happen to you is to be born to a high-status mother.

Rachel often set up OMs for me to have with different women. Like Cheryl, these were women who had a scheduled sales appointment with Rachel right afterward. It became obvious that OMing with me was part of the sales process. After all, an orgasmic state makes you want to say "Yes! Yes! Yes!" to anything. But I figured I was simply helping these women overcome their fears and live in accordance with their desires.

Any OMs that Rachel set up for me were unusually sensational. As with Cheryl, they felt like sex. I almost always got an erection. Some of these women were my type, but many weren't, and I still couldn't help getting turned on.

There were many women in New York with whom I had occasional Makeouts. Without consciously realizing it, I began choosing to spend more time with women who happened to spend a lot of money with OneTaste. I had greatest desire for and best sex with women who happened to be Rachel's coaching clients. I had a particularly electrifying connection with Cheryl, Rachel's favorite coaching client. It was as if Rachel could control my arousal with her approval.

During the next House Meeting I noticed Rachel grinning at me.

"I've been hearing some good things about Ruwan," she said.

"What are they? I want to hear good things about Ruwan," said Andrew.

Rachel ignored him and winked with both eyes. I guess I made momma proud.

She scrunched her jeans down to the ankles.

Rachel had a different kind of grace. The bones of her rounded back protruded through bare skin as she hopped on one leg to get her pant past her heel. Now she was naked. Afternoon sun illuminated the translucent ends of her auburn hair.

Even though she was only five-foot-two and six years older than me, it was hard to feel like anything but a child in her presence. Being twenty-five made me an adult out in the 'real world.' But here, in the Morellino, I was one of the kids. Her kid. The fact that I was sitting on her elevated bed and piddling my feet only added to the dynamic.

"So let me get this straight," she said while looking through her dresser drawers. "The bitches won't leave you alone, and that's freaking you out, huh?"

I shrugged. She smirked. She began yanking clothes from the drawers. In moments, the carpeted floor was covered with her designer dresses, tops, and yoga attire. This was what most of our 'mentorship sessions' looked like.

She turned to her closet so that she faced me full frontal for a moment. I tensed. She didn't look at me directly but had a grin on her face. I knew that she knew that I was trying not to look at her breasts. This had to be a test. But I couldn't tell if passing the test meant looking, or not looking.

"And it was fun at first, but now you're getting diminishing returns on pleasure."

"I guess."

"Got it." Rachel rose from the shoe pile holding two matching pumps. "You know, I was thinking about you last night..."

My heart fluttered.

"I was thinking about how far you've come, considering where you came from." Rachel moved over to her makeup mirror. "You have a lot of Orgasm now. So you're like a magnet for women who want Orgasm."

She slipped on a black cocktail dress.

"These women aren't willing to do the work to have their own Orgasm. So they are trying to steal yours. They think *you* are the Orgasm. They are trying to claim *you*." Rachel leaned into her vanity to touch up her eyelashes. "But you are not the Orgasm, Ruwan. You're just standing in front of the doorway to the Orgasm."

She adjusted her hair. Then for the first time this afternoon she turned to look at me. Warmth filled my insides. Something about her attention always felt so good.

"Listen to me, Ruwan. This is something you always need to remember. Women are going to try to use you as a backdoor way to get Orgasm for free. They will try to marry you. They will try to get pregnant by you. They will suck you dry if you let them. But you must never let them. You can date, you can have Makeouts, but always guide them to walk through the front door themselves. You are not the Orgasm. You're just a *messenger* of the Orgasm. Do you understand?"

"I think so."

I would look back at this conversation many times. Over the following year I'd replay it each time my sense of reality jerked forwards and back again. I would consider all the decisions that led me to this peak, and the consequences that led thereafter.

But in this moment, I questioned nothing.

I had no fears or doubts.

For in this moment, I was plugged into a power much greater than myself.

"Thank you, Rachel."

She smiled. "You're welcome Ruwan. You're one of the good ones."

Rachel winked at me with both eyes, because she couldn't do it with one. She about-faced and called in her signature baby voice,

"Janey! I ready to go downtown and make some money!"

MOST OF THE TIME I spent with Rachel was as her personal chauffeur.

I'd drive her to in-person sales meetings, VIP OM trainings, or to the dentist. Sometimes we'd talk, but most of the time she'd be on the phone doing sales calls or trading info with another member of the Exec Team.

Some of it was gossip of who's sleeping with whom. Other times they were more pointed progress reports. Some OneTaste staffers were given the missions to seduce celebrities in different cities. An executive from CrossFit had recently been seduced and would become one of their biggest public supporters. Priscilla, OneTaste's CEO, was arranging a mass OM-training for the staff at the CrossFit Headquarters in Santa Cruz. Other celebrity targets would be revealed in court years later.

"You know everything you hear in this car is confidential, right?" Rachel would say.

I'd nod.

If there was such a thing as "limbic resonance," Rachel and I had it. I'd turn down the air conditioner a moment before she shivered. I knew when she wanted to stop for food before she had to say it. I knew when she wanted music and at what volume. As in an OM, I could feel her desires in my body. I was basically hooked into her limbic system.

When she did sales calls on the phone, I'd lay on her bed and take notes. Occasionally, she'd mute her mic and explain what she was doing.

"This guy is trying to Top me, so I'm taking my finger off. Never continue a conversation unless you're in control... If they don't surrender you can't help them."

Rachel called this shared time my "training." But it wasn't training in the sense of learning skills. Everything Rachel explicitly taught me wouldn't even fill one double-spaced page. The real training she gave me was implicit, changes in feeling and behavior... like training a dog.

As Daniel pointed out months earlier, like heat on the body, the emotional vulnerability of OneTaste meant we were vulnerable to being remolded.

Most skill acquisition at OneTaste was implicit—unconscious copycat behavior. Most people who went on to teach for OneTaste would speak in Nicole and Rachel's unusual stop-and-start cadence. Abby and I were called to teach some intro events, and we spoke in the same way. Much later I'd learn that this was an NLP technique known as *Open-Looping*—a way of leaving a listener with incomplete information so that they couldn't help listening more eagerly.

No one taught us to use this technique. No one told us to change our senses of humor, or body language, or ways of flirting. But we all changed, without having to be told.

Non-cult outsiders often ask, "How could you be so impressionable?" Even in the federal court, thirteen years later, Nicole and Rachel's attorneys would repeatedly ask witnesses, "Well no one forced you to do X, Y, and Z, right? You were a conscious adult who could make rational decisions, RIGHT?"

But we weren't. If you stay in a cult dynamic long enough, you cease to see yourself as an adult. In small, gradual steps I had come to defer my better judgement to that of my teacher. This allowed me to do things that I would regret later.

But in this was also a gift. As with all things in OneTaste, the light and dark were blended.

Rachel gave me a kind of love I hadn't experienced before. Love with *unconditional approval*.

Under this spotlight, all my shortcomings were forgiven. A lifetime of insecurities disappeared. It was impossible for me to feel shame— how could I when my emotional-spiritual authority asserted that I was a "good one"? I could be reset. Reformed. Reborn.

All I had to do was love her back.

What the guru really gives the disciple is an opportunity for devotion. The disciple projects perfection onto the guru, and in return receives (at least the perception of) unconditional approval. This allows the disciple to re-enter the hyper-receptive state of a child. The disciple can clear his slate and release his wounds.

Outsiders get confused by this. They point out that it really wasn't "unconditional"— that it, in fact, made me dependent. OneTaste taught "love" as a technique— to make people feel belonging and euphoria so they would pony up money and eventually their lives. It was Hooking. It was manipulation.

All those things are true. And it's also true that in my months with Rachel I developed a love for myself and a trust in life that I could only theorize about before.

Rachel would prove to be no saint over the next months. Years later, when the FBI opened an investigation of OneTaste, they'd question me about Rachel. I wouldn't hold back in sharing about her sins. More would come out in the criminal investigation. But that didn't change anything. Even as a false idol, she changed my life.

To this day, Rachel Cherwitz has had as positive an impact on me as anyone in the world. And for that I'm eternally grateful.

I DECIDED TO UP-LEVEL my devotion.

I felt I was spreading my energy too thin. I cut things off with all the women I had Makeouts with. I decided to keep my energy in the Morellino. And only give it to women who were also serving the Orgasm.

My world became particularly small and safe in this time. Rachel as my mom. The other residents as my siblings. And OneTaste as my purpose.

But the real world did still call me.

I often convinced myself and others that I wasn't in a cult because I still saw my pre-OM friends sometimes. I even convinced some of my college buddies to try the How To OM class, but none stuck with it. Roger had gotten serious with his date from Barnard and they'd sometimes invite me out to talk about my "crazy clitoris thing" with her friends.

One day, a friend of ours from college was visiting New York and wanted to do mushrooms with us, like old times. I felt weird about joining, but I knew they would really judge me if I didn't. We ended up tripping in his rented AirBnb in Midtown.

Around two a.m., I sat up from under a blanket. Only a desk lamp was on. All my buddies were either passed out or still hallucinating in dark corners. The room looked scary. I heard a voice.

Go home. Now.

Despite having taken a few grams of psilocybin just hours ago, somehow I sobered up and took a cab back to Harlem.

It was close to three a.m. when I arrived back at the Morellino. I quietly entered apartment 2E. There was an orange glow coming from the Womb room. Lila had left her salt lamp on. As I opened the door, she sat up like a spring-loaded action figure.

"I felt you coming," she said.

When I saw her, I loved her. I didn't ever want to go out into the real world again.

I told Rachel about this.

"It's good you listened to that voice," she said. "If you didn't, you'd be Whacked a long time."

Whacked meant being so emotionally distraught that you couldn't function. It happened when a person tried to enter levels of sensation beyond their range or tried to contradict the Orgasm.

"The Orgasm is entering its biggest peak ever," Rachel said. "Most aren't going to make it through the Portal. But I'm glad you are."

MOST DID NOT MAKE it through the Portal.

Rachel became increasingly frustrated at Bonnie's inability to 'Parent.' She fired Liz and sent Bonnie back to Austin. By the seventh immersion of CP6, there was a clear and growing divide within the class.

Over the summer, each major OneTaste city had invited certain CP6 students "to go deeper," meaning probationary employment with the company. If you were useful, they found a use for you. Those who were attractive and articulate were invited to take part in sales—usually the *Hypervolatile* types. Those who were focused and organized were invited to help with production—usually the *Fixed*.

But some stopped at the threshold. Others simply weren't invited. And anyone who didn't "make it through the portal" was treated differently. Everyone received massive love and attention when they entered OneTaste. But to continue receiving that drug, you had to give them one of their valued currencies.

"OneTaste runs on two currencies: Money and Orgasm," Nicole said.

Money was the material currency of the masculine world, she explained. It paid for stuff.

Orgasm was the immaterial currency of the Feminine. It could only be felt, because it was feeling. It was the source of enthusiasm, joy, desire, and courage. It was what made music good, or art beautiful, or an experience meaningful.

OneTaste staff joked that they were "paid in Orgasm". That was why staff members were willing to work for bare subsistence salaries, and probationary employees like me were willing to work for nothing at all. We really did live at a "higher level of sensation" than the rest of the population. Sex, connection, highly vulnerable communication— basically what *muggles* tuned into Netflix for— was a part of everyday life. We lived in a reality show, where nothing was staged, and every moment was true authentic humanity.

But money was still necessary to exist within the greater world. Therefore OneTaste needed its business to keep the lights on and its people fed. OneTaste sales was basically a currency exchange. It traded good feelings for cash. Sales was a finite game OneTaste must play to serve the infinite game of our high-sensation lifestyles.

"If we make some money, great! If we get some ass, great! But they are all just in service to keeping the infinite game going," Nicole said.

The class cheered.

Amongst those who "didn't make it through the portal" were those who decided to drop out for financial reasons. Like me, many students were spending a thousand dollars per month that they didn't have.

Rachel always said that anyone who left angrily had been overcome by scarcity fears and blamed OneTaste to justify it.

"Those who reject their freedom must then demonize what had made them free," she said. "People usually keep their Orgasm for about six months after they leave. But then it disappears. You'll see."

I was glad that I had made it through the peak. But my unpaid credit card bill was now more than a few months of income. The first time I couldn't cover my bill, back in January, it was extremely anxiety provoking. But now a certain peace had come over me.

There was no foreseeable way for me to pay it off soon. So I might as well surrender and trust the Universe. I figured this was the "Abundance Mentality" Rachel spoke about. And if I bailed now, then I would be in all this debt for nothing. If I stayed, maybe I'd become Enlightened or make a lucrative career from all this. At least I still had my day job.

That evening, I was fired.

My employer had been trying to get in touch with me all day while I was in the immersion. I got back to the Morellino in the late evening and called him from the rooftop. He had finally gotten around to reviewing my work and noticed my quality and output had tanked, basically since I joined OneTaste.

I had gotten this job as a content writer the previous summer when I was still with Lisa. I showed up to the interview coked out of my mind, kind of hoping I wouldn't get the job because that meant I would have to spend less time with her. I demanded that I work from home four days a week. This was at a time when remote working was rare. Mistaking my confidence for competence, he accepted. When I moved to the Morellino in March, I demanded I work from home full time. He also accepted. But now, he had understandable buyer's remorse.

A part of me was relieved. I had felt guilty that he was basically paying me to study Orgasm while I crammed eight hours of work for him into about forty-five minutes each morning. But now I was in trouble. With no income, my credit cards were going to be maxed out soon. My heart was pounding. I couldn't take a full breath.

Downstairs in the PHC living room, Lila and Sergio were drawing tarot cards. Sergio could feel my feelings before even looking at me.

"Hey dude…. Whoa. What happened?"

I told them my troubles. As I spoke, I realized this was the wrong crowd from which to get sympathy. Sergio worked as a minimum wage janitor while also working full time for OneTaste. Lila kept her life savings in an envelope under her pillow. Me complaining about only having a few grand of credit left probably sounded like a millionaire complaining that he could only afford a fifty-foot yacht.

"Ruwan, this is a great opportunity," Sergio said. "The Universe is giving you a chance to let go of your attachment to money. If you surrender, the Orgasm will take care of you."

"Orgasm doesn't pay rent, Sergio."

"You would be surprised, Ruwan. I used to be like you. I used to think money was important to be happy. Then I learned to surrender to the Orgasm, and it's taken care of me since."

I felt too defeated to argue.

"So how do I surrender?"

"We can do a sex magick ritual," Lila said. "Come, I'll do it with you."

I was just desperate enough to give it a shot. Lila took me by the hand and led me up to the Birdy Nest.

Apparently, a sex magick ritual looked just like an OM.

"You just stroke me," Lila said, "and I'll hold the intention of abundance for you."

Under any other circumstances I would have laughed or rolled my eyes. But even if there was a one percent chance this did something, I guessed it couldn't hurt.

I did feel better afterward. Lila claimed that our sexual energy was now going to attract abundance to me because *like attracts like*.

"So what do I do now?" I asked.

"Just be grateful and receive what's coming."

The next morning my money fears returned.

I did my best to "sex magick" during the immersion's morning OMs but worry caused my breathing to constrict. After the OMs I curled up in one of the white leather armchairs in the Bank Street space and tried to get off on it.

A firm petite body climbed into my lap. It was an OMer from the Midwest with whom I had hardly spoken. She cuddled me and massaged my chest right where my breathing was constricted.

Suddenly, she sprang up and left.

I rubbed my eyes open and saw Rachel standing over me. She was wearing platform heels, white jeans, and a blazer. She smiled love down at me. Light from the floor-to-ceiling windows made her silhouette glow white.

"Hi Ruwan," Rachel said.

"Hi."

"I spoke with the Exec Team about you. You've been officially hired by OneTaste."

My chest expanded. I wasn't sure if Rachel knew I had gotten fired. But I did know she was the one who pushed for me to be hired by OneTaste. I knew that she was my connection to the Orgasm.

"You're going to get twenty percent of New York's revenue," she said.

My jaw dropped. OneTaste New York sometimes brought in as much as thirty grand per week.

"Thank you, Rachel."

"My pleasure, Ruwan. You're one of the good ones."

And with that she winked at me with both eyes and walked away.

"HAVE YOU HEARD THE one about the Scorpion and the Frog?" Nicole said.

"So, a scorpion needs to get to the other side of a river but cannot swim. He sees a frog and says, 'Would you take me across the river?' The frog says, 'No way. I know you. If I let you on my back, you'll sting me and I'll die.' 'But if I sting you while on your back, we'll both drown,' says the scorpion. That made sense to the frog, so he lets the scorpion on his back. Halfway across the river the scorpion stings the frog and they both begin to drown. The frog says 'Why'd you do that? Now we're both going to die.' The scorpion responds, 'Because it's my nature'."

Sounds of recognition came from the crowd.

Nicole showed us a mini documentary about the Stanford Prison Experiment. The Stanford Prison Experiment was a thing where students were assigned to play the roles of prisoners or prison guards in a closed environment. It had to be shut down after six days because the students began to take the roles far more seriously than expected.

I had seen it before in psych classes in college. Those who hadn't seen it before gasped. But this time it made me feel hopeful about humanity. It confirmed that people were neither good nor bad, but we tend to act in accordance with our social incentives—the "game."

Nicole's point, I assumed, was to show us about how someone's reality and identity could be changed so quickly.

Before Nicole left the stage, she singled me out. I was so caught off guard that I didn't realize she was talking to me at first.

"Yes, I mean you, Ruwan," she said. "I want to acknowledge the shift in you. Sometimes we only see a small shift in people. It's remarkable seeing how you are showing up in the room now as a man. I want to mark this moment in your language center so that you can start from here."

"Thank you."

The highlight of this CP immersion was the Sales Demo.

Sales demos were like Orgasm demos, but everyone kept their clothes on. The staff treated it with the same reverence. Chairs were aligned perfectly. The Back of House was still. The room was completely dark except the stage. Under the spotlight were two chairs facing each other. Rachel sat in one of them.

"I need a volunteer," Rachel said.

Many hands shot up.

"We're doing this for real," she said. "Who ACTUALLY wants to get stroked?"

Some hands went down.

"Lila," Rachel said.

I got a sinking feeling when Lila took the stage. She was wearing a short black skirt and broken floppy sandals. She sat on her hands with her elbows flared out, leaning forward with her knees knocked in. The broken sole of her sandal flapped as she wrapped her ankles around the chair legs.

Rachel sat with her legs wide open, her platform wedge heels planted firmly on the ground.

"So," she said, "What do you want me to know?"

Lila sighed and her face turned red. It was clear why Rachel picked her. Lila always got off on the stroke.

"I feel... kind of lost."

"I see."

Rachel looked down at her even though they were the same size. She was perfectly still. "You're heartbroken."

Lila nodded and her posture collapsed. Abby reached over and took my hand.

"That's understandable," Rachel said. "You feel as if your friends went off and left you."

Lila nodded.

"What do you want?" Rachel said.

"I want... I want to be a part of it."

Rachel sat taller. "So, you want to join the team... You want to be the *backbone* of New York."

"Yes!"

Abby and I glanced at each other.

"So you want to take *Mastery* so you can become the backbone of New York."

"Yes!" Lila's limbs externally rotated. She was still sitting on her hands, but now her posture more resembled Rachel's.

Mastery was OneTaste's new six-month program, Rachel explained. Each month it focused on an advanced skill application of Orgasm into sex and into life. It was six thousand dollars. I knew Lila didn't have six thousand dollars.

I yelled in my head, don't do it, Lila. *Don't do it.* But it was too late. She was getting off too hard. The room was getting off with her. That was the real magic of a demo. When a Turned On woman is in Orgasm, everyone can feel it in their bodies. Almost half of the remaining CP class would sign up for Mastery that night.

"So," Rachel said, "how do you want to pay?"

STAGE 6:
EXCITEMENT

Swelling into form. The subject prepares for action.

"The body wakes to a spark, a reckless hum that promises everything and demands nothing but surrender."
~ Anaïs Nin

BOOM! BOOM! BOOM!

"Police."

I was pretty sure I heard that wrong. It was six in the morning. Lila was stuck to my left side. I waited for another knock before I peeled myself out of bed and checked the door.

A tall cop and a short cop stood in the hall. There was a dead body in the alley behind the Morellino, they said. They wanted to check our windows. I let them in.

I told Lila to cover herself and she pulled the blanket over her face. The tall cop entered our Womb room and peeked out our window.

"Not here. He fell from higher up," the tall cop said.

The short cop grunted. Before they left, he took a long look at the stacks of blankets, pillows, hand towels, jars of lube, and latex gloves that lined our hallway.

We spoke about it at the Team Meeting.

"I heard it was a guy from the next building," Andrew said. "He was on the roof and he fell off."

"I heard he jumped," Tanya said. "He killed himself because he was depressed."

"Tanya!" Jane said. "How the hell would you know that?"

Tanya crossed her arms and looked up and away. "Well, that's what I heard."

"Okay, there's a lot of energy in New York right now," Rachel said. "Mastery is making everybody feel a little crazy. It's important for us, the holders of the Orgasm, to be super grounded."

We started selling the new Mastery program some weeks ago. OMers were flocking to sign up. There seemed to be a new euphoria flooding the New York Community. OneTaste moved a couple more staffers to New York from the West Coast including another CP6 student named Rose, to run production. Rose had to go through various acts proving her devotion including writing a public declaration that Rachel later referred to as the "Rose Program." It came up in court years later.

Us new hires for Team New York worked from seven a.m. till past midnight every day without losing a beat of enthusiasm. The only explanation was that we truly were "charged up with Orgasm." Some of course, were able to handle the energy better than others.

"That means being conscious of where you are," Jane said. She glared at Tanya, Lila, and Tanisha.

The last few weeks the three of them had been walking into the wrong apartments. Each floor of the Morellino had identical layouts. Dr. Tanisha kept walking into apartment 2C thinking it was PHC. Yesterday, Lila and Tanya walked into PHE thinking it was 2E.

"Yeah I was wondering why we put up random photos of some family," Tanya said. "But I did like that we had better furniture and a rug."

"You should have walked out of there right away!"

"I didn't know. And hey, I'm not the one who bled all over their carpet."

"It was just a drop," Lila said.

Jane put her palm to her forehead. Lila turned red. She had been free-bleeding and left a menstrual stain on the carpet. Free-bleeding is a thing that witches do that often ruins furniture.

"The neighbors are starting to complain," Jane said. "The building management said they are going to evict us if we keep walking between apartments without clothes."

"I was wearing a towel!" Tanya said.

"A towel isn't clothes!" yelled Jane.

"Hey!" Rachel snapped. "We're going to take the energy levels downnnnnn. We're all going to get this within the rails. Do whatever you need to do today to get grounded."

Everyone dispersed. Rachel put her nose in her phone.

"Hey Rachel," I said.

"Yes, Ruwan."

"So Abby is sales, Rose is production, and Lila is the backbone... What exactly is my role?"

Rachel smiled down on me even though she was four inches shorter. "Your role, Ruwan, is to keep the women turned on."

She winked at me with both eyes then began to turn away.

"Wait, seriously," I said. "I am just supposed to OM all day?"

Rachel sighed.

"Ruwan, we're grooming you for leadership. One day you will run New York. So I need you to be aware of everything. Make sense?"

"Oh," I said.

She didn't wink at me this time. Instead she smiled in such a way that made my chest expand.

"Which reminds me," she said, "there's someone I want you to stroke today..."

THERE WAS NO "WORK-LIFE" separation at OneTaste.

There were no official work hours or even workdays. Every morning, we did our practices. Then we had a Team Meeting. Then we were supposed to do what "felt right" to serve the Orgasm. Seven days a week.

"Weekends are for people who don't love what they do," I explained to a new OMer.

Working at OneTaste was all about feeling good. If someone was tired or overwhelmed during work, it was totally acceptable to stop what you were doing to go to another yoga class, do more fear inventory, meditate, have an OM, or even have a Makeout. In fact, attempting to do work when you didn't feel good was considered "masculine" and therefore incorrect.

"It has to feel good to be good," was one of our adages.

We were tasked with generating five thousand dollars per day. This meant selling at least one Mastery or Coaching Program—CP7 was starting soon in San Francisco, and CP8 was to begin in New York in March. We were given no instructions, but to simply make it happen. Abby did this by cold calling each of the few thousand people who attended TurnON New York in the last year. I'd stroke her in between calls.

Lila and I tried the most random ways of generating leads. Before every TurnON event, we'd go to Washington Square Park handing out white balloons with provocative sayings and the TurnON event details on it. I recorded street interviews in Union Square where I asked people about their sex lives. We didn't track metrics or have a clear plan. We just did what felt right.

"Sometimes you'll invite a hundred people to TurnON and none of them will show up," Jane said. "But then twenty new people you didn't invite will. *Energy in. Energy out.*"

The only thing that actually generated sales were personal connections. A lot of our sales meetings looked like gossip. We'd report to Rachel all the intel of who was sleeping with whom and see if a sale could be enticed through multiple touch points. One of us might invite someone to an OM or Makeout then "casually" mention Mastery. Another might trigger an insecurity in that same person at TurnON. All of this was designed to make them want to buy.

"We're lions. And lions hunt as a pack," Rachel would say. She'd often play us video clips of lions savagely chasing down prey together.

We generated multiple Mastery sales almost every day many weeks in a row. A large part of it was from the Sister Goddesses and their lovers who made up a huge part of the New York OM Community.

We were euphoric. We got up before seven each day and worked till well after midnight with boundless enthusiasm. It was probably the excitement of money rolling in and our esteemed roles, and the fact that we were all in our early twenties. But of course, we assumed our energy came from the "Orgasm" we were generating. Even at night, we'd stay up laughing and playing. Each night felt like a slumber party.

"The Morellino is like summer camp for grownups," Abby said one night.

As if in a hamster wheel hooked up to an alternator, we were all expelling energy with the assumption that it was doing something useful. We were trained to believe that if we "followed the stroke," desired results would follow. So Abby made her calls. Rose planned event logistics. Lila, as "backbone," mostly cooked our meals and kept the apartments clean. I did a lot of stroking, and schemed ways to generate more leads.

We were on the stroke. We assumed the good feeling would last forever.

THE ONLY PERSON I didn't see much was Dr. Tanisha.

She was technically part of the sales team, but over the summer she had been doing very important research over at Rutgers University.

The study was testing the hypothesis that "self-stimulated orgasm" was neurologically different than "partnered orgasm".

First, they had female subjects enter an MRI machine and bring themselves to orgasm. Then had their partners reach into the MRI and stimulate them to a second orgasm, to compare the brain activity. Most of the participants ended up being OMers. Apparently, it's hard to find normal people that want to get off twice while inside of an MRI.

We heard that the study so far was very promising. During solo orgasm, the women's amygdalas were still active—that was the part of the limbic system responsible for threat detection, what Nicole called the *vigilance center*. Whereas in partnered orgasm the amygdalas were quiet.

This validated Nicole's adage that "You can't take yourself out of control"— Women could only enter deep Orgasm when contained by a competent other.

OM was ready for the mainstream.

One morning meeting we were told that, in addition to Mastery, we were to focus on selling a new event called the Orgasmic Meditation Experience, or OMX. It was a three-day conference about Orgasm, health, and wellness, directed at the greater personal development community. It was in three weeks. Each city was expected to sell at least two hundred tickets. Rachel expected New York to outsell the rest.

"Nic got this idea from the Transcendental Meditation community," Rachel said. "They have a huge dome in Iowa where they set the record for the number of people meditating at once. Nic wants to create a one-thousand-person OM Circle."

"Wow that will be so much energy!" Lila said.

Rachel smiled and nodded. OMX would bring together all the OMers from around the world, while introducing newcomers to the cutting edge of sexuality and human connection. There would be talks by Nicole, famous speakers in health, wellness, feminism, neurology, mindfulness, and the unveiling of Dr. Tanisha as America's next celebrity doctor.

"We're launching T's career!" Rachel said.

"Tanisha's a doctor!" Lila said.

"Yes, and she's under a lot of stress," Rachel said. "So everyone do what you can to support her." She turned to me. "Ruwan, I want you to make sure T is feeling good."

I texted Tanisha to OM.

"Actually, there's something else you could help me with," she wrote back. "Come to my room."

She was sitting on the bed with her laptop and a bunch of papers. RnB was playing in the background. She cleared space for me to sit.

"This book has been stressing me out so much," she said. "I don't know where to start."

There were many tabs open on her browser.

"What's it supposed to be about?"

"Priscilla actually wants me to write two books," she said. "One is my story of finding Orgasm, like 'How Tanisha Got Her Groove Back.' The other is on the science of Orgasm."

"Oh I have an idea!" I said. "For the story one, you can make it eight chapters, one for each of the Stages of Orgasm. Like Climax can be your divorce, then Resolution can be finding OM…"

She stared at me blankly.

"Or not…"

We decided to look at the science one first, as she was going to present about the Rutgers research at OMX. She already started the PowerPoint.

"Feels like something's missing," she said.

Half her slides were about the Rutgers study, half were on Nicole's philosophy of connection.

"Wait, you're talking about two different kinds of 'orgasm'," I said.

She stared at me blankly. There were red capillaries in her big eyes. She had either been crying, or not sleeping, or both.

"Your Rutgers study is about climax, *little o*. The philosophy stuff is on connection, *big O*."

Tanisha was a doctor. She was articulate and charismatic and had a great ability to recite verbatim. But somehow this semantic distinction went over her head.

"Um, can you just fix it?"

I figured she needed a transition slide. I quickly made one. It was a flow chart of words that connected the two definitions of "orgasm." It was vague and the words didn't quite fit on the slide. I figured she or someone would edit it later.

Tanisha and I began meeting regularly in the afternoons. Sometimes we'd OM. Sometimes she'd just ask me things. I looked forward to it. When she was cold, she was really cold. But when she was warm, she was really warm. She did feel like a big sister. And I liked being a helpful brother.

"Hey Ruwan, what's a *biohacker*?" she asked me.

"It's someone who finds ways to optimize their body. Like a hacker who finds ways to cheat a computer system, but you find ways to upgrade your biology."

"I was just interviewed on this podcast by some guy who used that word like every other sentence. This Dave Bulletproof Man…"

"Dave Asprey, The Bulletproof Exec?"

"You know him?"

"Yeah! He's the reason I drink butter coffee."

"That is so. So. Gross."

OneTaste had a big PR campaign for the new face of Orgasm. Tanisha was scheduled for a podcast circuit to be interviewed by many people I used to follow, such as Chris Ryan who wrote *Sex At Dawn*. I liked helping her prepare.

One afternoon, I found Tanisha in the PHC kitchen drinking a glass of milk.

"Hey T, would you like to OM?"

"No," she said. She was in cold mode.

"Oh, okay."

"Actually, can I ask you something?" she said.

"Sure."

She showed me a document on her laptop. It was a contract between her and OneTaste about writing the books. She wanted to know what I thought of it.

"It looks like this gives OneTaste all the rights to whatever you write," I said.

"So that's bad right?"

"It's not good."

"What should I do?"

"Renegotiate? It looks like OneTaste will get all the money from your book and be able to do whatever they want with your image."

"That's bad."

"It's not good."

Tanisha went back to her room with her glass of milk.

She was taking a risk sharing that with me. It was Collusion. But I was her only option for a second opinion. The senior staff would have gaslit her. Lila was too up in the clouds. Abby was sort of her rival as posterchild. And anyone outside of OneTaste wouldn't get it.

A few hours later I got a series of angry texts from Priscilla, OneTaste's CEO. She didn't like that I was helping Tanisha with her book.

"That is not your role!" she said.

"I thought my role was to keep the women turned on," I wrote back.

"No, your role is social media!" Priscilla said. "And production!"

The next day we each got an email outlining clear bullets of what our roles were. My new role was to produce four videos per week for the OneTaste YouTube channel. And help Sergio move boxes.

OMX WAS TO BE OneTaste's big break into the mainstream.

Three days. Thousands of attendees— both existing and future OMers. And a record-breaking one thousand nest OM. I didn't want to miss a second of it.

"The Orgasm has entered the Excitement Channel!" Rachel said.

After years of being a fringe sexuality company, OneTaste had finally passed the peak and now was ready to enter the world of mainstream personal development, Rachel explained. Nicole was invited to teach OM to Tony Robbins' 'Platinum Members' who were mostly A-List celebrities. I had heard from an OMer who used to work for Tony, that Platinum Members paid ten percent of their income yearly.

I was thrilled to be a part of something so big. But one week before OMX, I had a family reunion cruise in LA. It was a big deal for my family. My mother grew up in poverty in the Philippines and was the first of her eight siblings to come to America and make it into the middle class. That all my aunts and uncles now had the means to go on a cruise together was a generational achievement. But I felt bad I was missing out on the OneTaste happenings.

"You feel guilty that you're going to miss out, huh?" Jane asked me. "I know how you feel. But don't worry. Family is important too. The Orgasm will still be here when you get back."

Some of my cousins were aware I was doing some sort of spiritual sex thing based on my Facebook posts. But no one talked about it. Bringing up high-sensation stuff like that was antithetical to Asian-American culture.

But they noticed I was different. Even my parents didn't recognize me when they met me at the airport. My aunts used to call me "the autistic cousin" because I never spoke at family gatherings. But now I was the most eager to connect.

I tried to engage my fourteen-year-old brother in vulnerable conversation. I apologized for being closed off when we were growing up. I expressed my desire to be closer from now on.

"Um, this feels weird," he said. "I think I have a headache."

Only my uncle was willing to discuss my new lifestyle after a few drinks. He was a journalist in Hong Kong. He told me it would make a good story should I ever want to write about it. Eventually one of my cousins was bold enough to join in and ask me about OM.

"That's interesting... But kind of weird isn't it?" she said.

"Yeah, it's a cult!" my uncle said. A few beers later he added, "See, that's what happens when you're too strict on your kids. They end up in a cult, like Ruwan."

By the end of the cruise, I was disappointed that my new connection skills didn't translate so well to enjoying time with my family. Emotional vulnerability was simply a foreign concept to them. So I was even more eager to get back to my other family.

When we got back to land, my phone kept crashing from the number of text messages. I had been offline for five days. I had missed over two thousand group texts.

iMessage threads were a big part of working for OneTaste. There was a thread for every city, a thread for the worldwide team, a thread for the sales team, a thread for every production event, a thread for expressing emotional needs, and ones for all committees. Android users were expected to get an iPhone if they wanted to stay on the team.

Some messages were important announcements, directives, or celebrations of big sales. But most messages were flirtations— emojis, and memes. If you were on a thread you were expected to respond immediately to "stay connected." If you couldn't, you were expected to announce what you were doing and for how long.

"*OMing. Offline 22min,*" was a common message on the thread. So was, "*Bathroom. Offline 10min.*"

I was happy to return after "*Family reunion. Offline 5 days.*" Team New York arrived in San Francisco a few days before OMX to help lay the groundwork. We were welcomed by our West Coast counterparts like extended family. They felt like our cousins. Team New York was my siblings. It was an odd feeling after leaving a literal family reunion.

Most of us camped in one of the living rooms in 1080 Folsom. Lila and I fooled around with one of the San Fran residents on one of the couches while other staffers snored on cots next to us. Around midnight she and I drove to the Oakland airport to pick up some of the London staff, slept a few hours, then got up at four-thirty to launder and dry the new OMX staff t-shirts— we'd have to do this every day for the next three days, since there was only one shirt per staffer.

OMX was the ultimate sales event. Hundreds of people were OM-trained each morning, if only so they could participate in the thousand nest OM. Many OMers were enrolled in Coaching Program 7, to start soon in San Fran. And even more were enrolled in Mastery.

Rachel had me give John all the info on women from the New York Community so he'd know how to flirt in order to sell them. Mixed in with the talks and panels were dance breaks on the main floor. During one of these breaks, I saw John connecting with Xena. I remembered that punch-in-the-solar plexus feeling. I was glad I didn't have that anymore.

On Saturday, the keynote was "The Science of Orgasm" by Dr. Tanisha.

She captivated the audience. She made them laugh and nod at all the right times. I was proud of her. She shared how the Rutgers experiment was finding that yes, there was a major difference between partnered and self-stimulated orgasm. It was proof that we really did need each other. And proof that the OM practice delivered something vital to our nervous systems.

Halfway through the slide deck she pulled up a flow chart. It was vague and the words didn't fit on the slide. It was the one I made for her trying to connect the different definitions of "Orgasm." It looked ridiculous on the giant screen. Bullets of sweat formed on my forehead. I thought for sure someone would have edited it. I should have thought it through better. I held my breath.

A collective awe came over the crowd. Affirmative sounds popped up. They loved it. They loved her. Somehow it all made sense. I exhaled.

OMX was a huge success. OneTaste had hit a new level of prestige. Orgasm had infected the hundreds of newcomers. Almost all attendees were impressed by the pristine attention our staff put on everyone. Many journalists attended and we expected them to put out positive write-ups.

OneTaste always recommended people "Come down pleasurably" after a big event. The idea was that we cultivated a ton of Orgasm and sensation. If we didn't find a pleasurable way to bring our energy back down, our bodies would find an unpleasurable way to discharge. Staffers and students who ignored this advice were well known to end up in fights or even car accidents after OneTaste events.

So after the last day was packed up, almost everyone ended up in bed with someone. I spent a few high sensation hours with Cheryl right after the event was closed. She and I had reconnected on the dance floor. Lila spent some time with her ex who lived in 1080.

But not everyone was coming down pleasurably. When I got back to 1080 that night, Dr. Tanisha was standing catatonically in front of Rachel and Priscilla who seemed like she had just been yelling. It seemed that the more OneTaste elevated a person in public, the more they cut them down in private to ensure submission.

"Hey T," I said.

Priscilla glared at me. "Ruwan, it's not your job to..."

"Let him be," Rachel interrupted. "He knows how to handle her."

Priscilla frowned. I led Tanisha to the upstairs lounge.

Two residents were just finishing up an acupuncture session. We had the room to ourselves.

"Would you like to OM?" I asked.

Tanisha slowly shook her head. Her eyes were glossy.

"Can we like, just cuddle?" she said.

We laid down and I held her. I put a hand on her chest. She was trying not to cry. I could feel it in my own eyes.

"Do you want to make out?" she said.

"Okay."

It was a particularly unsexual kiss. We really did feel like siblings. She was my big sister going through a hard time beyond my comprehension. I was her little brother doing my best to console her. She wept. Then finally took a full breath.

"It feels different between us," I said.

"I think we've become friends," she said.

"Cool."

I had been naked with this woman multiple times. But this was by far our most intimate moment—cuddling with clothes on, calling each other "friends." Sometimes sex is a block to connection.

Monday morning, we had a team debrief in the new OneTaste headquarters.

OneTaste San Francisco had moved out of the small office in 1080 Folsom and acquired a huge event space in an office building. It was on Market Street, right across from the Twitter headquarters.

OMX was the biggest revenue weekend in OneTaste history. Many people signed up for CP7 which would start soon in San Fran, and Mastery which would begin in November in New York. OneTaste would soon make the top ten lists in *Inc. Magazine* for "Fastest growing female-owned companies" and "Fastest growing companies in Health and Wellness."

There was one result that wasn't so favorable. A journalist from *Gawker* wrote a piece titled, "My Life with the Thrill Clit Cult." It wasn't scathing, just cynical. The author did try OMing during the weekend and seemed to love it. But she had called OneTaste the 'C' word.

Via the worldwide iMessage thread, we were told to not mention the article to Nicole. The Exec Team was trying to protect her from it.

"Nic is very sensitive," they said.

Theresa once told me that Nicole used layers to protect herself from the public. People were not allowed to be physically close enough to her to touch her—for when you touch someone, they feel human to you. Only the Exec Team had direct access to her. If she engaged with someone, it was always on her terms.

The layers added to her mystique. They amplified the Halo Effect—people could project omnipotence on to her.

But it worked both ways. She was also separate from reality.

At the next CP6 Immersion, Nicole gave a talk called "The Fucker and the Fucked."

All Nicole lectures were recorded. A clip of this talk eventually became one of the most watched clips on the OneTaste Youtube channel.

"We have this misconception that power is in isolation," she said. "Everyone wants to be the fucker, and no one wants to be fucked. But to be a good fucker, you need to get fucked first."

I remembered Theresa's email to me about how suffering is not a virtue. But then I thought about how Theresa was literally alone and had far less money and power than Nicole and OneTaste. Nicole's framework was simply more believable— of course one grew by entering discomfort.

"Being the fucker is not the dominant position," Nicole continued. "The power is in being fucked. You learn to fuck well by being fucked. When you become a good fucker, you never have to worry about money again."

The high of OMX didn't last very long.

Many signed up for CP7 and Mastery shortly after OMX, then sales dropped off. We had saturated the market.

After a string of twenty-thousand dollar revenue days, OneTaste corporate gave New York the daily revenue goal of ten thousand dollars. Now we were struggling to make five. Even if we sold a quarter of the newcomers at TurnON on the How To OM, a great accomplishment, that still would barely make two grand in revenue.

The Team got upset with me when they found out I hadn't yet signed up for Mastery. I told them I was deep in debt and couldn't afford it. John texted me from SF, "don't you think it's inauthentic to sell people on Mastery when you're not doing it yourself?"

He had a point. I applied for a new credit card and signed up.

We were all crashing. Whatever had fueled our enthusiasm the last months was gone. Rachel said we had wasted our Orgasm. Whether that was true or not, we all needed somewhere else to go to recharge.

Abby began spending more time with her longtime non-OneTaste boyfriend. I found my escape with Cheryl. She and I began sleeping together again after OMX. Cheryl was still Rachel's coaching client, and a potential Mastery sale. So Rachel approved of me missing Morning Practice to spend time with her.

I liked Cheryl a lot. She was funny and smart and our physical chemistry was off the charts. But I had to admit, a large part of why I stayed at her place once a week was simply to get a full night's sleep. I knew Rachel was expecting me to get her to do Mastery.

I asked Andrew what he thought of the way OneTaste played with people's emotions to make sales. He told me that he's seen a lot of people go through OneTaste over the years. The ones that grew the most were the ones that dove into the intensity and let it work them. The power was in "getting fucked."

The next day he quit.

He told Rachel he loved the practice and loved OneTaste, but he got the message that he needed to do his own thing. Rachel looked heartbroken but didn't fight him on it.

Shortly after, I wrote Rachel an email with the subject, "Ruwan wants to get fucked." I declared my intention to do whatever it took to grow and serve the Orgasm.

"Oh my!" Rachel wrote back. "This is great. Let's do this."

I had no idea what I was asking for.

LOVE TRIANGLES WERE COMMON in OneTaste.

Sometimes it was two women with one man. Sometimes it was two men with one woman. But the type of person who was shared was very different than the ones who did the sharing. You never saw someone do both.

As Daniel pointed out months ago, Anxious-attached and Avoidant-attached people behaved differently in OneTaste. In any love triangle, it was typically two Anxious-attached people sharing an Avoidant.

Anxious people were drawn to dynamics where they never quite got their needs met. This made them perfect students for OneTaste, who always "left them wanting more." This made unavailable (Avoidant) people particularly attractive. Though consciously heartbreaking, longing was their subconscious comfort zone.

Avoidants were drawn to dynamics where more was being asked of them than they could possibly give. This made them ideal employees of OneTaste, who would drain them of everything they had. This made always-available (Anxious-attached) people particularly attractive. Though consciously exhausting, being always desired was their subconscious comfort zone.

I was of the latter category. My relationships with Lila and Cheryl both developed into "serious" ones. When I wasn't slaving for OneTaste, I was spending time with one of them.

One interesting thing about dating two very different women concurrently was seeing how different parts of my personality came out.

Cheryl was older than me and had a high-paying corporate job in the "real world." With her, my more "feminine" side came out. When we went out, sometimes to restaurants I couldn't afford, she always paid. Like the movie trope, but reversed, I was her Manic Pixie Dream Guy who nudged her to do crazier things, such as quit her job and move into an Orgasm Residence.

Lila, on the other hand, was barely connected to earth. Since she was so deep in her feminine, my traditional masculine side came out with her. When we went out, which always had to be framed as a 'LeadGen' opportunity, I'd end up paying. I was as broke as she was. But I still had room on my credit card. She was the one always encouraging me to feel more and think less.

Managing their jealousies became its own job. Every time I saw Cheryl, half the evening became talking through jealousy feelings. Then the next morning, I'd have to do some of the same with Lila. I asked Rachel about what to do.

"They both need to learn how to let go of their attachments," she said. "Remember what I told you. They are using you as a backdoor to the Orgasm."

Cheryl eventually signed up for Mastery and CP8. Rachel indirectly gave me credit for it. Rachel seemed to approve of me spending even more time at Cheryl's. I got more sleep this way. But Lila began to suffer even more.

"You're not even a player in this game. You're just the soccer ball," Jane once told me.

In reality, I wasn't in a relationship with either of them. I was in a relationship with OneTaste. Though my feelings for each of them were genuine, they were mini-games inside the game of OneTaste. Relationship drama such as this was shuffling furniture on the Titanic. It kept us emotionally occupied. It gave the illusion of free will. But our destination was already decided.

ONETASTE MOVED JOHN FROM San Fran to New York.

When he arrived, he gave me an expensive-looking shirt that he said didn't fit him anymore.

"I keep hearing a lot of good things about you," he said. "I think we're going to be good friends."

I looked up to John. He was a few years older, more experienced in OM, was always composed and seemed to carry a lot of wisdom. And unlike many other leaders in the OM

Community, he had options outside of OneTaste. He used to work for Apple but chose to be here.

Rachel encouraged us to spend more time together. It seemed that he was a part of my training.

John offered to do a coaching session with me every morning at six am before Morning Practice. We'd go into the building's storage basement and he'd ask me confrontational questions to help get my "Beast" out. We did a practice called "Withholds," a practice where you shared thoughts you've held in for some reason. It was kind of like a one-on-one HotSeat that got straight to the point.

It was October. Our breaths would make frosty clouds as we yelled in each others' faces. By the time we went back up for morning practice we'd usually be sweaty. It felt good to do "man stuff" for a change.

One afternoon, John pulled me aside.

"Hey Ruwan there's something I have to tell you," he said. "So Lila and I had an OM... and that led to a Makeout... and that led to a little bit of sex."

"Oh thanks for letting me know," I said.

"How do you feel?"

I checked my solar plexus for a punch-in-the-gut. Nothing. Maybe I had successfully learned to 'get off' on jealousy, I thought.

Later that day, Lila pulled me aside.

"Ruwan, I have something to tell you."

"You boned John?"

"Yes." She blushed an embarrassed shade of red. "But it only lasted a minute."

"Ah, that's why he said, 'a little bit'."

"What? Anyway, how do you feel?"

"Fine."

"What? Why aren't you jealous??" Her face flushed into an annoyed shade of red.

I wasn't sure at the time. But it probably was because I felt more devotional attachment to OneTaste, and John by proxy, than the actual woman I was romantically intimate with.

One evening John asked me to take him speed dating as he heard it was a thing I used to do. On the train ride he told me his story. He was one of the first employees at the Palo Alto Apple branch and received a bunch of stock. By his mid-twenties he had everything he wanted: money, a cool car, a hot girlfriend. He and his girlfriend started taking OneTaste classes together. On a OneTaste retreat at Lake Tahoe, Nicole asked him what he had to offer the group. He said, "money." Nicole told him to go home.

"I didn't understand the Feminine," he said.

In OneTaste, his girlfriend wanted to open their relationship. She ended up leaving him for a OneTaste staff member from Philadelphia.

"I found out this one afternoon," he said. "I was driving around the Mission in San Fran with Rachel. Every block I'd stop the car and bang the steering wheel yelling 'Fuck! Fuck fuck fuck fuckkk!!' Rachel was just there with me. She held space while I burned through my shit."

Years later, I'd realize this is what they did in Chinese prison camps—Cause extreme distress then save you from it, creating deep attachment. These were the same camps where the term "brainwashing" comes from.

"I ended up sitting on Nic's bed—that's when she still lived with everyone in 1080—and just burned through my shit. It was horrible. But Nic just loved me up." High-up staff referred to Nicole as 'Nic.' It was a status marker to say you were on friendly terms with her.

"Wow."

"Yeah, around that time I realized that all I wanted was to devote my life to the Orgasm."

"Wait, you're a lifer??"

Lifers were OneTaste staff that committed their lives to OneTaste. There was no explicit contract, or even declaration. But it was usually obvious who was. These were people who made it clear they had no intention to go back out into the real world. But unlike John, they usually had no money or other desirable options.

"Yes, I am."

"But... you can actually be successful outside of all this. I thought you were just doing this for a bit then... but what about your job at Apple..."

"I've completed that cycle," he said. "This is my path now."

I knew my brow was furrowed, but I couldn't help it.

"You've only seen Nic on stage, so you have a different view of her," he said. "Nic is the homegirl. When she lived with us in 1080, her door was literally always open. If you ever had a problem, she'd invite you to sit on her bed... she'd be in her pajamas and no makeup... and she'd just feel you."

We continued our 6am "icebox" coaching sessions. They were one of my favorite parts of the day. I began to wonder if being a OneTaste *lifer* could be a good path for me. John was clearly happy and had qualities I was seeking.

One Sunday, the Team went out for brunch. Rachel was on the West Coast helping with the first CP7 immersion. I got a series of texts from her while our food arrived.

"This boys club needs to stop," she wrote. "You and John have been colluding."

"I don't understand," I said. "He's just been coaching me."

"No, Ruwan. He's been pulling you away from your Orgasm. It stops NOW."

I saw John at the other end of the table hunched over his phone. He hadn't touched his Eggs Benedict. I knew he was also getting downstrokes from Rachel, much harder ones than mine.

Without discussing it, we stopped our morning coaching sessions. He and I didn't speak directly again for months.

I participated in Dr. Tanisha's study with Cheryl.

But it turned out, it wasn't Dr. Tanisha's study at all. Though she had the title of "doctor," she was still in residency. Far from "America's next celebrity doctor," she was just a research assistant to PhD sexologists, Barry Komisaruk and Nan Wise.

I was shocked. A sane person would take this difference between perception and reality as a reason to start questioning everything. But I was not a sane person. Instead, I decided to further push what I previously believed.

So I set Tanisha up with a speaking gig at the philosophy salon that I used to attend.

I had been going monthly up until I was hired by OneTaste. It was kind of like an underground TEDx event, where many New York-based authors, thought leaders, and artists would present their work. It was co-facilitated by the ginger anarchist whom I met at my How To OM class. He hadn't OM'ed since.

"Hey so I've been following your journey on Facebook," he said. "Has your sex life really become that good?"

I wasn't sure how to explain it to him. Orgasm really wasn't so much about sex when you got into it. It was about living a higher resolution reality.

"Yeah," I said.

I was proud to unveil Dr. Tanisha to this crowd. She had all the credentials that would impress a group of intellectuals. And she had killed it at OMX just two months earlier.

She did that same exact presentation that she did at OMX. She recited the same words with the same facial expressions. She made the same jokes with the same timing. But this was a very different crowd. There were no OMers trained to get off on everything. There was no BOH staff to provide Social Proof. The salon instead was made up of intellectuals, filmmakers, psychotherapists, and philosophers skilled in critical thinking.

By the midpoint flowchart, she was panicking. Arms crossed and brows furrowed in the audience. The same quotes that received cheers at OMX got groans here at the salon. She had lost the crowd. I wanted to throw in the towel and shield her from the blows.

During the following Q&A they picked her apart. They pointed out her inconsistent definition of 'Orgasm.' She didn't have a clear response. Someone asked if her definition of 'connection' was related to Marxism. She went catatonic.

Tanisha was a doctor. She wasn't a pundit. At some point I turned around to answer the rest of her questions for her. But it was too late. She had been beaten down.

As soon as the talk ended, Tanisha grabbed her things and was out the door. I walked out with her and hailed her a cab. I noticed she had a suitcase.

"Where are you going?" I asked.

"Ohio, to visit my family."

"When will you be back?"

"I don't know."

Her face was blank. I wanted to hug her and tell her everything would be okay. But awkwardness and our winter coats deterred me.

"Hey T, you did really well tonight. It was just a tough crowd."

She looked at me with her big brown eyes. Her pupils were pinholes. I felt tears in my chest.

"Goodbye Ruwan. Thanks for everything."

"Bye Tanisha. See you soon."

"Yeah."

She got in the cab. I never saw her again.

WHEN A MID-RANKING CHIMPANZEE is dominated by the alpha, it often takes out its aggression on those of lower status.

Nicole blamed Rachel and the Exec Team for the drop in sales. Rachel took it out on her direct subordinates. With Tanisha gone, that meant most of the blame was put on Abby. Abby took it out on whoever she could.

Jane once told me that "Women who OM sometime act like men. Every strokee wants to prove she has the most lit up pussy."

The tangible evidence of this was sex and sales. And no one was making sales.

The fact that John had slept with Lila first was a big deal in the female-female competition within the Morellino. Abby began making biting comments against the rest of our team, especially against Lila. When I tried to defend Lila, Abby started taking it out on me.

"What's going on between you and Abby?" Jane said to me one day.

"I don't know. She's just being mean all of a sudden."

"Yeah, she's been Topping the shit out of you... you can't let her do that."

"I thought I was supposed to get off on stuff."

"Ruwan," Jane sighed. "You're the only man here. The women are tumesced because you're not handling them."

"I don't know what that means."

"You need to be more dominant!"

"Oh."

"Didn't the pickup artists teach you how to be dominant or something?"

"I wasn't good at that part."

I was surprised at what I was hearing. I thought 'domination' was some sort of patriarchal construct that we were supposed to avoid. One of my draws to the OM Community was that I thought in the 'feminine' world, I wouldn't have to learn how to be 'alpha.'

I was very naive.

"Wait, I thought all that mattered was connection," I said.

Jane smirked her disappointment.

"Women need to be handled," she said. "And you need to learn how to do it."

Theresa had told me about the guy who was the "only man Nicole ever let Top her," Om Rupani. Since OneTaste's New York's recent resurgence, some women in the OM Community had been OMing with him. I got in touch with him to learn about power dynamics.

He lived in a brownstone in the Sugar Hill section of Harlem, walking distance from the Morellino. We met one afternoon in his front parlor.

His entry way was lined with plants. When I knocked on the door, it swung open. Om's bassy voice invited me in. He had a lot of antique furniture. He had a lot of cats. He was sitting in his front parlor petting a cat on his lap. The drapes were drawn so that a shadow cut across his body. I wondered if good Doms needed to look dark and dramatic.

"So what's up?" Om said.

I asked him about Topping and I asked him about Dominance. I had my notebook out, of course, to capture everything he said. He didn't show much emotion, but it was clear he didn't want to be interviewed. I put my notebook away.

"If leather and whips and chains are your thing, that's all fine and great," Om said. "But they are not necessary for domming. I can top anyone from my pajamas."

I noticed he was in his pajamas.

"You'll find that the kink realm is more about healing than pleasure, though even practitioners don't always realize this," Om continued. "Many fetishes are related to past traumas. We tend to eroticize our pains because it's a way to reclaim parts of our psyche that we've become disconnected from. We take what we used to hate or fear and combine it with immense love and pleasure..."

He shared his connection to OneTaste. He was involved in the first iteration of One-Taste New York five years earlier with Theresa. He developed a Dom-Sub relationship with Nicole but took his distance at some point.

"You all have chosen to Bottom to Nicole," he said. "She strokes you, and you get off. She's the ultimate Dom. All you OMers submit to her because you trust her to handle you... We must have positive feelings about our Top. You must think she is interesting, capable. That perception elevates her to a higher level of mastery."

"I still don't totally get what 'dominance' is. Like, Nicole said that you were the only man who was able to dom her. How do you dom someone like that?"

"I was able to top Nicole because I saw her as a normal person," he said. "That woman has a hard job. All day people are treating her like a god. She doesn't get to relax with other people. Most my interactions with Nicole were just like this," Om said gesturing between him and me. "We'd just hang out. She could finally let her guard down because I didn't need anything from her. I didn't need her to be something. It must be exhausting being that woman."

One morning in PHA, Abby made a biting comment at me before our sales meeting started. I tried throwing it back at her. Abby was about to throw another insult at me when Rachel interrupted.

"No, no, no! Whatever *this* is," Rachel said pointing to us, "it stops now. The two of you are to go have sex. And you're not allowed back to work until you have."

I got tunnel vision. In a lifestyle where surreal events were common, this still was a shock. Abby and I meekly did as told, as we had been trained to do over many months. But even for us this was strange.

"Our boss just assigned us to have sex," I said to her as we entered PHC and walked to the Birdy Nest.

"This is so crazy," she said.

Meanwhile, Lila broke down weeping in PHA. She was already in a state of constant stress from our love triangle, plus the ever-increasing responsibilities of being the "backbone of New York." Any time an Exec Team member came to town, she had to give them a massage.

Rose broke down crying too. She was probably the most outwardly composed of the four of us, but had been breaking down in different ways over the last month. Her responsibilities had also increased. Rachel had Rose be the strokee when Rachel OM-trained New York celebrity men. Whether or not they stuck around OneTaste was the measure of how much Orgasm Rose "gave" them. She also had to clean Nicole's bedroom. Since no one else was allowed there, it was framed as a special privilege. In reality, that meant Rose had to pick up used condoms.

Rose would frequently "climax," which meant hiding in the bathroom to cry. Lila would be sent to talk her down, then I would be sent to stroke her. We kept an OM nest in the bathrooms for this purpose. Twice, Rose tried to escape the Morellino in the middle of the night, but was intercepted by Sergio. Each time, we spent the following morning having an intervention. We love-bombed Rose. Then Rachel guilt-tripped her for wanting to leave.

Rose later said this was the moment she knew she had to leave. But in OneTaste, nothing was ever that simple.

Abby and I sheepishly returned to PHA twenty minutes later, after a very awkward encounter. Lila and Rose had already recomposed.

"Good," Rachel said.

I still didn't understand 'how to be dominant.' But this wasn't it.

A LETTER CAME IN for me that looked like a check.

I opened it excitedly. My eyes got wide.

I owed the Marine Corps ten thousand dollars.

"You were in the Marines?" Jane smirked.

No, I said. I enrolled in their Officer Candidate School while in college because I hoped military training would help me become confident. Plus, they gave me a monthly stipend. But after earning my commission, a mushroom trip showed me that I didn't want to kill people. Since I didn't serve, I had to pay that money back. I had kept it saved for a couple years, but once I got fired from the marketing firm and I hadn't heard from them, I figured they forgot, and I spent it. Now the bill was in.

Thankfully, I was owed a good amount of money from OneTaste.

We had been working for months and still hadn't been paid. I partly didn't notice because the pace of life had me lose track of time. And when I did remember to ask, Rachel would get annoyed, and I'd drop it. But now it seemed like the right time to bring it up again.

"Hey Rachel, so when are we getting paid?"

"You need to learn how to speak about money without all this charge!" she snapped then left the room.

After a few more brushoffs I spoke with Abby and Lila about it. Abby agreed with me that it was pretty messed up for us to go so long without being paid.

One evening I put my foot down. The whole team was hanging out in PHC. In a partially rehearsed monologue, I laid out that we were owed a few months of wages, and asked when we'd get paid.

I expected Abby, Rose, and Lila to chime in with me. Instead, I got crickets.

"Aw poor Ruwan is stuck in money scarcity," Rachel said.

I noticed I was sitting alone on the floor. Abby, Lila, and Rose were cuddled on the couch with Rachel. John and Jane were off to the side. The room seemed very long and everyone else was far away.

"What do you want?" Rachel said, Her tone shifted from teasing to sharp. "You already live in such fat abundance of Orgasm."

"I'm not trying to be greedy, but I need to know if I can manage my life here, or if I need to leave and find a real job!"

"If you do, it will be Compensatory Behavior," Rachel said. *Compensatory Behavior* was Nicole's term for anything you do to avoid following your real desire.

"Don't worry Ruwan" Lila said, "pray to Archangel Michael and he will provide for you."

I frowned.

"Oh Ruwan doesn't want help from angels, Lila" Rachel said. "Don't worry I'll pray to Archangel Michael with you."

Everyone laughed. Even Abby. Rachel had somehow captivated the room and framed me as a crazy person. I didn't understand. But I knew that if I said anything else, it would be twisted to make me look more crazy.

Once the spotlight was off me, John took me aside.

"Hey Ruwan, I just want you to know I understand the spot you're in. I was there for a long time," he said. "You want the Orgasm to prove itself to you, and then you'll surrender. But it's the other way around. In my experience, when you trust the Orgasm, it will take care of you."

I went up to the rooftop by myself. The courtyard was surrounded by a short brick wall with a wrought iron fence on top. I climbed onto the wall. I looked down on the Harlem streets. It was freezing. Slices of warm light came up the stairs and out through the top bedroom glass doors. I could hear everyone laughing below.

In OneTaste, I was framed as crazy for wanting money. Outside of OneTaste, I was crazy for ever being in such a position. I was completely alone in my reality. I did feel crazy. This is why most people drink the water.

Later that night I asked Abby about what happened.

"Yeah, she Topped the shit out of you," she said.

"No I mean, why didn't you back me up? You haven't gotten paid either."

"Honestly I don't know," she said. "It just felt good to laugh. I'm sorry."

Eventually I got a message that next week the Exec Team would talk to me about my money concerns. But this week was an important event that required everyone's focus.

OVER THE PREVIOUS MONTHS, OneTaste had been doing a secret project in Los Angeles.

OneTaste had been working with a pornographic production company to make sex education videos. The first one was to be unveiled, as the final big promotion for Mastery, which would start in the month.

It was officially titled, "Oral Sex for Her Pleasure." Internally, we referred to it as the "Cocksucking Demo."

In it, Priscilla did a video demonstration on how a woman can derive pleasure from giving oral sex. It was a skill that Nicole would be teaching in Mastery.

We hosted a "film premier" for the video instead of TurnON one Wednesday. I was tasked with getting dinner for the team at Chipotle before the event began. I had a stack of reimbursement receipts from similar trips. I had to open a new credit card to just to cover my "work expenses."

As I exited Chipotle with two full bags of burrito bowls, a small woman in a giant coat tugged on my shoulder.

"Can you buy me some food?" she said.

Her eyes showed a lot of pain. Of course, I said. I waited on line with her. She was sixteen, she said. She moved out of her parents' house to live with an older boyfriend. He turned out to be abusive and kicked her out. Her parents wouldn't take her back. Now she was living in a women's shelter. She had a stain in the middle of her front teeth. She ordered the biggest size of burrito with guacamole.

"Guac is extra," the server reminded us.

I shrugged.

On paper, this young woman's net worth was higher than mine. Hers was zero. Mine was about negative twenty thousand. But I had credit cards. And I had Orgasm. Maybe my scarcity-mindedness really was just in my head. Maybe I was just being ungrateful.

Before I could get back to the venue, I saw an OMer sitting on a stoop. It was Sally, the Sister Goddess ballerina, who also taught the Alexander Technique.

"Ruwan, can you sit with me for a second?" she said.

"Sure."

She told me she had been considering taking Mastery. Her boyfriend, who sometimes came to my Men's Group, had an Exploratory with Rachel recently. He just sold his car in order to take Mastery. I knew many of the details already. Part of being on the OneTaste sales team meant sharing personal notes about anyone and everyone in the OM Community. I heard they had opened their relationship, Sally began sleeping with Sergio, and her boyfriend was now desperate to win her back.

Ironically, she was now jealous of him and wanted to take it too. She also felt Mastery would help her flourish as an artist and as a woman. But she promised herself that she wasn't going to take any more personal development courses.

"Ruwan, I'm over twenty thousand in debt from Mama Gena courses," she said. "I don't know what to do. You've gone a lot deeper with OneTaste. Is it really worth it? I mean, no offense, but all you guys working for OneTaste kind of look like stressed out zombies…"

I tightened up a little but tried not to show it.

"I figure if I leave now, I'd be acting out of fear," I said. "I'd still have all this debt, and I'll always wonder what could have been. And… it has been my experience so far that if you serve the Orgasm, it does take care of you."

I wasn't sure about what I had just said. But it seems the best way to get someone to defend a position is to challenge them there.

THE FILM ITSELF WASN'T what I expected.

It was less instructional, and more art film. It opened with Priscilla sitting cross-legged in a bright white background. She read from a diary.

"Dear Women," she said. "I am a woman who used to do oral sex for *him*. I did it to be a good woman. Maybe I fucked up, or I wanted him to think I liked him, or for a new pair of shoes. Then I learned of Orgasmic Meditation which led me to a new possibility…"

The film cut to her performing fellatio on a male staffer. It was done "softcore" with nothing more explicit shown than the back of her head over his crotch. Cinematic shots showed their fingers embracing, his facial expression, and a zoomed out shot of them on a red couch in an angelic white photo background. There was some voiceover of how she was using his anatomy to pleasure her mouth, but no other instruction.

The final shot was of her on the couch, addressing the camera with the flushed cheeks and glow that showed she was feeling a lot in her body.

"I do it for me, and he gets exactly what he wants," she said. "I look forward to the day that every woman in the world does oral sex for her pleasure."

There was a huge ovation when the lights came back on. Many women had tears in their eyes.

Abby did the sales pitch for Mastery, sharing how one of the six monthly immersions would focus on "how to get off from giving head," as shown in the video. Many signed up for Mastery that night. Over one hundred students would be in the inaugural class.

Sally was one of them. John credited the sale to me. I received a bunch of kudos from staff members around the world, many of whom I had never met. Sally had been labeled a "hard sell." Many salespeople had already struck out trying to close her. Apparently, I had found the right stroke to push her over the edge.

THIS SEEMED LIKE THE right time to ask to get paid again.

I finally got a meeting with Rachel and Priscilla in apartment 2E. Rose, Abby, and Lila were there too, but didn't say much. This time I tried coming in with more data. I had a list of everyone who signed up for Mastery in New York. Twenty percent of all that revenue meant we should have received a huge payout.

"Well Rachel technically closed all those sales," Priscilla said.

"We were told not to close ourselves, but to fluff for Rachel," I said.

"And you all are part-time employees so all you're owed is twelve-fifty per month."

"What?! We literally work from seven am to midnight every day!"

"Practices don't count as work."

Rachel looked at me with sympathy. Priscilla was the bad cop in this setup.

"You have to ask yourselves," Priscilla said, "am I really doing this for the money??"

Priscilla was once the founder of a major men's clothing startup. I heard she was booted because she was caught embezzling funds. Depressed and suicidal, she ended up meeting Nicole, who "saved" her, then hired her as OneTaste's CEO.

"Believe me, I'm not trying to get rich working for OneTaste," I said. "I just have bills to pay!"

"We all do!" Rachel chimed in. "You think we're keeping all the money for ourselves??"

I knew that was true. Rachel, despite personally generating over four million dollars per year in sales, received the same twenty-five hundred per month as everyone else.

Rachel then said that she and Priscilla shared a bank account. Nicole would periodically put funds in it, and they had to decide between themselves how they spent it. I wasn't sure if she meant literally or figuratively.

"If you're really worried about money, then you can get a part-time job," Priscilla said.

"I thought that was *Compensatory Behavior.*"

I looked to Rachel. She said nothing.

This wasn't a game that could be won with logic. I was "stroking for climax" so of course I was getting a contracted reaction. I had failed to read between the lines. I took a deep breath and changed my tone.

"Listen, I really love serving the Orgasm," I said. "And I want to continue doing so. What I need to feel safe here is to know I can cover my material needs."

Priscilla softened her attack. Rachel seemed to approve of my stroke. After more discussion we came to an agreement. Rose had financial support from a family friend so she was willing to defer her income to help the Orgasm. Lila was happy to receive the twelve-fifty per month. Abby and I would share commission from any sales where we directly spoke to the person before they were closed by Rachel. The commission check came out to about twenty-five hundred for three months of work. In total, less than two dollars per hour.

SOME DAYS LATER, ROB Kandell called Lila and I together.

"You've been let go by OneTaste. You'll each receive three weeks' severance minus tax, seven hundred and forty-four dollars."

Lila and I looked at each other and smiled. More sane people would have demanded much more. But we were just grateful to have received anything.

"How do you guys feel?" Rob said.

"Honestly, I'm relieved," I said. "It hasn't felt so good to be on the team."

"Good."

We were a part of a mass firing. OneTaste had to let go of almost all the 'tier three' people hired with us back in August. Only a few of those early hires stayed on. Abby was one of them.

Jane mentioned that OneTaste was in financial trouble. They had made a huge amount of money for a couple months—high high five figures a day selling Mastery, CP7 which just started in San Francisco, and CP8 which would begin next April in New York. But they'd increased their spending along with the huge increases in revenue, assuming the sales would continue rising forever.

On top of that, OneTaste's balance sheet seemed to also function as Nicole's personal account. OneTaste paid for her to have a home in every city, including the loft bedroom in PHA. Every so often my car, the "OMmobile," would be unavailable because Nicole would take it to visit a lover in Connecticut. I heard from someone on the bookkeeping team that there were periods where Nicole didn't draw a salary but instead had OneTaste pay for her life as a business expense. Later, a forensic accountant would find that a salary was being funneled to Nicole's mother, whom no one had met.

I was back to having no income and no life direction. But I wasn't worried. These months of OMing had given me a totally different lens on reality. I had come to "trust the stroke." If I did what would feel best in every moment, then the next best thing would work itself out.

It had to feel good to be good. It didn't feel good to work for OneTaste anymore. But it still felt good to be in the OneTaste world. My life was still as interesting as ever.

Something would work out.

BEING "LET GO" DIDN'T actually change my day to day.

I still attended Morning Practice as a resident. Rachel still invited me to sit in on the Team Meeting. I still OMed a lot. I still attended TurnON. I still ran the OneTaste Men's Group. The only difference was that I wasn't contributing to sales.

Rose finally made her escape from the Morellino one night. Similar to Tanisha's departure, Rachel showed real sorrow but tried to hide it. She brought in more people to fill the void.

A CP5 graduate from San Fran named Heather recently quit her job to come volunteer with the New York Team. She was also John's longtime primary partner and no doubt was tired of hearing of all his Makeouts in New York from afar.

Arjun, the self-made millionaire, and his girlfriend Winter moved to New York too. He was still wary about OneTaste and didn't want to move into the Morellino. So he found a way to be "halfway in" by getting an apartment across the street. Winter had a dog, a large Belgian Shepherd, and pets were forbidden in Orgasm Residences as they "sucked up energy." Arjun and Winter began volunteering their time with OneTaste New York all day. They paid me to run their dog around Central Park every day.

I had started coaching some younger guys in the OM community over the last couple months. One asked me if I was still "in" OneTaste.

"I'm still in the community, I just don't want to be in the company," I said.

"But it seems like you do OneTaste stuff all the time," he said. "Why not get paid for it?"

I remembered saying the same thing to Abby months ago. But I forgot her answer.

The only real difference in not being an employee was that there was no pressure on me to make sales. All the pressure previously placed on the whole team was now solely on Abby. She was expected to OM with any man off the street and sell them courses. She started saying no to OMs, and often was chastised for it. A TurnedON Woman was supposed to get off on anything. We could see her wilting day by day. One afternoon she was so stressed by Rachel's yelling, that she climbed out of the OMmobile while Jane was driving down Frederick Douglas.

Rachel called an emergency House Meeting. The only people in the Morellino were the OneTaste staff, Lila, and me. The meeting started like an intervention. It was all about Abby, and how she had been "off" lately. She had been feeling crazy, she said. We all sat in a circle while Rachel laid into her.

"You have Survivor's Guilt," Rachel said. "Your friends were dropped and you're the only one left."

"I just feel so terrible all the time," said Abby.

Abby was on the threshold of a big breakthrough, Rachel explained. Abby's fears were taking over to prevent her from evolving. That's why she had been so resentful lately. That's why she'd been unable to sell. That's why she'd been lacking in Orgasm.

"You have a virus," Rachel said. "We're going to get it out of you."

This wasn't an intervention. This was an exorcism. A "Killing."

It didn't take many strokes to kill Abby. She had already been in *fight-or-flight* for weeks. At the same time, she was devoted to Rachel. Rachel knew all her secrets. Abby went from resisting, to crying, to dry heaving, to silence. When she finally looked up, her eyes were completely blank.

"There's my friend!" Rachel said.

My conscience was screaming. I felt the impulse to stop it. But at the same time, I rationalized maybe this was good for Abby. Everyone in the room was nodding as if so.

"Your brain perceives learning and pain as the same thing," Nicole always said.

The next day, Abby was transferred to OneTaste San Francisco.

ONE TASTE MASTERY STARTED A few weeks before Thanksgiving.

OneTaste advertised Mastery as a course that would teach you how to bring Orgasm into sex—essentially to master sex. Each monthly immersion would focus on a different skillset. The first immersion was on "energetics"— how to manipulate sensation without physical touch. The second was on oral sex—how to get off on giving, as shown in Priscilla's video. The third was on anal play and power dynamics—which, funny enough, went well together. And so on.

But the opening night seemed more like church.

Nicole opened with a lecture about "Sex as Transmutation" referencing a chapter in the self-help book *Think and Grow Rich* which spoke of using sexual desire to manifest creative ideas. Nicole's take was that sex was the most direct access to the divine. The last couple CP6 immersions, Nicole had been revealing how she did occult magic rituals as a part of her growth practices.

The highlight of the evening was a demo. One of the selling points for Mastery was that Nicole was going to do the demo as a *strokee* for the first time in years.

The staff ushered everyone to their seats. Abby was one of them, in New York for the weekend to help as Back of House. The staff seemed even more serious than in regular demos.

Normally Nicole would walk on stage to a contemporary rock or hip-hop song. Almost every OneTaste lecture started with everyone getting up and dancing to rev up the energy of the room. But for this demo, she entered with angelic choir music. She wore a pink gown and walked barefoot to the demo table. They were framing her as the Messiah.

Demo models were usually trained to lie perfectly still and release their energy only as vocalizations of pleasure. Nicole as the demo model was much more theatrical. Her body spazzed and every limb tensed as if she was being electrocuted. Her moans were not rhythmic, but ecstatic, dramatic. This felt more like a show.

Across the room, Abby gave me a look that said, "*This* is what jumping the shark looks like."

Days after the immersion, she quit. The pressure finally got to her again. We heard she "ran away" in the middle of the night back to her parents on the East Coast. We were told she wasn't able to "make it through the portal," meaning she couldn't handle the next level of growth. She wasn't to be trusted, and must be avoided or else she might infect us with her resentment.

"Abby rejected her freedom, so she now must demonize what had made her free," Rachel said.

THE FOLLOWING WEEKEND WAS the final CP6 Immersion.

I was glad to complete it. My life had become so much more interesting, that the CP immersions felt boring in comparison. I still believed in "living in Orgasm," but I also wanted to re-engage with the real world.

The only exciting part of this final immersion was that each student got to have a private five-minute conversation with Nicole. She scanned me and told me what she saw in me: that I was torn between the realities of becoming a powerful man and being liked by others.

"Right now, you're so in the middle that you're not really going to fit in, and you're not going to be a powerful man. And you're going to have to move the needle to one of those to have any kind of peace. And my guess is that with the level of magnetism you have, you can't peacefully move to this one, though some part of you thinks that you can. So you are going to have to lay out... How are old are you?"

"Twenty-five."

"I'm forty-five... When I was your age I had a life where I was perfect... Top ten percent in the United States in grades, I had an art gallery, everything was right and I was already tasting the emptiness... I was getting so much external validation and I was tasting the emptiness and I thought, 'Oh my god, I'm going to be forty-five years old one day and I'll be totally empty, with an art gallery. Who cares?'... See right now, you put your attention out there to see the outcome, and you're going to have to put your attention in here," she pointed to her heart, "and ask yourself, 'Am I being true to you?' And that's going to have to be your only compass."

"Thank you."

"I hope you do it." Nicole nodded and smiled. "You did a video once..." She leaned forward and her eyes lit up. She said in a loud whisper, "I loved that video. You are so gifted."

Maybe it was too soon for me to leave.

That Thanksgiving I visited my family in Queens. I was never close with my immediate family. Even living just one borough away, I only saw them on holidays. Turkey day was normal, other than my little brother saying, "Dad told me not to end up like you." My cousins laughed. I had long been the black sheep.

The next morning, however, was an intervention. My father, a physics professor turned computer programmer, had prepared a Powerpoint. Slide by slide, he went through all the information available online about OneTaste— the Gawker article, various angry FourSquare reviews about 1080 Folsom in San Francisco. He was sure he was going to enlighten me about the "cult" I was in.

But I had many months of experience fluffing intellectuals exactly like him. I had also been making videos for the OneTaste YouTube channel and could explain the OneTaste philosophy in a non-weird way. I had handled every possible logical objection to OMing, and had enrolled countless guys in How To OM classes who initially made cult accusations.

The secret was the improv comedy adage, "Yes, and...". OneTaste taught this in most of their communication classes. You don't try to fight opposing arguments. You agree and show that it's in fact part of a bigger picture that they were unaware of. Like an offensive lineman, you stay light on your feet and so they are contained while also having nothing to push against.

"Always stroke people in the direction they are going," Rachel always said.

After about twenty minutes, my dad was out of ammunition. I even left on warmer terms than usual. When I left, I couldn't help feeling a bit like Rachel when she dominated someone with love. I simply had the stronger limbic system.

Arjun had the idea to make his own OM House in Jersey.

I thought it was a great idea and began discussing it with him.

I was still on the main Team New York text thread. At first it seemed like a nice gesture from Rachel to "keep me connected." But I realized all the notifications were just distracting my attention. I asked Rachel if I could be taken off.

"Why?" she responded.

"Because I don't want to be on the Team anymore."

"Why does that feel so horrible?" she said.

I felt bad for making her feel bad. I was confused. My conscience told me not to be involved with the OneTaste business, but I still wanted the benefits of the community. And I still wanted to make Rachel happy.

The following weekend Rachel demanded to have a meeting with Arjun. Afterward, he told me he couldn't do the non-OneTaste OM house anymore.

"Because of Rachel?" I asked. "Did you explain to her we weren't trying to compete, just do our own thing?"

"Nah, it wasn't about that. We mainly talked about you."

"Me?"

"She really loves you. She was afraid I was taking you away from her."

Instead, they offered Arjun the "game" of buying the failing Harlem yoga studio and running it with OneTaste. He and Jane ended up managing it together.

A few days later Rachel got me a job. There was a Sister Goddess, new to OMing, who owned a cafe in Brooklyn. Rachel convinced her to take me on as her personal assistant. A part of me realized this was Rachel's way of keeping me in her rails. Another part just felt grateful to have a job.

What I didn't realize is the few months of working for OneTaste had totally changed my sense of work. The fact that my new employer was an OMer didn't help. She looked up to me as a former OneTaste staff member and experienced OMer. This led to a strange dynamic.

Though my official role was to help her manage the cafe, much of my time was spent coaching her through emotional challenges. I had her read me her Fear Inventory. I let her vent about personal things. I even invited her to OM each morning.

"Is this okay?" she asked as we left the cafe at eight am to OM at her apartment down the block.

"Well, you're the boss right?" I said. "And you have to feel good to do good."

It only took a few weeks for her to fire me. She listed all ridiculous things I did as an hourly employee— leaving in the middle of the day to take yoga classes, suggesting we OM instead of actual work. I just nodded. All I could hear was, "I am not ready to live by desire, so I'm going to use logic to demonize it."

The job showed me I didn't really want to re-enter the "real world". At least not on real world terms. But I needed money and I didn't want to work for OneTaste.

There had to be another way.

THE LEASES ON PHA and PHC were almost up.

The Morellino building management refused to allow Jane to renew them. They were tired of complaints of us walking between apartments in our underwear. That meant all the staff was going to move into 2E. And all the non-staff had to go elsewhere. Rachel was heartbroken about it, but it had to be done.

I took it as a sign to finally create my own thing. There had to be a way to live by all the principles of Orgasm without being tainted by the OneTaste business. I told Lila we needed to do some sex magic to manifest the new house.

"What house?" she said.

"The Brooklyn OM House!"

"Where's that?"

"In Brooklyn!"

In a manic frenzy, I texted every serious OMer in New York who wasn't on the OneTaste staff. There was a whole stratum of people who wanted to live the Orgasmic Life without being controlled by OneTaste.

"But how?" she said. "We have no money and no jobs."

"If there is desire, there is a way."

Many people immediately texted back their interest. Arjun, his girlfriend Winter, Elma— my first OM partner, Sergio— who was still just a volunteer and wasn't allowed in the staff apartment, and several CP6 graduates and serious OMers enrolled in the upcoming CP8.

That night I had a dream about Nicole sitting on a park bench. I walked up to her and punched her on the shoulder. She smiled.

"You don't have to use force for me to feel you," she said.

THE NEXT DAY, ARJUN found a few listings in Bushwick.

I set up appointments. Lila, Arjun, Winter, Sergio, Elma and I went to see them that night.

The first apartment was a ground level place and included a storefront. All the bedrooms were in the back. There was a basement that would have been perfect for a practice room or event space.

"It's practical," I said.

"Too cold," Lila said.

"Yeah, it's too masculine," Arjun said. "Everything is efficient, but the energy doesn't really flow."

The second apartment was a three-story split-level over a car dealership. It must have been built section by section because each room had a different style. They had random nooks and closets that would have been great for hide-and-seek.

"It's unique," I said.

"The energy is chaotic," Lila said.

"Yeah, too feminine," Arjun said. "I already feel watery just being here."

The third apartment was a duplex on a side street near the M Train stop. You walked into the kitchen and common area which was surrounded by three bedrooms. Downstairs were two more rooms and another common area— perfect for OM Circles. It had a large backyard.

"It's just right!" Lila said.

"Yeah the energy is good here," Arjun said. "Feel the floors. They are solid."

Lila, Sergio, and I began stomping on the hardwood flooring.

"Please don't do that," the realtor said.

We signed the lease an hour later. The building was managed by a Russian Jewish leasing company. Their office was above a bar they owned under the M Train's above-ground tracks. The manager frowned that no one except Elma had a job—she taught math at a private school. Arjun logged into one of his bank accounts and showed the figure.

"Oh very good," the manager said. "Go have a drink downstairs on me."

The five of us got drinks. I hadn't had alcohol in almost a year. We all held our glasses but felt too awkward to take a sip.

"Shall we set an intention?" I said.

"We're going to create a house of badass witches and wizards here in Brooklyn," Arjun said. "People will feel it on us and ask, 'What's with those people?' and others will say, 'They are from the Brooklyn OM House.'"

"The Brooklyn OM House!"

"A-men."

"All the women!" said Lila.

We clinked our glasses and sipped. All five of us frowned. Lila and Winter spat it back in their glasses.

Sergio and the girls began discussing decorating options. Arjun and I had a minute to talk by ourselves by the bar.

"It's been interesting being in bed with OneTaste," he said. "I don't think the Harlem yoga studio will ever make money. But it's been worth the investment for what I'm learning."

"Like what?" I asked.

"OneTaste doesn't know how to run a profitable business. But they know how to run people," he said. "Jane told me, 'The secret to running a community is to make it look like a democracy but act as a dictatorship'."

"Is that what we're about to do?"

Arjun squinted his hawk eyes.

"The real question," he said, "is do people actually need free will to be happy?"

I remembered how Rachel told me she was going to take away my independence.

"Maybe not," I said. "I mean, even a dog walker needs to dominate the dog for the dog's sake. It's not to power trip over the pet. It's that the only way to keep the dog safe from running into traffic is to control the dog's reality. And it's not like we're doing it for selfish gain. We're just trying to have a happy magical community."

Arjun smiled slyly. "We can tell ourselves that."

Stage 7: Play

The Plateau phase. The subject can do no wrong.

"You ever see that movie *Samsara?*" Lila asked.

We were cuddling in our new bedroom in the Brooklyn OM House.

"No," I said.

"It's this spiritual documentary," she said. "They show these monks who spend their whole lives making huge mandalas in the sand. They place each grain of sand till it's perfect. Then as soon as they are done, they clear it away and start over."

"Why?"

"That's just what they do."

Sergio's footsteps shuffled up the basement stairs.

"Morning Practice, five minutes!" he called.

Doors opened and the yawns of sleepy OMers filled the house. We were all in the nests before Sergio's meditation app rang it's familiar gong.

"And begin..."

We did two OMs per usual. Every so often, OMers from the community would be waiting outside the apartment before seven to join the Brooklyn Morning Practice.

"And… time!"

From her nest, while wiping off excess lube, Winter would direct the morning chores. She was the House Mom, an official position which gave her free rent. Two people would cook breakfast for all, while the rest of us cleaned the House: mopping the floor, wiping down every surface. By seven fifteen the entire house was spotless. Then we'd eat a five-course breakfast.

Split ten ways, our rent came out to just four hundred ninety. Just like in the Morellino, we paid three fifty to a house fund that covered breakfast and dinner Monday through Friday. Each day of the week one room-couple was assigned to cook dinner for the house. So for eight-forty a month you had a place to sleep and ten meals a week.

I was sure we had created utopia. It felt like my first euphoric months in the Morellino, but without being tainted by OneTaste business practices. I had the idea to make a YouTube reality show about our house. Episode one became sort of a commercial for why people should move into OM Houses.

"I'm grateful for all this abundance!" Winter said mid-episode. She put the standard eggs, bacon, kale, and French presses of coffee on the table. "We have the best food, a beautiful home, because we pool our resources! And we get to live with all our friends!"

Out of the ten of us, only Elma had a real job. Arjun was independently wealthy and supported Winter. The rest of us found a way to make ends meet however we could. Sergio still worked janitor gigs while volunteering for OneTaste. Lila worked as an art model at NYU and sometimes got gigs as a backup dancer. I had a few coaching clients, but money came in randomly. The other residents, relatively new OMers who were enrolled in the upcoming CP8, found some ways to get by. Money was rarely discussed.

Coaching Program 8 would begin in New York City in April, so a lot of OMers from around the world wanted to move to New York to study full time. But unlike with CP6, there was no official OneTaste residence where students could live with staff. Each immersion, CP8 students would pay fifty bucks a night to sleep on a yoga mat in our living room. And there was a long waiting list of people who wanted to move in full-time.

Every Sunday we had a house meeting. We attempted to run our first meeting "leaderless" but that didn't work. As the most "highly trained" person in the house, I ended up running them. On the surface, this meant facilitating people's shares and making sure we hit all the points on our agenda, such as who would do what weekly chores or what kinds of snacks we should order. But in practice, this meant *stroking the room*.

As in the Morellino, the excitement of house meetings came from people working out intense emotions in full sight. Only this time, I was the stroker. Like Rachel, I often ended up doing impromptu therapy, conflict resolution, or even giving people life assignments for their growth. OMers were trained to be vulnerable, connectable, and to get off on anything.

Initially, I took my leadership role reluctantly. Someone had to make certain decisions for the group, such as the sleeping assignments, which we rotated every other month or so. Technically we put them to a vote, but they always ended up being what I suggested. OMers liked being inside someone's rails because it allowed them to go deeper into their feelings without worry. They could enter the magic receptivity of Child mode. But for that to be possible, *someone* had to hold the Container.

I began taking more initiative with directing our reality. I always felt our "shares" took too much time during house meetings, so I suggested that instead of sharing with words, we all put our hands in the middle for ten seconds and feel each other "energetically." We called it *Syncing Up*. It was meant jokingly, at first. But as many things in the OM world, repetition made it seem real. When new residents would move in, they'd "sync up" as if it was an important spiritual practice. Even I started to believe we were really merging our energies. It felt that way. But as I was beginning to forget, you can convince yourself to feel anything.

Across the East River, OneTaste New York had also found a new home. The Morellino management were so eager to be rid of OneTaste that they let Jane out the 2E lease early without penalty. The staff moved to a cramped two-story in Midtown West with three of the four bedrooms underground. It became known as "The Bunker." It was too small to host community events, so our Brooklyn House became the New York community's social hub.

Rachel and the New York staff came to visit the Brooklyn House a couple times to watch *Game of Thrones* "as a family." I knew that this was partly so Rachel could check if we were still aligned with OneTaste. But I didn't mind. It felt good to get her stamp of approval. It felt like we were dubbed a vassal within the greater OneTaste kingdom. That gave me more hubris in how I ran the house.

I began pushing the envelope with how much I could get people to do. I gave people nicknames, which became like their special identity within our house. When someone was overwhelmed, I'd give them an unusual task to do which seemed like a Zen lesson, but really was some random thing I made up on the spot—I learned that from Rachel.

One time a new OMer from a small town called me saying he felt inspired by OM life, but was nervous about going all the way in.

"It sounds like you're spending a lot of your life waiting for time to pass," I said. "Sometimes you need to make a bold move."

He quit his job, sold all his belongings, and moved into our house.

I wasn't trying to gain anything. I wasn't trying to domineer. It was just fun to see what I could get away with. The more certain of my reality I seemed to be, the more others wanted to subscribe to it.

Another time, the Brooklyn residents went to volunteer as BOH for the How To OM class. A relatively new OMer came to me distraught. His face was completely red.

"Ruwan, I'm whacked. I don't know what to do."

"Come here," I said.

I put one hand on his chest and another on his forehead. I pretended like I was channeling energy into him. I told him to close his eyes so he wouldn't see I was laughing.

"Wow, Ruwan, I feel completely better," he said a minute later. His face had returned to normal color.

I was just messing around. I knew this was likely auto-suggestion—his blind trust in me gave him a placebo-like effect. But also, a part of me liked the idea that maybe I really did have superpowers.

Without intending it, I had created a mini-cult within the cult.

This was not unique. It was part of the concentric circles of influence throughout the OneTaste community. People like me ran non-staff houses. We still took indirect direction and sought approval from teachers like Rachel. Rachel had her immediate cult in the New York staff and serious students. City leaders like Rachel, in turn took direction and sought approval from Nicole. The main reason I had authority in the OM Community was this indirect connection to Nicole.

It's a funny thing when a group of adults readily defer to you. I was still one of the youngest residents in the house. Only Winter was younger than me. But with some of the residents, especially the new ones, I could feel they treated me like a Parent. I felt like everyone's dad.

Arjun was also one of the leaders of the house. He ran our finances and logistics. But he was so often caught up in jealousy drama with Winter, that he often ended up in "Child mode." That left me to sort out everyone's drama.

If there's one thing I learned at OneTaste, it's that changing people's minds—whether to empower them or control them—follows the same exact principles. This power to change minds, desires, perceptions of reality, is neither good nor bad. Only the application makes it so.

But regardless of the intention, power is intoxicating.

One Sunday, we had a particularly chaotic house meeting. It was a web of emotions involving interlocking love triangles and triggered childhood wounds. Somehow, I was able to verbally stroke everyone to harmony—that is, get everyone to confirm the same reality. We ended the three-hour meeting in sleepy laughter.

We weren't explicitly taught how to change people. It was part of the hidden curriculum. I learned it while in the field of someone who could do it much better.

Shortly after the meeting, I received a text from Rachel.

"I heard you had an intense house meeting," she wrote.

"We did," I said. "I thought of you a lot. I realized I learned how to run meetings like that from you. I'm grateful."

"I'm really proud of you, Ruwan."

My eyes started tearing. The physical response started before I realized the emotions.

"I'm crying all of a sudden," I wrote with a sobbing emoji. "I don't know why."

"Because you can feel how much I love you," she said.

Prior to OneTaste, I had never cried as an adult. I had finally been able to this year, once in a CP6 immersion exercise, and once in the Morellino, but it still wasn't something that came easy to me. And yet with six words of praise, Rachel was able to get my face leaking.

Love is a complicated emotion.

"I want to tell you something," she wrote. "We're going to give you TurnON Brooklyn. You're going to lead it with Heather. OneTaste is going to invest in setting you guys up. But we're going to give you the autonomy to act on your own."

That was an offer I could say yes to. It was an offer I could not say anything but yes to. I didn't see the irony of being 'given autonomy' till much later.

"Thank you, Rachel."

"You're welcome, Ruwan. I love you."

"I love you too."

And just like that, I let her hooks back in me. I knew how the game was played. But like Odysseus and the Sirens, I wanted to keep hearing the music.

ONETASTE DECIDED TO DO OMX again.

OMX2 was going to be even bigger and more mainstream. It was held in a much larger facility, a Masonic temple in Oakland. The goal was to get a two-thousand-person OM Circle. In addition to a full three-day speaker lineup, there was also an OM training every hour.

This time they got even higher profile speakers including feminist author Naomi Wolf and the writer who mainstreamed the dating coaching industry, Neil Strauss.

OneTaste took pride in the fact that their Back of House staff and volunteers were the most attentive and empathic hosts possible. New students always noted the special attention they received. Any time a real-world celebrity or VIP came to OneTaste, this was done tenfold.

Every VIP needed a "handler." Handlers were officially supposed to drive and accompany the VIP to and from wherever they had to go. Unofficially, we were supposed to ensure the VIP had a good time. Even less officially, we were supposed to ensure the VIP had a very positive view of OneTaste.

Lila was assigned to handle Naomi Wolf. I was assigned to Neil Strauss.

"I'm nervous," Lila whispered to me as we drove to the SFO airport. "What do I talk to her about?"

"I don't know. Just be normal."

I read Neil Strauss's book, *The Game*, as a freshman in college. He told the story of starting as a shy awkward nerd, finding the "secret society of pickup artists," and becoming a confident ladies-man. It gave me hope that one day I too could be confident, and even inspired me to hire my dating coach over a year ago. Millions of awkward young men around the world looked up to him as an example of someone who really transformed himself.

He looked very normal in person. I picked him up from the airport the Friday morning of the event. I told him that his book was my entry into personal development. I told him I was going to write a book about my journey too.

"Make sure you write everything down," he said. "One thing that helped me was that the whole seduction community was online in forums. So I had all these field reports already written that I could use for my book. The thing is you might remember what you did, but you won't remember how you felt."

Neil was charming and likable. Though I wondered if he was just "running game" on me.

"So as a member of OneTaste, you can only have sex with other people in OneTaste?" Neil said.

I knew he was really asking if OneTaste was a cult. He was also gauging how brainwashed I was. I wanted to tell him that OneTaste was definitely a cult, but a good one as far as I was concerned. But I wasn't sure how connected he was to Nicole, or what would get back to her. This was a test. But I wasn't sure if passing the test meant admitting, or not admitting.

"No, we can have sex with whomever we want," I said. "But if anything, OM women are better in bed." That seemed to be a good diplomatic response. "But there are a lot of guys in the OM Community who probably wouldn't get laid outside of it," I added.

Neil had no follow up questions.

As a feeling-based production, OMX2 left a lot unplanned.

We had a fleet of Escalades rented to pick up and drop off VIPs from their hotels. Each handler knew their VIP's schedule, but often there weren't enough vehicles. This led to massive schedule delays and chaos on Friday. Someone needed to take control.

"If you notice something that needs to be done, then you're the one to do it," Sergio always said.

I put together all the schedules and assumed the role of dispatcher. I made sure there was always an available Escalade and driver. This meant I often ended up handling various VIPs myself.

Lila didn't work out as Naomi Wolf's handler.

"I think I fucked up," she said.

"How?"

"She was talking about feminism and the patriarchy, and I don't know I got nervous and started blabbing."

"About what?"

"Um... the reptilian overlords."

I decided to handle Naomi myself. She was there partly to promote her new book *Vagina*, which covered various elements of female sexuality, including OM. She was there with a filmmaker who was shooting her documentary.

She had a lot of questions for me.

"The most notable thing about OneTaste men is how they pay attention," she said. "I'm not used to men paying attention to how I feel so closely. It's refreshing but also uncomfortable. I didn't know men *could* pay attention like that."

I shared with her my view that this was OneTaste's great service to the world. If all men could learn to be so attentive, most societal problems would be gone.

"I'm just wondering when the men are going to ask for theirs," Naomi said to her videographer as they got in the backseat.

"Actually," I jumped in, "OM doesn't require reciprocation because men get a benefit from giving. That's the whole *stroke for your pleasure* thing. It trains our intuition through moment to moment feedback. That is arguably as good, if not a better, benefit than what the woman gets."

"Oh, that's interesting," Naomi said.

Naomi interviewed me for her documentary. She had interviewed a few different staffers so far, but felt they mostly spoke in jargon.

"By the way," Naomi said. "I saw you speaking with Neil Strauss. Can you connect me with him? I want to interview him."

"Sure."

"That's the guy who teaches men to sleep with women by putting them down," she said to her videographer. "It's called *negging*."

I drove Neil in later that afternoon. There was a press conference for Nicole and all the VIP speakers. There were a few major media outlets there. Most of the experts answered questions in systematic sound bites. But Nicole and Neil were on a different wavelength than the rest. They side-stepped every question and turned it back on the journalist.

"I learned how to do that from Bob Dylan," Neil told me afterwards. "When I started in journalism, I'd sit in all these press conferences with big musicians. Bob Dylan never answered a question straight. He knew they were just looking for a soundbite and he never gave it to them."

I told Neil that Naomi wanted to interview him.

"I don't know. I heard her interviewing Priscilla in the green room. It sounded like she had an agenda to make OneTaste look bad. She probably just wants to paint me as a manipulator. What do you think?"

"I think it would be a great opportunity to educate people who misunderstand men."

"My book was about male insecurity," he said. "But people don't get that. They saw 'picking up women' and made a bunch of assumptions. Many critics of *The Game* didn't even read it."

"But won't you be fine if you just answer with the truth?"

Neil paused. "She has the editor. The person who controls editing can make the truth whatever they want."

NAOMI AND NEIL DID get to dialogue after all.

The second to last event was a Q &A panel with the three keynote speakers: Nicole, Naomi, and Neil. It was the only event of the weekend where all the seats were full—there was no concurrent OM Circle.

Each of the three speakers had their own audience and questions. Neil's fans were men who wanted dating advice. Naomi's fans were women who wanted feminist commentary. Nicole's fans were OMers who wanted to know about Orgasm. And in an audience this big, there were trolls.

"This question is for Nicole," said a young pimply guy. "I have this intensive training to be a life coach. It's fifteen thousand dollars, would you like to buy it?"

Both groans and laughs came out of the audience. Many people were upset at the hard sales by staffers throughout the weekend. There was a sales pitch after every single session. Every staffer was primed as a Fluffer.

Nicole began to sidestep the question and turn it into a joke, but Naomi cut her off.

"I think he raised a good question," Naomi said. "Why is the OneTaste Coaching Program so expensive?"

About a third of the audience cheered. From backstage, I could see the faces of the first floor of the audience. The room was divided. Naomi had her faction. Nicole had hers. And there was a group that was either neutral, confused, or there to see Neil.

"Because that's a good price," Nicole said. She went one to list some of the benefits of the program. Then she invited the next question.

"Wait hold on," Naomi said. "As a journalist, I think this is good to discuss. Why is OneTaste, a wellness company, so heavy-handed with their sales?"

Naomi's audience cheered. Nicole straightened her posture and her affect became coldly composed. She deflected the comment in a way that made Naomi look foolish. Nicole's audience cheered.

A public conflict, no matter how subtle, is very different than a private conflict. Nicole and Naomi were not debating a point. They were fighting for control of the collective reality. The winner of this dispute would determine "the truth" of how most remembered today.

Naomi made a biting comment at Nicole. Naomi's audience cheered.

Nicole threw it back at Naomi. Nicole's audience cheered.

The tension rose.

Then Neil cut it with a joke at Naomi's expense. It was an innocent joke on the surface, but it made it clear that he was on Nicole's side. Naomi looked flustered. Neil and Nicole's combined audience cheered. They had the majority of the room.

Naomi still tried to fight with logic. Her points were reasonable, but in contrast to Nicole and Neil, she looked like a stick in the mud. I remembered how Rachel made me look this way when I first complained about not getting paid.

The panel ended and Nicole made a closing statement.

"One day, very soon, we'll be able to say Yoga, Meditation, and Orgasm in the same sentence," she reprised.

The music turned on and she led everyone in dancing. Three-fourths of the audience got up and danced in place. Naomi ran off the stage and Neil exited quietly.

"I've never seen this before," Neil said to me, looking out from backstage. "I've been in so many men's workshops, and you would never see something like this... dancing."

"Yeah, I guess it's feminine *state-pumping*." I was referring to a term in Neil's book where he noted how many dating coaches would trick their students into thinking they had a transformation by having them run around and high-five each other.

"I've been so impressed by the level of service here," Neil said.

"Yeah they really train us to notice every detail."

"So what's your plan in life?" he said.

"I want to help men. So working in OneTaste is very in line."

He nodded and his expression became more serious.

"One day you'll have to find your own voice."

I wanted to tell him I wasn't *really* brainwashed. But I wasn't sure how.

MONDAY MORNING, WE HAD our closing meeting at OneTaste HQ on Market Street. Each person checked in with how they felt.

One woman on the staff said, "One of my friends said, 'Wow you guys work so hard. They must be paying you really well!' and I said, 'No, we're all volunteers. Actually, most of us are paying to be here!'"

Everyone laughed.

"That's beautiful," Nicole said. "Remember, OneTaste runs on two currencies: money and Orgasm. Muggles won't understand what it's like to be paid in Orgasm. But you all do."

Every cell in my body was tingling. I couldn't deny that I did get paid in a certain currency.

OMX2 didn't do as well in the other currency. Some people signed up for Coaching Program 8 and the next Mastery which would be in San Francisco. But the aggressive sales practices didn't pay off. The OneTaste salespeople *overstroked* the attendees. They did unveil a new program, The Nicole Daedone Intensive (NDI), which was two weeks with Nicole. It cost twenty-thousand. A few longtime OMers signed up.

Nicole praised Rachel and her new protege, a young CP7 graduate. Nicole ceremonially announced that Rachel would be moving into a consulting role, and her protege was the new Head of Sales. Everyone cheered.

The meeting ended with Priscilla and Nicole sharing the vision for the next peak. There would be more media coming out. Nicole's vision was coming true. Very soon we'd see yoga, meditation, Orgasm in the same sentence.

"And that's a debrief!" Sergio yelled.

Everyone laughed and began to disperse.

Nicole stood, adjusted her skirt, and said in a voice that was quiet but still cut through the room,

"And next meeting we'll announce Ruwan…" she said and winked at me.

I RECEIVED A CALL from Priscilla when I got back to New York.

Priscilla had big visions for OneTaste Media, she said. She wanted me to be a part of it. OneTaste had tried a few different spokespeople in the last years such as Dr. Tanisha, but they hadn't worked out. She said I was the only person who could translate OM concepts into normal language.

"I want to make you the *Male Voice of Female Orgasm*," she said.

Priscilla shared that the video instructional series, which included the "Cocksucking demo," was a huge flop. They burned seven hundred thousand filming them and made back only a few thousand in online course sales. She wanted me to write an e-book specifically for men to learn to OM. It would be called *The Ignited Man Manifesto*.

The contract was like what they gave Tanisha— OneTaste would own all the intellectual property in perpetuity. But they were going to pay me five hundred bucks. I needed the money.

She also created a publication called *Orgasm Daily*.

"It will be like Huffington Post, but for Orgasm," she said.

I'd be an Editor-At-Large. I had written a few pieces for the OneTaste blog and they received a lot more traffic than other posts. She wanted me to write three articles a week. I wouldn't get paid, but she'd encourage the sales team to provide me with coaching clients.

Technically, anyone who graduated from a Coaching Program was in the "Certified Coaching Directory." One of the selling points for CP was that the OneTaste sales team would enroll coaching clients for you, based on who would be a good fit.

But with hundreds of graduates from now seven completed CPs, hardly anyone ever received clients from OneTaste. Most clients went to OneTaste staff, who didn't get paid for it since they were on salary. But some clients went to people who OneTaste wanted something from. Priscilla basically told me I'd be pushed to the front of the list.

Om Rupani said that Nicole would often say, "A woman will buy you for the cheapest price she can get."

I had raised my price a bit. But I was still being bought.

NICOLE HAD BECOME BOLDER with the recent mainstream attention.

As a parable about forgiveness, she shared about how her father was a convicted child molester who used her as a little girl to ensnare victims.

"My father had too much love to give for this world," she said. "He was so expansive and fourth-dimensional that he couldn't confine himself to the arbitrary laws of the third dimension."

As with all Nicole talks, it was recorded and put on YouTube. Years later this clip would be scrutinized by media and prosecutors. But in person, no one batted an eye about it. Anyone who made it this deep in was so well indoctrinated that this just seemed like the next level of accepting the dark side within us.

Nicole's next book was called *Unconditional Sex*. It was a follow up to her previous best-seller, *Slow Sex*. For *Unconditional Sex*, Nicole was having sex with a different man every day of the year. The goal was to prove she could truly love and orgasm with anyone—it was the ultimate "get off on anything" experiment.

As a Left Hand Path, OneTaste was always about going into "difficult sensation." With her increased hubris, Nicole repurposed a new term for the OM Community— *Aversion Therapy*. Officially, aversion therapy was a controversial form of treatment where pain or discomfort was introduced to deter a bad habit, such as nail-biting or smoking. In OneTaste, it meant diving into whatever made you feel bad, and getting off on it.

In theory, it wasn't that different than the self-help cliche, "Do what scares you the most." But in practice, this meant doing sexual acts that repelled you, specifically with people that repelled you. Anything you resisted was seen as an area where you haven't yet learned to get off.

Many women were encouraged to sleep with old men that creeped them out. They were then celebrated as a woman who was able to "overcome her preferences." No one pointed out that these previously sexless men often ended up spending a lot of money at OneTaste.

At the final Mastery Immersion, Lila raised her hand to ask what she should do about her jealousy. She and I had been in an open relationship now for almost a year, and although she was in support of it, she was constantly burning with jealousy. Nicole told her that she had been putting too much energy into me. She told Lila to follow the Unconditional Sex protocol and sleep with a different man every day.

Lila tried, but only made it three days.

"It made my heart hurt," she said.

After this Lila decided to go on a road trip with an old friend of hers. She said she needed a break from OneTaste, which meant a break from me too. Before she left, she groomed a replacement. She convinced Sally, the ballerina, to move into our room.

"He's yours now," Lila said.

CP8 WAS ONETASTE'S BIGGEST program yet.

Over one hundred fifty students were enrolled from around the world—including a much bigger cohort from Europe. OneTaste London was as big as New York. There were also growing communities in France, Netherlands, Denmark, and Germany that were comparable to OneTaste Austin in size.

Every immersion, the Brooklyn OM House's living room was full of sleeping bags of incoming students. Often they stayed for awhile after the immersion. Every month new full-time residents were moving in and out. It was always interesting hearing how they funded their lives.

A nineteen-year old woman from London said she was an almost homeless drug addict before finding OneTaste. A OneTaster had approached her on the street and invited her to TurnON London. She showed up drunk, and belligerently said it was a cult. But she kept coming back. Sarah, the Head of OneTaste London, helped her get sober. When Coaching Program 8 was pitched she immediately decided it was her path.

"But how did you pay for it?" I asked.

"With Orgasm," she said.

When she expressed her desire to do CP8, Sarah encouraged her to ask a wealthy man in the London OM Community to pay for her. She asked a doctor in the London community and he said no. So she asked him for something he could say yes to— an OM. Apparently, it was a very intense OM.

"After we OMed he was like 'I don't know why, but I suddenly want to pay for your Coaching Program,'" she grinned. "And he wrote me a check for eleven thousand quid right there."

"So he changed his mind just from stroking your pussy?"

She shrugged. "Men are so funny. They can be so mean but make them feel good and they do anything that you want." She paused and put a finger to her purple-painted lips. "I wonder if that's bad karma... Oh well, I suppose I'll find out."

She essentially did a currency exchange— She gave him Orgasm. He gave her sterling pounds. It was the oldest profession. But somehow OMers figured out how to get a much better exchange rate.

This was applied *Hooking*. Even though we were told not to do it, it was becoming a common practice in the OM Community. Younger OMers, especially women, were encouraged to ask men to pay for their OneTaste courses as a "game"— an uncomfortable challenge for such a woman to grow. After all, asking someone for a large sum of money was vulnerable.

It was also a way for a woman to prove how much Orgasm she had. A check for eleven grand converts to a lot of "get off."

"Women who OM compete over their Orgasm the way boys compete over who has the biggest muscles," Jane had said.

I asked Arjun what he thought of all this. As a guy with a lot of money, he was a prime target for getting Hooked.

"What makes a person Hookable is that they have pre-existing loops within them that the hooker can attach to," Arjun said.

"You mean insecurities?"

"Or trauma, pain, loneliness— something that hurts so bad you're willing to suspend your better judgement to make it go away... Same as addiction."

"But if you're aware of the manipulation, then you're safe right?"

"Knowing how alcohol works doesn't stop you from getting drunk," Arjun said.

ONE MORNING, I RECEIVED a call from a Florida number.

"Hi Ruwan, I'm calling you to make amends."

It was Lisa. I hadn't heard from her since she went to the detox center. I hadn't thought of her in almost as long. She apologized for taking advantage of my kindness and playing with my emotions. She was nervous.

"Um, so you're the first person I called," she said. "Did I do it right?"

"Oh, so what I'm your practice amends?" I joked.

She didn't laugh. I probably was. I told her she did great. But she could try being more vulnerable next time.

"Are you still doing that orgasm thing?" she said.

"Yeah."

OneTaste would have loved her. She was the exact kind of deep-feeling, emotionally contagious, hypersexual, hyper-volatile being that OneTaste celebrated. And she had

Hooked me pretty good. Our short relationship was one of the most emotionally intense of my life. Now it felt like someone else's memory.

Everyone wants to be connected to something bigger. It can be a substance, an ideology, a community, a mission. We want to come home to a place where our perceptions are confirmed, our actions have meaning, and we can feel loved. And if we don't have that, we'll go for the first person or thing that can provide it.

That afternoon, I told Arjun we needed a new project. Creating the Brooklyn House was a big success, but now that it was stable, we needed a bigger game. He and I came up with an idea to create a cafe that ran by Orgasmic principles. We'd only hire OMers with performance art backgrounds (there were many). On the surface, we'd be serving food and coffee. But under the surface, we'd give people a "transmission" of sensation and vulnerability.

"People will leave our cafe and wonder why they felt so good there," Arjun said. "When people are ready, we can invite them to 'go deeper'."

We laughed. We were half-serious. Little did we know, running feel-good restaurants was actually a very common enrollment scheme used by cults all over America.

A couple days later, I received a message from a 415 number, San Francisco.

"Hey Ruwan, this Nicole. I wanted to check in with you about things."

"Hi Nicole."

Unless you were high-up in OneTaste, or spending tens of thousands with them, it was rare and special to get a direct communication from Nicole. On the one hand, she was an 'open book' who freely shared her email address and phone number. But it wasn't common to get a response from her, unless there was a good reason.

"I imagine you must be feeling a lot with everything that's been going on lately."

I had no idea what she was talking about.

"I'm alright actually. I'm working on some fun projects."

"Oh? What kind of projects?"

I told her about the idea with Arjun. I waited for Nicole to respond, but she went silent.

Lila emerged from our room with phone in hand. She was packing for her trip.

"Hey Nicole just texted me," she said. "She said 'you must be feeling a lot with everything that's been going on lately.'"

We compared texts. Nicole must have known we'd do so. Why would she want us to know we received the same message?

Everything is a communication.

Minutes later I got a text from Rachel, inviting me to tea. As her former chauffeur, I knew that tea invitations always had a deeper meaning. If it was a potentially confrontational meeting, then there would be more than one staffer there to make sure they controlled the reality by majority. If it was a peace-making mission, it would be just Rachel.

I met Rachel at the cafe she suggested in Midtown. Sarah, the Head of OneTaste London, was there.

"Oh hi Ruwan," she said then turned to Rachel. "Do you want me to stay?"

Rachel scanned me, then smiled. "No, it's alright."

Rachel was warmer and more smiley than I had seen her in awhile. She asked me about my relationships. I told her the magic between Cheryl and I had fizzled out since she decided not to do CP8. Rachel seemed pleased. I told her Lila was leaving on a trip to Texas. I was single again.

"And what are you working on these days?"

I told her about the master plan with Arjun. I assumed she already knew about it, since she and Nicole shared all information about everyone.

"I see," was all she said.

When we hit the peak, she hugged me warmly and said she had to go. Our entire tea meeting was barely the duration of an OM. This was a reconnaissance mission.

When I got back to Brooklyn, Arjun was concentrating on his phone.

"OneTaste just offered me a game," he said.

He showed me a series of text messages from OneTaste CEO, Priscilla.

They offered him to buy OneTaste New York.

OneTaste had jumped strata in the last few months.

Mastery was five grand, CP was fifteen, NDI was twenty. Their next offering would be seven figures.

OneTaste unveiled its "Affiliate Program." They were selling each of the major branches to dedicated students— San Francisco, Los Angeles, New York, and London. The idea was that each city would operate independently, running their own How To OM classes. OneTaste corporate would still run Mastery, CP, and NDI, but compensate the cities for the students they enrolled.

Arjun showed me some of his text exchanges with Priscilla. She asked him for a million dollars. He said no. So she asked him for two million. The price changed along with her strokes. She praised him for his "readiness" to take the next step. She challenged his masculinity. She tempted him with the adventure of working directly with Nicole and being "the Holder of the Orgasm" in New York.

But when Priscilla finally showed him the financials, it made no sense. Based on the proposed compensation structure, the New York affiliate would barely be turning a profit. "Desire-led business" meant no budgeting or projecting. If it wasn't for the fact they had the most motivated staff that they barely paid, they'd be in the red. The currency of Orgasm doesn't show on a balance sheet.

Arjun said no.

Besides, he had more on his mind. His relationship with Winter was at an all-time peak of drama. Winter had been suspicious of OM at first. Arjun had dragged her into it, along with opening their relationship. He paid for her CP8 so she would get to have her own experience.

And that she did. She blossomed under Nicole's spotlight. She was exactly the kind of young, beautiful, well-spoken woman that OneTaste could use. At a CP8 Back of House meeting, the staff listed all the CP8 students who could one day be hired. Winter was highlighted.

"She's completely impressionable!" John said to Rachel. "She has this incredible ability to repeat verbatim!"

As Arjun had hoped, Winter did 'find her Orgasm.' That meant she took on lovers and developed the insight to pick him apart in arguments. This meant ever-escalating chaos that the rest of the house became subject to.

Drama like this wasn't unique in the OM community. If anything, it was implicitly encouraged. The belief that "pain leads to growth" meant the more drama in your relationship, the more you must be learning. The Left Hand Path was framed as superior in this way.

"In Taoism they say that muddy water becomes clear in stillness because the sediment sinks to the bottom," Nicole would say. "But then you can't drink it... So instead we stir up the water so the sediment comes out. So the water is clear, and you can drink."

One evening, in a moment of jealousy, Winter locked Arjun in their room and refused to let him leave. Winter did Muay Thai. Arjun had fibromyalgia. He was a prisoner. Sergio and I had to save him by unscrewing the hinges off their bedroom door.

Arjun had enough and broke up with her. It didn't seem significant. OM relationships started and ended dramatically all the time. But for some reason, Rachel took special interest.

She called for a "Special Meeting" with the Brooklyn House one afternoon. We sat around the table and checked in as always. But when it got to Winter and Arjun, Rachel revealed why she was there.

The two of them had a soul contract, Rachel said. They had found each other to help each other awaken. This was not a time to pull back, but to lean in. She said they had to get married.

Arjun took the stroke and pulled off a ring he wore.

"Will you marry me?"

Winter made confused expressions, then nodded. Arjun slid his ring over her finger. There was an awkward silence.

"Yayyy!" cheered Sally and we all joined in.

In a way that only made sense in a Rapid Changing Reality, we whipped together a full-on wedding in twenty-four hours complete with bachelor and bachelorette rituals. Many OMers came including some OneTaste staff. We had a full band, Indian wedding regalia, and Arjun even flew in Winter's sister last minute. I wrote a poem about the sacred silliness of "going with the stroke." OneTaste recorded it and turned it into a promo for CP9.

The party continued until eleven pm which was very late in Orgasm time—we all had to wake up for morning practice. The wedding was episode two of my YouTube reality show. It ended with a shot of Winter cutting a slice of wedding cake.

"I have a forever playmate!" she said.

Two weeks later, they broke up again.

But this time, it was on very different terms.

From the day after their wedding, Rachel took Winter on as her personal protege. As John said months earlier, Winter really was impressionable. She transformed into a mini-Rachel. She got her hair cut in a bob identical to Rachel's. Rachel gave her hand-me-down clothes to replace Winter's previous hippie-wear. Winter adopted Rachel's facial expressions, phrases, and vocal tone.

Bonnie wasn't able. Abby wasn't willing. But Winter was both willing and able to execute on everything Rachel instructed.

Despite their "soul contract," Rachel decided Arjun had been holding Winter back. Winter had to "live her own life," and Arjun had to "earn her back."

Arjun was wrecked. Winter was getting colder and colder. She would post to the OMHub about her thrilling Makeouts with other men. Arjun spent all his waking hours figuring out how to win her back.

The irony was that he wanted to break up with her just weeks before. But the public declaration and ritual of the marriage ceremony made him attached.

All the while, Priscilla was trying to get him to buy the New York affiliate.

He decided he needed a "new game."

He found an apartment in Manhattan and decided to make another OM Residence, specifically for people who wanted to directly work with OneTaste. This was his way of showing his devotion. The address was 365 First Avenue, so from then on it became referred to as '365.' He and Sergio moved there along with other OMers that wanted to be closer to the staff. Rachel and the staff turned their attention to this group.

This left me in Brooklyn with no "rails." Like when Rachel left the Morellino to Bonnie, the residents and I began doing unusual things for the sake of being unusual.

We did alternative forms of OMing. We explored spiritual ideas such as reading from the self-help book *A Course in Miracles* that a temporary resident had left in the house. Sally and I tried practicing advanced skills we learned in Mastery like climaxing from giving head and reading each others' minds.

I searched for other ways to find "Orgasm." I started taking Tai Chi classes with an old man in McCarren Park. We practiced Push Hands, the competitive form of Tai Chi where you try to feel your opponent's center and off balance him. My instructor was surprised I picked up the feeling part so quickly.

"Most people can do the movements, but have trouble feeling the other persons' energy."

I didn't tell him I had thousands of hours of practice doing this with women's genitals.

I also began taking Meisner acting classes. The Meisner method believed good acting came from "authentic reactions." So students would meet at weekly practice sessions where we paired off to practice—like an OM Circle. Students who hit it off would arrange times to practice in private. Naturally, some of these practice sessions turned into Makeouts.

On the one hand, I found that OneTaste did not have a monopoly on the things I used to find magical—sensory and emotional intuition. On the other hand, I realized I was just trying to recreate what I had in the OM Community, but without the OM Community.

I wanted a bigger game, too. I just wasn't sure what that should be.

NICOLE HAD BEEN SPEAKING more about Magic.

Her CP8 lectures frequently mentioned her practice of doing occult rituals. She idolized the British occultist Dion Fortune who wrote novels with ritual magic principles embedded inside. Her famous books, *Moon Magic* and *The Sea Priestess,* were about an unwitting man who is seduced by a wise female witch to do her bidding. He is deceived and has his life turned upside down, but it is later shown that it was all to his benefit— by surrendering to the Feminine, he accesses superpowers.

I wanted to know what Om Rupani thought of it. I had continued visiting him periodically to learn about Dom/Sub stuff. Sometimes I'd bring Sally, and he'd coach me on how to dom her in scene. But most of the time we talked about OneTaste.

"Nicole has made pacts with some dark entities," he said. "There's no way a regular person gains that much power without having otherworldly allies."

"Wait, you're talking about spirits? You really believe that?"

"I'm Indian, we believe in everything," Om laughed. "But we also believe that you should let spirits be. They have their world, we have ours. If you make deals like that, you're asking for trouble."

"What do you mean by other worlds? Like when OneTasters talk about the 4th Dimension?"

"I have no idea what OneTasters talk about these days," he laughed. "But for example, I have a brother who is schizophrenic. For forty years he's been speaking to people that only he can see. Other people will look at him and call him crazy. But if you listen to his conversations, they are very real to him. He has real relationships. He has a very rich life in that world. He can see our world too, but he prefers not to. He sees it as a nuisance. He just wants to get back to his people."

"So to him, that's the real world, and our world is just a bad dream?" I said.

"You could say that," he said.

Om crossed one leg and leaned forward. He was surprisingly flexible for a big man. "Your former colleague came to see me by the way," he said. "The one with the pretty green eyes... She's on the warpath against Nicole. She wants to ruin Nicole for whatever OneTaste did to her. I told her that was foolish. Nicole is like a bear in the woods. Don't try to take on a bear. If you see the bear, just go a different way. If you avoid her, she probably won't care if you exist. But do not try to fight the bear. Because you will not win."

"Is this what Nicole means with the Lao Tse quote?"

"What quote?"

"*The Left Hand Path is best never started, but once started must be completed.*'"

"That sounds true. But I doubt Lao Tse said that," Om chuckled. "There's nothing evil about the dark arts. They go into the lower three chakras: that of survival," he pointed down, "sex," he pointed to his genitals, "and power," he touched his belly. "Other spiritual paths denounce the lower chakras because one can get stuck there. Anything built solely on money, sex, or power will not last. OneTaste meddles with the first two chakras in an unclean way. Survival must be secured before sex."

"Like in Maslow's hierarchy of needs."

"OneTaste's problem is they switch the first and second chakras. People try to cultivate sex at the expense of their own survival. Then they must use their sex in order to survive. The whole organization is built on unconscious prostitution."

I wasn't sure I believed in the whole 'dark entities' thing. I had a bad view of their ethics. And I wasn't clear on when I should leave this organization that had given me so much and yet had a very dark underbelly.

But I was still sure of one thing:

Nicole had a power nearly indistinguishable from magic.

And I still wanted that.

PRISCILLA KEPT STROKING ME to join their game.

After months of praising me without success, she switched to the guilt tactic.

"We've given you so many privileges," Priscilla texted. "So I feel sad when I see you off doing your own thing."

After OMX2 I had gotten a content-creation gig for a sex advice website. Priscilla was upset that I was putting energy into something besides OneTaste. Apparently, the Editor-At-Large gig came with strings attached. She hinted I would no longer be getting coaching clients from OneTaste.

"We only want to work with people who are willing to commit to OneTaste for the very long term," she wrote.

A moment later I received a text from Sarah, the Head of OneTaste London. She was the "good cop." I assumed Priscilla and Sarah were sitting next to each other while they texted me.

"You know we want you on the Team," Sarah said. "You say you don't. What's your deeper desire then?"

I closed my eyes. I saw an image of me sitting on a mahogany chair, sitting across from Nicole. She was speaking while I wrote things down in a notebook.

"I want to write a book with Nicole," I wrote back.

"Well then you should tell her that," wrote Sarah.

I emailed Nicole the idea to help her write her story. She wrote back immediately "Yes." This would be my last project with OneTaste, I decided. This world had given me so much, but I didn't want to get stuck here forever.

Over the last year and half of OneTaste lectures, Nicole had peppered in anecdotes from her past.

At twenty-five she was a PhD candidate in general semantics and owned an art gallery called "111 Minna." One evening her place was vandalized. She found herself crying on the floor of the gallery when some strangers with dilated pupils showed up and wordlessly cleaned up her space.

They invited her to live with them in their LSD house. During this time she met Richard Bandler, the co-creator of neurolinguistic programming (NLP). For one year, Nicole did LSD daily and didn't speak a word. This was when she transformed into the current version of herself where "every word she spoke was intentional."

Later, she discovered DOing which led her to Welcomed and Morehouse. She had an infamous meeting with Vic Baranco where she said she wanted to take his seat when he died. When he did pass, the Morehouse people didn't accept her, so she and Rob founded OneTaste.

I wrote some narrative scenes of her story and sent it to her.

"Damn, Ruwan. You're alright," she wrote back.

She said our book should be a parable of a young man— me, learning about the magic of the Feminine from a wise older woman— her. It would be like a Dion Fortune novel. We agreed to meet in Bryant Park to discuss the project.

"I just had a meeting with John," she said, sitting down. "Did you hear he bought the LA affiliate?"

"I heard something about that."

"Isn't it amazing? To have a man like that as the face of Orgasm in LA? And Sarah and some others are buying San Francisco."

"Yeah, that's cool."

I wondered why Nicole was volunteering this information to me. Everything is a communication.

"OneTaste used to be set up for initiates, people who wanted to live like monks in full service to the Orgasm," Nicole said. "But you know what? Most people don't really want that even though they say they do. Most people on the staff don't really want that. So now with the affiliate program, those who want to make money and be in the world can do that, and those who want to live like monks can live like monks."

Nicole sat up straight and looked at me from stillness. It was my turn to speak.

I fumbled around explaining my vision of the book.

"...Anyway, I could really see this book spreading Orgasm to a lot of people," I concluded.

Nicole tilted her head down. She drew in a slow breath as if through a straw.

"So basically you're asking me to give you power," she said. "The problem with giving someone power is that they can use it against you."

She scanned my eyes. Her tone shifted.

"The only reason I've agreed to meet with you," she said, "is that I believe you're still fifty-one percent on my team. Up until this point, for whatever reason, you've decided to stay in school."

I was at least ninety percent on her team, I thought. I still saw her as an Enlightened being, my guru. My only hard line was not committing my life and getting devoured like so many others.

"You're at a crossroads," Nicole said. "It would be so easy for you to do the Neil Strauss thing and sell out and make lots of money."

"I honestly do want the money and fame that could come from a book," I said. "And I know that these superficial desires can lead me astray. Isn't there some way I can ensure that I..."

Nicole interrupted me with a slow shake of the head.

"You're at a crossroads," she repeated. "It's going to be like this at every peak. At every moment, you'll have to make this choice. And the deeper you go, the more compelling it will be to turn your back on the Orgasm."

I didn't want to be a sellout. I didn't want to retard my growth or power. But I didn't want to be a monk either.

"My hope for you is that you will be able to look past all that and stay connected to what is truly gratifying. You know, out there..." Nicole gestured into the fuzzy background, "*they* want to know all the magic tricks. But there's really only one trick: Unification. And when you're in that place, there's only one thing to feel, and that's gratitude."

I still wanted what Nicole was selling.

"My only concern with you is how quickly you're trying to go *out there*," she said. "I spent ten years... well, fifteen total... but counting truly deep, deep practice, ten. Ten years of heavy practice before I even thought of trying to create something out there."

"Thank you, Nicole. I just really want to do a good job here."

Nicole smiled and craned her neck. "Thank you for letting me see you finally." She nodded towards my heart.

I hadn't kept track of the time. But the peak was felt and we both stood up.

"Oh one last question," I said. "Is there anything you don't want me to write about you?"

Nicole squinted and looked away. "No I'm an open book," she looked at me with eyes both soft and sharp. "But... I wouldn't ever want to hurt the people who are close to me. You know, Reese lost a lot of friends in Silicon Valley by associating with us. I wouldn't want anyone I love to suffer because of what I choose to write."

"Got it. Thank you again, Nicole."

Her expression became big and bright. The background blurred around her. She took two steps away then looked back over her shoulder.

"You know what, Ruwan. You're alright."

She winked then disappeared into the crowd.

STAGE 8: STILLNESS

The timeless moment of clarity. The subject prepares to descend into the next peak.

ONETASTE HAD CHANGED ITS image.

Last year, Nicole had been offered an opportunity to create a reality show about OneTaste. It would cover life in 1080 Folsom, the practice, and behind the scenes of the Orgasmic Meditation company. It would have been the biggest coverage the company had received by far. The Exec Team was very excited about it.

But Nicole refused. According to Rob, she was afraid to lose control of the narrative around OneTaste. She was afraid of how OneTaste would be portrayed. So she decided to go "big" in a different way.

Rather than soften for wider appeal, she decided to become bolder, more insular, more niche. *Unconditional Sex* and "Aversion Therapy" were parts of this. Speaking about occult practices was another.

"We're finally big enough that I can teach what I really want to teach," Nicole had said.

This is what OneTaste would now be offering in their next program.

"Magic School" would be the first time OneTaste directly addressed the occult. It was a coming out party of a sort. I decided I had to be there.

Nicole stopped responding to my emails after our meeting in Bryant Park. I figured she was testing my commitment. Like the bumbling protagonist in the Dion Fortune novels, I would make the pilgrimage to receive the gifts of the goddess.

But I decided I wasn't going to pay for it.

OneTaste owed me money because they continued using my car when I moved to Brooklyn. Jane had quit OneTaste back in February and no one had been paying me the monthly rental. They owed me five thousand, the price of Magic School.

If there was anything magical that I had come to believe, it's that when useful coincidences appear, you're on the right "stroke."

Heather had moved to New York with her car and I was getting tired of paying for parking. She wanted to ship it back to her sister in the Bay Area. I told her I'd drive it for her. I also told her we had reached a peak with TurnON Brooklyn. It was time to pass it on to some of our regulars.

"Are you sure we're doing the right thing?" she said when handing me the keys.

"Super sure. It hasn't been on in months. Don't you feel lighter now that we've let it go?"

"Yeah, I guess. It just feels funny. Shouldn't we have told OneTaste?"

"No, they gave us autonomy. It's up to us what we do with it."

"I just feel like they're going to be upset when they find out."

"That's okay. It's better to ask for forgiveness than permission."

Little did I know, this move created a whirlwind behind the scenes. OneTaste had been monitoring my commitment levels. Twelve years later, subpoenaed text messages would come out between Priscilla and Nicole about this:

"My guess is they are planning their own thing. We will need to get strategic with Ruwan fast," Nicole texted to Priscilla.

"Yes," Priscilla replied. "He is currently under contract with us which has protection for us."

This road trip was to be the first time I spent more than a week apart from OneTaste in almost two years. My intention was to surrender to the will of the Universe completely, to listen to every voice and whisper even if it didn't make sense. If I wanted to re-enter the real world, I needed to stop using OneTaste as my surrogate to spirituality.

One of my coaching clients, Leopold, happened to be on his way to Burning Man. I offered to drop him off on the way. He had founded a startup some years ago that was acquired by Google. He became Google's "chief ethicist" and was working on some secret project.

We had three weeks till Burning Man, and a few more days till Magic School, so we decided to take the long southern route via country roads whenever possible.

Brad's band had booked a gig down in Raleigh, so he caught a ride with us down. It was strange having a pre-OM friend in the car with a post-OM friend. Brad just wanted to have normal conversation.

"Yo everyone is having babies," Brad said.

"I don't think any of my friends have had kids yet."

"What do you mean? We have the same friends!"

He named a few of our high school acquaintances who had kids.

"I had no idea that anyone from our class even got married."

"You living under a rock? They're all over Facebook."

Brad showed me his Facebook feed and it was full of baby photos from our mutual friends. I hadn't seen any of their posts in years.

I opened my Facebook feed. It was almost all posts from OMers: OneTaste announcements, vulnerable shares about emotional turmoil, selfies of TurnedON people. About half of the posts were from Rachel.

"Social media algorithms customize your feed to show more of what you click on," Leo said. "So if you click on baby photos, it shows you more baby photos. If you click on OneTaste stuff, it shows you more OneTaste stuff."

He explained how our brains can only keep track of a limited number of human interactions, known as *Dunbar's Number*. So even though we "know" our social media feed is only a small sample of the population, to our social brain, it feels like "everyone."

"They've known this in advertising for a long time," he said. "If you see an ad seven times it seems like it's 'everywhere' so 'everyone' must know about it. But with modern tech, it could be just targeting *you*."

I knew my world was filtered differently than the "normal" one. But I was sure I was part of the early adopters. It felt like OM was catching on at such an accelerating pace that soon everyone was going to be OMing, they just didn't realize it yet.

"You're going to see a lot more of this in the next Presidential election," Leopold said. "Candidates are going to target specific demographics with different messages so that people will have very different views of reality, even when it comes to hard facts.

I scrolled down on my feed till there were less OneTaste posts. There was a new Facebook feature where they showed "memories." Two years ago today I was at a music festival with Lisa. I didn't recognize myself in the photo. My hair was many inches shorter. My muscles were bigger and my posture was stiffer. I looked both older and more childish. My smile was tense. Drugs and numbness used to be my normal.

We dropped Brad off in Raleigh and Leopold and I continued on.

Leo came to OneTaste to get better with women. He was innocent and intelligent, maybe too intelligent. The Feminine was completely foreign to him. He got confused and upset at irrationality. John sold him on coaching with me saying that I was also once analytical but now knew exactly how to read the Feminine. I had been coaching Leo for about a month.

Last week, Winter asked him to have a Makeout. I knew that she was likely doing it to fluff him to buy a course, and I told him that. I also told him to go for it. It would be good for him to experience a woman with a lot of Orgasm.

You become a good fucker by getting fucked, Nicole said.

"I didn't like it at all," Leo recounted as we drove west out of Raleigh. "She's really hot, but it felt so mechanical. She took off her clothes and mine immediately. It felt like all I was to her was a dick, lips, and fingertips."

This was a somewhat common way to have a Makeout in OneTaste. "Following the sensation" sometimes meant going straight for what felt the best.

"Well, at least she didn't try to sell you something afterwards...yet," I said.

"That's so fucked up that they use sex to make sales."

"Well, they believe that you can't make someone do anything truly against their will. So all sales is helping someone do what they wanted to do, because if they really don't want to do it, no sales techniques will work. So they feel all sales techniques are fair game."

"That's simply not true," he said. "I've seen many salespeople tell themselves that to reconcile putting pressure on people, but it's wrong. My research shows how much the mind can be manipulated. It's so easy to overcome someone's free will."

Leopold was working on a self-directed project on how technology can warp people's minds and emotions. He would later turn it into a very popular TEDx Talk, Netflix documentary, and speaking career about the negative effects of social media.

"So they are basically prostitutes..." he said.

"Not exactly," I said. "Because they don't receive any money. OneTaste salespeople go so hard because they believe that their path to spiritual growth is to help people go deeper into OneTaste."

Leo shook his head. "It's such a cult."

I cringed at the c-word. It felt refreshing to share my analyses of OneTaste with someone. But at the same time, it felt blasphemous. I partially feared this collusion was going to limit my growth.

We stopped in Gatlinburg to see why Johnny Cash loved it so much. We stopped in Chatanooga, Tennessee and slept in a hotel made from a train car. The whole city smelled like feces because the sewage leaked into the river.

We stopped in Jackson, Mississippi because Leo wanted to see "America's poorest city." Some girls we met invited us to the Jackson State Fair that night. We ended up crashing with a couple of gay artists who lived in a repurposed factory building. Across the street was Mississippi's only abortion clinic. Our hosts believed the rest of the state was brainwashed.

We decided to couchsurf in New Orleans and stayed with an artist in Bywater. There were already five other couchsurfers in sleeping bags all throughout the one-story house. When we arrived, a guy from Wisconsin was arguing with a man from Lithuania over which William S. Burroughs novel was the best.

Our host was a tall, flamboyant, gay man. He told us he was moving to Brazil to build an artist community in two days because he received a "sign from the Universe."

"What exactly do you mean by 'sign'?" Leo asked.

"Child, please."

Over dinner, our host told us that this wasn't the first time he moved countries on short notice due to a "sign." He used to be an executive at a major music label in Toronto, when three different strangers told him he needed to go to Dubai.

"After the first one, I was like, 'Child, please, I don't know anyone or any-*thang* in Dubai.' But then a second person came up to me later, a total stranger, and said the same thing. Then a few days later a third person came to me as I was leaving my house for work and said, 'You really need to go to Dubai.' So I got my job to transfer me to that office."

"Who were these people?" I asked.

"They were messengers of the Divine," our host said. "When I was in Dubai, I went out with this man. And you know over there, they're progressive for the Middle East, but it still ain't easy to be a gay man… He came home with me, and all of a sudden his face and his voice changed. He told me I had to get out of Dubai immediately. I had to quit the music industry and go back to New Orleans."

"Did he say why?"

"No, then he just left… I tracked him down the next day and asked him about it. He didn't know what I was talking about. He was a married man and said he had never seen me in his life."

Leo and I gave each other a look.

"So what was the purpose for you to go to Dubai then?" Leo asked.

"Child, please. When the Divine tells you something, you don't question… I don't know what *would* have happened if I didn't listen to the signs. But I know I'm in the right place and I have my angels with me."

We drove out the next morning, aiming for Austin, Texas.

"You didn't believe his story did you?" Leo said.

"I mean, it's probably more accurate to write off synchronicities as a coincidence," I said. "But then your life will be dry and meaningless. But if you choose to make meaning from events, and those meanings inform your actions, then they really will have meaning… even if it's self-fulfilling prophecy. And that's a much more enjoyable way to live life."

"So you're telling me that if I hired three actors to tell you the same ominous message, I could get you to do anything because you'd think it was a sign from the Universe."

"Um…"

"What you're calling 'faith' is just making yourself vulnerable to manipulation. If you just saw some of what I'm uncovering in my research… Big tech companies have teams of experts figuring out how to manipulate people's attention… I *wish* I could just live in the moment like you, but in today's world, you can't. If you don't keep your guard up, someone is going to manipulate you."

"One could say that true faith then is trusting that even if I get manipulated, everything will still turn out perfectly in the end," I said.

"Do you really think that's true?" he said.

"I don't know. But at this point I have to find out."

IN AUSTIN, LEO REALIZED at our pace he'd miss Burning Man.

He decided to fly from there. Austin had a big OM community, so I figured I'd hang out a bit. I received a big welcome from the team at TurnON Austin. They all knew me from OneTaste's YouTube channel.

"It's like we have a celebrity with us," one of the facilitators said.

I reached out to Bonnie and we spent an afternoon at Barton Springs. She had left OneTaste employment some months ago. She didn't want to talk about it. We took a selfie for Facebook and immediately received a comment from Rachel, "So sweet."

She had started seeing an acupuncturist who had many patients who were OMers. He told her to stop OMing immediately.

"He said all OMers have burnt out kidney meridians," said Bonnie. "We run way too much sexual energy. He said if I didn't become celibate for awhile I might cause irreversible damage."

Though she was a key member of the Austin community, not OMing meant ostracization. She had been sorting through her experience since.

"Abby came to visit me a few weeks ago," she said. "She is still really fucked up. She has PTSD symptoms. She might be traumatized for a very long time."

I asked Bonnie what she thought of OneTaste now.

"They have a deep shadow. But I'm also grateful to them, to Nicole. Before OneTaste I had no concept of God. Now I do."

I CONTINUED WEST ON my own.

After Fredericksburg, there was nothing but desert and sky. America is a beautiful country, I thought. I made it to New Mexico that night and slept in the desert under the stars.

The next day, I reached Sedona and couchsurfed at a place called "The Top of Bell Rock Club." The host was an older guy who hosted people for free under the one condition that he takes them to the top of Bell Rock, a local red rock *vortex.*

"A vortex is a place that collects and circulates spiritual energy," he said.

"So it's like a chakra, but for the earth?"

"Something like that," he said. "Around the time I got my cancer diagnosis, the angels told me that I needed to take one thousand, one hundred, and eleven people to the top of Bell Rock. Then they will take me to heaven. Do you know about eleven-eleven?"

"Yeah," I said. Lila would always say we were in sync with the universe whenever the clock showed '11:11'.

"Good. Not enough kids your age do."

On the walls were photographs of the sky and a New York license plate that said, 'UFO LAWYER.' He was from Brooklyn too. He was a lawyer there for forty years. He came to fame in the seventies for being the only lawyer to fight the government about aliens.

"About aliens?"

"Yeah, I went to court five times to get them to release the Area 51 papers. They are still keeping them hidden."

"Keeping what exactly?"

"The aliens. Little grey men and their technology. The government is still keeping it hidden. We were making a lot of progress in the seventies. Every month there was a convention for UFO believers. There were sightings all over the country... But it's died down now. Now UFO conventions are just a bunch of old farts reminiscing about the good old days... For some reason all the sightings just stopped. We haven't had a good one in many years."

"Why do you think that is?"

"I don't know. The aliens stopped visiting us for their own reasons."

I wanted to raise the possibility that there never were any aliens. The sightings only 'died down' because people stopped confirming a false belief in them. But he was a nice old man, and I didn't want to hurt his feelings.

I hiked up Bell Rock with him right away. On the way up, he asked me where I was when the Mayan calendar ended two years ago. I had just started OMing and was doing mushrooms often with Roger. He told me he took a group to the top of Bell Rock that night, because he was sure that was the time and place the aliens would come back and take away the believers.

"We were dancing and singing all night," he said. "But the next morning, no aliens came, so we all went home."

"So how close are you to one thousand, one hundred, and eleven people?" I asked.

"I passed it a while ago," he said. "The angels must have reasons to keep me on earth longer. So I'm going for eleven thousand, one hundred and eleven."

He was a seemingly intelligent and lucid man. I wondered what could make him continue to hold on to convictions against contrary evidence. I figured at his age, it was probably too painful to admit that you had been believing in a false reality.

There was a young couple staying in one of the other rooms. We all went out for lunch together. The guy was an energy healer.

"I am ordained in the Twenty Two Rays," he said.

"What's that?"

"Well, you know the Violet Flame of St. Germain? That's one of them. Most people don't realize, there are twenty-one other healing energies just like that."

I wanted to tell him I had never heard of any such flame. I was pretty sure no one else had nor cared. But he was a nice young man, and I didn't want to hurt his feelings.

After he ate, he said a prayer then held his palm over his right side.

"I'm healing my liver with green energy," he said when he saw me staring.

I hoped I didn't sound like him when I spoke about OM.

The young lady was wearing a CrossFit t-shirt.

"You do CrossFit?" I said.

"Oh yeah, my mom has been doing it awhile, and she got me into it last year. I'm like, totally obsessed."

"I used to do CrossFit," I said.

"Oh so you left the *cult*?" she said. "My friends always joke that it's a cult. They are kind of right. It like, takes over your life when you get into it. But I think it's a good cult. Like, I really enjoy it. I need my fix. That's the worst part of this road trip. Sometimes we can't find a Box and I go totally crazy."

The guy groaned under his breath.

"Yeah, I liked the community aspect," I said, "A lot of my Marine friends were doing it. But I kept getting injured. I don't think doing that many reps of anything works for my body."

She nodded quickly. "Yeah, people only leave the cult when they get hurt."

I told them about Orgasmic Meditation. He frowned. She blushed. I told them about how CrossFit HQ hired OneTaste to teach the entire corporate staff to OM. Maybe they'd incorporate OMing in the Workouts of the Day one day. The woman asked for my card. When she got up for the bathroom, the guy came over and whispered.

"Hey, um, so this OM thing," he said, "can it, uh, help a guy if he, um, you know, has issues getting..."

"Yes, it can totally help with erectile dysfunction."

He flinched and I decided to lower my volume. He was one of those unfortunate souls who still experienced shame, I thought. I told him my story and he seemed relieved. We decided to stay in touch.

I stopped for the night in Vegas. My former dating coach's protege happened to be there for the weekend. He invited me to stay in the extra bed in his hotel room. I hadn't seen him in two years. I used to really look up to him. He was a little older than me and had done a ton of personal development work. But now he seemed lost and distraught.

He was in Vegas for a spiritual personal development conference on 'manifestation.' Our former dating coach said it was a stupid idea and forbid him from going. This caused them to split.

"I realized, I'm thirty-three years old now," he said. "Why the fuck am I letting some guy I hired to help me with dating, tell me how to live my life? Don't get me wrong, he definitely helped me with confidence and approaching women. But I don't owe him my life... And the thing is, I used to think if I could just be successful with women, then I'd be set. Dating is no longer a problem, but I'm still fucking lost. I wish figuring out life was as simple as figuring out women."

I shared with him my journey with OM. How it started about sex, but it really gave me a roadmap on how to navigate life. "Following the stroke" was the most practical approach to spirituality that I could have asked for.

"Sound like you have everything figured out now," he said.

I wasn't sure if he was being sarcastic.

The next morning, I continued to California and dropped off Heather's car with her sister. I stayed the night at the Santa Cruz OM House along with many OMers from around the world who were there for Magic School.

Magic School was a retreat for Players.

Almost every student was an experienced OMer who had done a CP, Mastery, or both. A few inexperienced men were dragged there by a woman. We all waited in the cul-de-sac outside of the welcome lodge of the Monterrey resort for the official start. OMers were always on time.

A handful of students recognized me from the OneTaste YouTube channel and the Orgasm Daily blog. But the staff seemed to be ignoring me. The New York staff in particular were avoiding eye contact. I had to stand directly in front of Rachel for her to acknowledge me.

"Oh, hi Ruwan," she eventually said when I became impossible to ignore. "What are you doing here?"

"I'm here for Magic School..."

"Oh great, Sergio will register you."

He greeted me in an unusually cold way. Something was off.

We were herded into the main auditorium. Nicole entered with music and dancing, and then went straight into her opening address.

"Lao Tzu said, *the Left Hand Path is best never started, but once started it must be completed,*" she said.

She implied that we all had already started on this path, so we better follow through or face the consequences. She spoke about how the modern world had lost its connection to ritual and ritual magic.

"An initiate is one who owns nothing but has access to everything," she said, quoting Dion Fortune.

"...and when we can get enough people living this way... The goal is Mytheria, the ultimate state of connection..." she said, then switched loops. "Gosh, if someone heard us right now, they would really think we're a cult."

The audience laughed.

I looked around for Arjun during the first lunch break but couldn't find him. I tried saying hi to Winter and some of the other staff but got the cold shoulder. Finally, I confronted Sergio.

"What the fuck is going on?" I said.

His grey eyes were wet with emotion.

"I'm mad at you," he said. "The biggest wave is coming. You do it better than any of us. And you're throwing it away. We need you. And you turned your back on us."

It turned out that it was a big deal that I had given up the TurnON Brooklyn event. Lower tier staff saw it as me being ungrateful for a privilege. Higher tier staff saw that I was trying to get direct access to Nicole without committing my life, as they had. These were violations of the game.

I wanted to explain, but we ended up hugging instead. He began to cry and convulse. I couldn't help tearing up too. He still was the only man who I could cry with. Just as abruptly he pulled away with disgust.

I had to find Arjun. I searched for him through the entire lunch break. I finally found him sitting in a dark corner in the welcome lodge. It looked like he had been crying for days.

"Hey buddy," he said softly.

I relaxed to hear a friendly voice. We hugged, but it was a weak one. I filled him in on my road trip, but he didn't seem to care.

"I bought in to OneTaste New York."

"What?!? But I thought…"

"Yeah. It's not a good investment… for money," he said. "But I had to go all the way in. It was the only way to get Winter back."

As Winter became Rachel's protege she got round the clock training, which largely involved pulling Arjun's heart strings. Rachel reminded her of their "soul contract." Arjun brought her to OM, and now she had to "free him from his ego." This meant going hot and cold with affection and sleeping with different men and rubbing it in his face so he'd be able to "burn through his shit."

That was the same phrase John used when he said he decided to become a Lifer.

Arjun knew OneTaste was going after his wallet through his heart. They Hooked him on the grand scale. But it didn't matter. Knowing how alcohol works doesn't stop you from getting drunk.

So he drank the water.

Arjun was one of five people who put in a quarter of a million dollars each to buy OneTaste New York. They got a better deal than most. OneTaste Los Angeles sold for two and a half million. I had heard that OneTaste London sold for three and half million, but later found out the real figure was closer to eight hundred thousand.

There wasn't much more to talk about. I stood up and looked at Arjun. He was staring into space. Abby had the same expression after she was "killed." He was a blank slate.

I was totally alone.

THAT EVENING WAS THE first of many rituals through the five days of Magic School. It was kind of a ritual sample platter. Different stations were set up around the auditorium and the students lined up to partake. One was by BDSM teacher, Cleo DuBois, where she pierced each students' chest with a needle. Another was with a thirty-third degree Mason, a friend of Nicole's, who led students to jump over a fire while saying "leap into life!" Only a real fire was deemed to be a hazard, so he set up a bunch of electronic tea lights instead.

The final ritual was with Nicole— a *puja*. Earlier in the year, the Brooklyn House attended a puja of Amma, the "Hugging Saint." In the same way, the Magic School class lined up to be blessed by Nicole. Except instead of hugs, it was sexual.

She did a little something different with each person. Some were slow and sensual caresses. Others were more raunchy groping. She pulled a man's face into her breasts. She dove her face into the cleavage of a woman. People like Sergio, who prided themselves in their sensitivity, left Nicole convulsing with sensation as they sat back in the pews. I knew enough to know such shows were partly theatrics. And at the same time, I wished to have as intense an experience.

On my turn, she grabbed my butt and pulled me into her. My shirt was off from the chest-piercing ritual. She ran her face and lips down my chest to my pants. I spasmed a little. After a few seconds, she looked up at me with bloodshot eyes. I remembered the dream I had where the Exec Team abducted me and Nicole gave me fellatio.

I was feeling a lot when I sat in the pew. I wasn't sure if Nicole really did deliver Orgasm into me, or it was the groupthink of the room, or both.

I guessed it didn't matter.

BEFORE DINNER ON THE second night, I went to the beach to think. I was hurting. Over the last twenty months these people had become my best friends, my family. All of them giving me the cold shoulder felt like a breakup, but times twenty. I remembered how Lisa convulsed on my bed when she was withdrawing from *blues*. I felt similar. I was in withdrawal from connection.

I sat on a dead tree trunk that had washed up on shore. It matched the feeling in my soul.

I knew that all the communications I had been receiving over the last months were coordinated— pressure from Priscilla, "good cop" messages from Sarah, disapproval from Rachel, sporadic attention from Nicole. Priscilla probably shared the most honest account: OneTaste only wanted people who were committed to them for the very long term... as in a life sentence.

Since my recent actions showed my lack of commitment, the only way I could remain in was to come back with full humility— I had to be humiliated. I didn't have money to display my commitment, like Arjun. I'd have to find some other kind of *expensive signal*, a un-fakable show of commitment. If I did that, I'd eventually be raised to exalted status in the community.

If my last couple years in the OM world were fun and meaningful, the next couple could be even more so. I'd write a book with Nicole, a parable of a young man learning magic from the wise witch. It would read like a Dion Fortune book— but real. And that would be my life. Forever.

But if I didn't serve penance, I'd be pushed out. I was too much of a liability otherwise. I would have to go back to the real world where I was a nobody. I didn't know what to do.

Someone sighed.

I hadn't noticed a man sitting on the other end of the dead trunk. He was middle aged, slightly overweight, hairy, and grey. I could tell he had been OMing awhile because I could really feel him.

I went over to put my arm around him. He began to weep. He put his face on my shoulder and sobs rattled out of him. I held him until the sun fully set into the ocean.

"Thank you," he said with a face full of snot. My shoulder was soaked.

The grey man didn't look so grey after crying. Color returned to his face, and he explained his grief as we walked to dinner. He and his girlfriend opened their relationship after she insisted they start OMing. Rachel told them to go on a '30 Day No Communication Break.' He signed up for Magic School to try to win her back. But she was ignoring him. As he and I sat here as bumps on the log, she was loudly fucking the man she came here with. But the sweaty grey man was committed to feeling through all these uncomfortable feelings. He thanked me again for holding space for him.

THE HIGHLIGHT OF MAGIC School was the "Priest Ritual." Nicole explained that, as in the Dion Fortune novels, men received real power when they surrendered to the

Feminine. In this ritual, OneTaste was going to unveil the seven "Priests of Orgasm"— men who had recently done the work to spread Orgasm through the world.

Nicole went behind the curtain, and ominous music began playing. A pair of snake dancers, that is, women who danced with snakes, came out in front of the curtains and did a semi-erotic belly dance with eight-foot-long green serpents coiled around them. I wished Abby was around to say how many times the shark had been jumped.

Then the music stopped. The curtains pulled back to reveal seven demo tables arranged in a semi-circle. On the tables were seven naked women with their legs spread open. They had black veils over their heads but it was clear they were Nicole, Rachel, and five other women from the Exec Team.

Then seven men came out: John, Arjun, Sergio, Nicole's new boyfriend— a lawyer in his twenties who had recently been hired as OneTaste's legal counsel, and three other men who had recently bought into the OneTaste affiliate program.

This was their initiation. They each began to stroke one of the women. Every few minutes a timer went off, and they switched to the next woman on the next table. The audience watched with the reverence of any demo. At the end of the ritual, the men were each given a necklace with a large ivory moon pendant— no doubt an allusion to *Moon Magic*.

Afterward, there was a social hour where many congratulated the new priests.

"My father is going to flip when he sees this," Sergio laughed. "He always said, 'Whatever you do, don't become a priest. They make no money'."

Some OMers asked me why I wasn't a "Priest of Orgasm." After all, I was the "Male Voice of Female Orgasm." I didn't know what to say. But I did know I wasn't chosen because I hadn't shown sufficient commitment. I couldn't help but feel massive FOMO.

ON THE LAST DAY of Magic School, Nicole stroked the room. This was my last chance. I chose my words carefully.

"Every time I feel I'm getting the stroke, I go for it and think, 'Yes, this is my calling!'" I said, "Then I pull on the thread and it seems to disintegrate in my hands."

Nicole looked annoyed. I couldn't tell if she was looking at me or through me.

"It's what I told you when we met in Bryant Park..." she said. "That was you wasn't it?"

"Yes."

"I wasn't sure because you're staring at me like an alien."

Nicole made a mocking face. The class laughed.

"The reason you're lost," she continued, "is that instead of surrendering to the Orgasm, you're always looking to profit from it. You're like an Orgasm pimp."

"I thought I had it for a second, but then I lost it," I said.

"That's because you have a fast-acting ego. I know you got it for a second because it looked like you were going to die."

She mimed a deer-in-the-headlights expression. The class laughed.

"So you need to decide, are you going to keep trying to pimp the Orgasm, or will you *commit your life* to something bigger?"

The 'right' response here was to *get off*, to make a grand show of emotion, a willingness to be stroked. I had done this dozens of times in OneTaste courses before. But something stopped me from doing that.

"Thank you," I said and sat back down.

Before Nicole turned to the next person, she made sure to show her disapproval.

After Magic School officially closed, I was waiting for my ride in the parking lot when a white Range Rover pulled into the spot in front of me. Two staffers loaded some suitcases in the trunk. Nicole got into the back seat and closed the door. A moment later she opened it.

"Ruwan," she said.

I walked up to her.

"Come give me a hug."

I did. I felt she was giving me energy but was unsure if I should open to it. There's a tradeoff between clairvoyance and the ability to protect yourself, Arjun had said.

"Will I see you on the other side?" she said.

"I hope so."

"I hope so too."

Then she pulled her tan legs into the Rover, closed the door, and told her driver to drive away.

THE NEXT DAY RACHEL invited me to come with her to TurnON Santa Cruz.

"They've been offstroke," Rachel said. "I need you to help me get them back in the rails!"

When we arrived in Santa Cruz, Rachel announced that instead of TurnON we were going to do a special talk by Rachel on "How to Have Great Sex." The event, like many OneTaste events, mostly consisted of stroking the room. Rachel improvised a whole show full of one-liners, jokes, and impromptu coaching. The event ended with sharing Intimacies.

"Um, this was interesting," a middle-aged man said, "but I don't see how we were taught how to have great sex... It seems like all night you've just been reading people and giving them therapy."

Rachel honed a laser gaze on him, then smiled.

"Let me guess," she said, "you don't have the best relationships with women?"

The man fumbled. "Um, no I don't but..."

"Yes I can tell. You want some *information* because you're disconnected from the Feminine." Rachel crossed her arms and leaned back in the chair. "Let me tell you something. Tonight was about *transmission*. I gave you *Orgasm*. I could have read the phonebook tonight and you all would go home and have better sex."

The man blushed. I felt a little bad for him. But Rachel did have a point, I thought. OneTaste courses were usually low on content, but everyone left feeling things.

After the event closed, we had a debrief. It wasn't a normal debrief about the event. It was more Rachel stroking each of us. She had some harsh things to say to the Santa Cruz facilitators. Then she turned the focus on me.

"And you, you've been off all night. You're one of the most highly trained people here. You should be an example to everyone."

I wanted to say I didn't know what she was talking about. But that wasn't true. Between the lines I knew she was continuing what Nicole had started at Magic School. She was pressuring me to publicly commit my life or leave.

Rachel moved on to the next person, a young woman from the Santa Cruz team with whom I sometimes had Makeouts.

"I feel like I have a lot of sight, but it's not acknowledged," she said.

"Oh well then tell us what you see," Rachel said. "Tell me what you see in... Ruwan."

"I see a warrior," she said.

"Oh him? Nooo," Rachel said. "He might *look* like a tiger, but he's actually just a vicious-ass koala bear."

Rachel dropped the humorous tone. "Ruwan has been on the threshold for something big, but he's afraid to go through the portal. He's being tempted to stop Waking Up. And if you can't see that, you can't see!"

No one spoke to me the rest of the evening.

The next morning, I took an Uber to the airport. Months ago, OneTaste would have made sure I was driven by a junior member of the staff. I sat by the gate and continued contemplating. I just wanted a sign.

My phone buzzed with a text from John.

"Hey brother," he wrote. "I know the spot you're in. I've been there and I want to send you some love."

My eyes teared up. When you're withdrawing from connection, the slightest hit has a huge effect.

"I know how difficult it is," he continued. "It's like you and your identity are standing on different sides of the fence. You're looking at what you thought was yourself, and he's looking back at you. You know you have a choice, but you don't know what the options are."

"I feel so confused."

"I know," John said. "It's because you're waiting for the Orgasm to prove itself to you so you can make a rational decision. But that's not how it works. Only when you commit will the Orgasm reveal itself. How's your faith muscle?"

"Weak."

John was typing. Then the dots disappeared. Then he started typing again. Then he stopped again. My eyes were getting cloudy from the tears.

"What should I do?" I texted.

"All I can tell you is when you hear the Voice, you have to listen to it," he said. "Don't question it. Just do. If you do, you'll find peace. If you don't, you'll stay Whacked."

"Thank you, John."

"You're welcome, Ruwan. I'm rooting for you."

STAGE 9: CLIMAX, REPRISE

Involuntary contraction followed by explosive release. The subject is ejected into a new reality, again.

It's not something I would recommend
But it is one way to live
'Cause what is simple in the moonlight
By the morning never is
~Bright Eyes (Lua)

EVERYTHING WAS WRONG WHEN I returned to New York.

I attended the OneTaste Men's Group that I had started. I had handed it off to John when I moved to Brooklyn earlier in the year and hadn't attended since. But I wanted to reconnect. Now it was being run by Arjun and Sergio at 365.

I didn't know any of the other guys in the Men's Group. No one knew who I was, or at least they acted like it. Arjun and Sergio were cold and snappy with me, and the rest followed suit. I tried lightening the mood with a dumb joke about passing the conch, but only received glares from Sergio and Arjun, followed by glares from the new strokers on cue.

"You're off," Sergio said.

"Uh, I was just making a joke," I said.

"You're trying to draw attention to yourself," Arjun said. His eyes were fierce and hawk-like.

He had completely changed in the week since Magic School. He cut his hair and replaced his hippie clothes with stylish ones. His ego had been reformed, in a OneTaste-approved shape. He took up more space. His back was straighter. His movement more deliberate. His tone of voice was more commanding. He even looked more muscular.

He had made it "through the portal." He was now a Priest of Orgasm. It only cost him a quarter of a million dollars.

I used my Intimacy at the end to question why Arjun was so hostile to me. That was a bad move. Starting with Sergio, everyone else's Intimacy share was how I was "offstroke" or "operating from my ego." The newbies weren't so savvy in *downstroking*, but they still found some way to get their jabs in.

So this is how it is, I thought.

I texted Arjun and Sergio a lukewarm apology after. I was willing to Bottom. I told them I genuinely didn't know what I did to piss them off, but I was sorry and was willing to get feedback. My ego cringed as I typed, but that was the point. I had to humiliate myself to feel connected again.

The only thing that feels bad is disconnection, Abby said.

They accepted my apology. But they didn't say what was "off" about me. Minutes later I got my answer. I received a text from Rachel.

"Just because you decided to stop waking up, doesn't mean you get to take shots at the men who are doing the real work to hold the Orgasm," she wrote.

I knew the three of them were sitting on a couch together showing each other their messages, discussing how to stroke me. A part of me wanted to call them out. But a stronger part just wanted to be included again. I didn't know where I belonged. Without my reference group, I didn't even know who I was.

THE NEXT MORNING, I felt a weird itch on the soles of my feet, like a sunburn.

After Morning OMs, I had a sore throat. By the end of breakfast, I had a fever. I went to bed and had a dream about missing a semester of school and not being able to graduate.

When I woke up my hands and feet were covered in reddish brown marks like chicken pocks. My throat was almost swollen shut, like there was a golf ball in it.

For the next few days I couldn't walk, talk, or hold things. It seemed symbolic. News of my strange disease made it through the OM community. I received a few 'good cop' messages from Sarah and John, wishing for my recovery. I received a downstroke through Elma when she returned from Women's Group at 365.

"I told Rachel about your disease, and she said, 'Well that's what he gets for saying no to his desire.'"

Sally eventually convinced me to see a doctor. She had to give me a piggyback ride to and from the cab. Thankfully years of sautés and pliés gave her sturdy legs.

"You're going to laugh when you hear the diagnosis," the doctor said. "You have *Hand, Foot, and Mouth Disease*." He waited for me to laugh, but I didn't. "Children get it a lot. It's quite rare for adults… Anyway, there's nothing to do but wait a few weeks. It will clear up on its own."

On the ride back, I noticed the church near the Brooklyn House was open. I had walked by it numerous times and never stopped to look. I made us get off there. Sally piggybacked me to the church pew. I got on my knees. I didn't know why. But when I closed my eyes, I felt the need to ask for forgiveness. I didn't know what for, or from whom. I just wanted to be forgiven. I began to cry.

I took out my journal and remembered one of my earliest lessons from OM. In big block letters I wrote, "DO WHAT MAKES YOUR BODY FEEL GOOD."

I decided to try Twelve Step. Many OneTasters, like Rachel, were addicts in recovery and referenced meetings as an important practice. I wanted to see what they were all about. Every morning I visited a different meeting. There were multiple meetings every hour throughout New York, so I decided to try as many as I could.

I visited one meeting in Hell's Kitchen with over seventy members. They were way livelier and more energetic than all the others. Everyone was hugging and laughing before the meeting even started. Many came over to offer me their numbers in case I ever wanted to talk. I noticed everyone was really well dressed. Most were quite fit. Many were bearded. And all of them were men. It was a gay men-only meeting. That was cool, I guessed. I could use a break from women.

That meeting had a speaker who was ten years sober. He shared a story of how challenging sobriety was, taking it one day a time, then one day he realized it was his seven-year anniversary. That day, his sponsor gave him a bag of marbles and said, "I always told you, after seven years, you get your marbles back."

I started bawling. There were many wet cheeks throughout the room. I felt an expansion in my chest that reminded me of my first TurnON events. At the end, they welcomed all the newcomers. I had to speak.

"I've been going to these meetings for a week, not sure if I belonged here or not," I said. "But when you told your story, I realized..." my voice cracked, "I just want my marbles back."

There was some laughter mixed with affirming sounds. I was both crying and laughing, too. I found myself hugging a man with huge delts and a thick beard. I dried my face on his shirt. I was highly impressed by its thread count.

As I walked out, I heard a voice.

You're done.

As always, I wasn't sure if I was just talking to myself. But then it said,

Tell Rachel. Now.

I texted her. I asked her if she would like to meet for tea. She agreed.

RACHEL AND I MET for tea in the West Village.

I picked a tea house that was Alice in Wonderland-themed. All the furniture was upholstered Victorian and the walls were lined with shelves of expensive-looking books.

"This place is so darling," she said.

She gave me a medium-length hug, not one that permeated my bones. I appreciated that she had come alone.

"One sec, I just need to respond to Priscilla," she said.

She slouched as she texted. She looked tiny in the high-backed chair. She stopped typing but kept looking at her phone as if waiting for a response. Everything is a communication.

I knew this was a tactic to Top me, to get the upper hand. That was okay. I was here for connection, not power. I was happy to Bottom. I ordered a small pot of white tea with rose.

Rachel put her phone down. I looked at it. She turned it over.

"So, what's up?" she said.

"Well, I feel like I've been in a revolving door with OneTaste for awhile now," I said. "And now I want out."

She looked at the back of her phone then back to me.

"Okay," she said. "What will you do?"

"The same as I've been doing, trying to get this coaching and writing thing going... I wanted to tell you in person. I wanted to tell you how grateful I am to you, to the game. I'm not turning my back, I just need to go my own way. I need to follow my purpose."

"And what's that?"

"To teach people how to feel, about Orgasm... I mean, right now it looks like writing my book."

"What's your book about?"

"My time at OneTaste."

Rachel squinted and cocked her head.

"It's basically the book I was going to write with Nicole... but by myself. And I know that I'm playing in dangerous territory."

Rachel's squint became a half-scowl. "What do you mean?"

"I mean... like I know that this could tempt me to all my ego triggers, like money and fame and stuff. But that's not why I'm writing it. This is how I will spread Orgasm."

"I see."

Our tea was served some minutes ago. I poured for both of us, but no one drank.

"Will you stay at the Brooklyn House?"

"For a couple months, maybe. The lease is up at the end of the year and there won't be anyone holding the house."

Rachel looked up and to the left, then down and to the left.

"I just wanted to say, I love you a lot, Rachel."

Rachel pursed her lips resembling a smile. Love is a complicated emotion.

"Are you happy?" she said.

"I'm getting there. I just know I haven't been happy for a while. I've been off my stroke. And then the other day, I heard the whisper that it was time to leave and that's when I messaged you."

I knew that she couldn't argue with my choice of words. I finished my tea cup. She hadn't touched hers.

"If you're happy, then I'm happy for you," she said.

We looked at each other. It was particularly mediocre eye contact, no intensity or confrontation, no intimacy either. She raised her eyebrows as if to say, "What else?"

"Okay, I'm going to go," I said.

"Let me give you a hug," she said.

It was a short hug, not like the ones where she'd envelope me with warmth.

Rachel said she'd stay here to take her calls. I said a final goodbye and she winked at me with both eyes because she couldn't do it with one. On the way out, I noticed there was no wear and tear on the books on the wall. They were all fake.

I WALKED CROSSTOWN TO the M train.

The cold was biting, but the bite felt good.

This was the right move, I thought. I was leaving on good terms. I expressed my love and gratitude. They couldn't possibly ostracize me when I was leaving in peace. I was a good player. And now it was time for a new game.

Get in. Immerse. Get out. Nicole said that all the time.

I walked through Washington Square Park. The sky was grey but I saw Lila and myself in every sunny corner laughing and handing out Orgasm balloons. I passed *La Colombe* on Lafayette and saw the Canadians and me philosophizing and trancing till our faces melted. I passed by Xena's apartment in the East Village.

Was my life experiment a success? It was hard to tell.

I was about thirty grand in debt. If I got an entry level marketing job and lived cheap, I could probably pay it off in two or three years.

Before I entered the subway, I saw I had a bunch of missed calls and a text from Roger.

"It's all over Roo. We're moving out. If you want your stuff come get it right now."

I called him. He was short of breath. He told me the apartment had flooded with septic water and the landlords weren't doing anything about it. A lawyer told them the only course of action was to evacuate immediately.

When I arrived, Brad was backing up a U-Haul.

"Roopadoop!" he said.

We hugged it out and went inside. The mood was somber. The apartment stank of feces.

"End of an era," Roger said. "It's all over."

"It's the over-est," Brad said.

They were taking this as a good time to enter new life chapters. Roger was moving in with his girlfriend. Brad was going to take his big shot at a music career by self-funding a road tour.

They offered me a beer. I refused.

They said the stuff I left was still under the stairs. The cardboard box was soaked. But the stuff on top was dry. It contained everything that was left of my pre-OM life, mostly drug paraphernalia from when I was with Lisa: Three cans of butane. Eighty-seven disposable razor blades. And a tinfoil pouch containing eight tabs of acid.

Make that six tabs of acid.

I don't know what made me do it, but I did. That sour buzz under my lip. The taste of nostalgia. I offered the rest to them, but they declined.

"Roo, you're still crazy," Brad said.

"Roo's the craziest."

I hopped on the M train at Houston Street. The LSD started hitting just as we were crossing the Williamsburg Bridge. The East River looked like a painting. I texted the boys a rocket emoji. They wrote back some pop culture reference that I didn't understand. I realized I was all alone.

I was no longer in the OneTaste world. But I wasn't in the "real" world either. My old friends couldn't possibly get me. And I couldn't pretend to be the person I once was. The train was full of the evening rush, but it felt like everyone was far away.

But the acid was giving me the giggles. So that was good.

Back at the OM House I flopped on my new bed which I shared with Elma. For nine months, I directed people to change rooms every month but never moved myself. Only last month, did Elma notice this. Everyone was mad that I 'manipulated them.' I no longer controlled the Brooklyn House reality.

Elma dressed our bed with a quilt with a mandala on it. It was rippling. I thought about the monks that made mandalas out of sand all day. I wondered if they entered a euphoric altered state through meditative focus. Or maybe kept doing it because they also had no money and nowhere else to go.

Someone opened and closed the apartment door. The bed stopped rippling. I couldn't let anyone know I was on drugs.

I got my computer and opened a folder of movies I downloaded a long time ago. I hadn't watched a movie in years. I picked *The Graduate* where Dustin Hoffman comes home from college, sleeps with an older woman, falls in love with her daughter, then storms the daughter's wedding to someone else and steals her away. The last scene showed them on a bus with the wedding party chasing them. They had an expression on their face that seemed to say "oh fuck, what now?"

"How relatable," I said out loud.

I attended my last TurnON New York on December 1st, my OM birthday.

I received a warm welcome from the staff. It felt like visiting high school after going away to college.

"The last two years have been the greatest decade of my life," I said in response to one of the Inside-Out prompts.

Everyone laughed. I was still a good Player.

Rachel brought me on as the final HotSeat. It felt like old times. I felt she accepted that I had graduated.

So the following Sunday, when Rachel said she wanted to attend the Brooklyn House meeting, I felt pretty good about it.

It had been about two weeks since I had tea with Rachel. Almost everyone in the Brooklyn House had started volunteering as BOH with OneTaste. It was a natural progression, as most of our new residents were in CP8. Even Sally, who had always been an enemy of Rachel, had made peace with OneTaste. Rachel invited Sally to read her Fear Inventory to her— one of the most intimate things two OMers could do with each other. It seemed like all was right in the world. I had also let go of my control over the Brooklyn House. I had suggested Elma lead the meeting.

But Rachel didn't come alone. She arrived with three of the seven Priests of Orgasm: Arjun, Sergio, and a third male staff member who would soon become Rachel's husband. She was expecting to do battle. Rachel sat at the head of the table. Her men in waiting spread out so one was at each side. Something wasn't right.

Also, Elma wasn't there.

"So Elma was supposed to lead this meeting. I'm not sure where she is though," I said.

"Elma is taking care of some stuff for Nicole," Rachel said. "She'll be here when she's here. Why don't you lead the meeting? You know how to do that. Don't you, Ruwan?"

I was sitting in the corner at the foot of the table. Sometimes I chose to sit in this 'low power' position when I led a meeting so everyone else could feel more authority in themselves. But that only worked because I already had the room. I didn't have the room right now.

"Okay," I said reluctantly. "Let's Sync Up."

The housemates all put in their hands. Rachel joined but made a face at Arjun mocking our Brooklyn ritual. The three men-in-waiting were completely stoic. The housemates for the most part seemed normal. We passed around warm eye contact and smiled, though mine was uneasy. Rachel didn't make eye contact with me.

"Okay, let's check in," Rachel said.

I wanted to tell Rachel that the point of Syncing Up was that we didn't have to do individual check-ins, but I didn't want to invite conflict. The first person next to Rachel was a new OMer, Greg, a computer programmer who came through TurnON Brooklyn. He had signed up for CP9 and moved into the Brooklyn House a month ago.

"I feel uneasy that there's so much OneTaste staff here. I don't trust you guys," he said.

"No. No! That is NOT fair!" Rachel said. "We are working our asses off to bring you Orgasm, to bring you this amazing life you live here. Yes, we make mistakes, but we're doing our best! Where were you before OneTaste? You're in heaven now compared to your old life. How dare you attack us like that."

"I... I... was just sharing what I was feeling," he said. He looked smaller than a minute ago.

"It was unkind. If you attack OneTaste, you're attacking me. And I'm not going to allow this anymore. This house has been off for a while now because you don't have any real practitioners holding it. That's why you're all off."

Rachel turned to the next person after Greg, a middle-aged woman. She was a longtime OMer who took CP6 but otherwise kept her distance from OneTaste.

"And I don't know why YOU are so resentful. I've been nothing but welcoming to you. I've been walking on eggshells around you, waiting for you to grow up into your power. But you resent me instead."

I wasn't sure what Rachel was referring to, but it was clearly the perfect killstroke. The woman's posture collapsed revealing a little girl inside who cowered when daddy yells.

"And you..." Rachel turned to me.

I straightened my posture to take the charge. Elma entered the apartment and sat down confused. Then she saw what was going on and took the cue to glare at me.

"You are running a practice house and right now you don't seem like a practitioner," Rachel glared at me. "If you want to go waste away all your Orgasm, fine. But if you put people who are under my care in danger, that I'm not okay with."

"I'm not sure what you're talking about."

"Ruwan, we're a dry house!" Elma said. "You broke the rules!"

"Oh, the acid thing…"

"Ruwan, LSD has been a huge part of my journey," Rachel said. "But you don't have the training to do it correctly. That stuff is dangerous. It can split your psyche. And if you do it the wrong way, you might never come back. And you're not powerful enough to hold other people in that field."

"I didn't mean to be on LSD in the House," I said, "But it's not like it affected anyone… I only brought it up after I came down. And I'm not trying to hold the House. I handed it over to Elma. I even met with you, Rachel, so we could have a peaceful parting. I felt like we had a loving split. Now I feel like you're acting like I'm trying to sabotage everyone or something."

"No, Ruwan," Rachel said. "Two years ago, you and I entered an energetic contract that said I would fight for your freedom forever no matter what. Then you decided you wanted out of that contract. That's what happened when we met for tea."

"Okay… so why am I being attacked right now?"

"C'mon Ru, just listen to Rachel," said Sally.

Et tu, Sally?

I realized what had been happening the last couple weeks. When it was clear I wasn't going to go back deeper into OneTaste, Rachel got to work to frame me as crazy. I had too much influence in the community. She had to make sure no one followed me out the door. So over the last weeks, Rachel planned to cut off my support. She captured the hearts and minds of the new residents by inviting them to do BOH. The others, she knew how to kill. Sally, she could disable with friendship. I was alone at the table. Anything I said could be reframed according to Rachel's reality.

Rachel came here tonight to delete me from the game. And she succeeded.

Checkmate. Rachel, you win.

"I've already felt that my time in the House was coming to a close," I said. "But it's now become clear that I need to move out sooner. I'll be out by the end of the week."

Rachel held her stare till she was clear I was not going to attack. Then she leaned back and flipped the oxytocin switch. The room exhaled. Greg lightened the mood with a joke. Only Rachel laughed. The Men-In-Waiting still hadn't made a sound.

Rachel told Elma to finish leading the meeting. Elma ran through all the logistical topics with very little group discussion. Greg tried another joke, but no one laughed.

"Alright, it's about that time," Rachel said in a sleepy voice.

Hugs were exchanged. I held my elbow like a child while I waited for Rachel to finish hugging everyone before she finally acknowledged me. I felt the impulse to apologize. But something in me said that was the wrong thing to do.

We hugged and she gave me the name of some guy she knew that guided LSD trips.

"Work with a professional if you're going to do acid. You're not powerful enough to do that on your own."

"Thanks Rachel."

"You're welcome, Ruwan."

I HAD ONLY A few days to find an apartment.

I had no income on record. Terrible credit. And no roommate this time who could cover for me on paper. But I had Orgasm, and a little faith that something would fall into my lap.

And it did. Literally.

I was invited to run an OM circle at a nudist party. The New York nudist society had some overlap with the fringes of the OM Community. Even though nudism wasn't explicitly sexual, most nudists dabbled in swinging, play parties, tantra, OM and anything deemed "sex-positive."

OneTaste highly frowned on all these activities, and even having OM in the same category. OM was about raising sensation through greater attention. Hedonism, or increasing stimuli, was seen as antithetical. I never would have attended such a party when I was a "Messenger of Orgasm".

After the circle, I was sitting in an armchair when a young woman climbed into my lap. Her name was Talia. She said she had seen me at the TurnON on my "OM birthday." She started OMing a few weeks ago and her life had been a crazy adventure since.

She wanted to go deeper. She wanted to move into the Brooklyn House. But she had a dog and a lease on her apartment.

"If only I could find someone to take my place...," she said.

We decided to switch places right away. Her place was a garden apartment in Fort Greene across the street from the park. Her rent was more than three times what I paid at the Brooklyn House. We agreed that I'd keep paying her OM House rent and she'd keep paying for her apartment. I just had to take care of the dog.

When you're on the stroke, things flow effortlessly.

THAT YEAR WAS ONE of the coldest winters in New York history.

The heater in Talia's apartment didn't work properly and it didn't dawn on me that I could ask the super to fix it. I no longer knew how to function in the real world. I tried to write my book, but spent most of every day under a pile of blankets clutching Talia's dog.

Like a hard moment in a mushroom trip, I felt there was something unpleasant I had to come to terms with.

I decided to make amends.

I texted Nicole first, "Hi Nic. I know I've been super far out, but I wanted to say I'm so grateful to you, now more than ever."

She responded immediately, "That feels so good. The door is always open. You're one of the good ones ;)"

I called Xena. The last time we spoke was over a year ago when I was on Team New York. She reminded me that she had asked me to have a Makeout. I responded by trying to sell her Mastery. I apologized. She forgave me. She knew I had become a different person in those months.

I reached out to Daniel. I hadn't seen him in six months or so. He was also living in Brooklyn. After leaving the Morellino, he fell in love with a Sister Goddess and moved in with her. We met for sushi to catch up. There was something different about Daniel. He still had interesting things to say, but the vigor was gone. It was like his inner fire was extinguished.

"People keep their Orgasm for about six months after they leave OneTaste, but then they lose it," Rachel always said.

Daniel said his girlfriend had recently dumped him for another OMer and he had just moved out. He had gained a lot of weight. He looked less like an enthusiastic puppy, and more like a grumpy dog.

A new Facebook group had been created by angry ex-OneTasters and he was active on it. He shared analyses of their manipulation tactics and ethical crimes. And how they promoted magical thinking. And how being in OneTaste makes a person go insane.

I mostly agreed with him, but I felt sad seeing him so cynical. He, after all, was one of the people who convinced me to view life more "magically." I suggested that if a little magical thinking led to a much better life experience, isn't that all that mattered? What about all the good times? What about Clark's Third, *technology indistinguishable from magic*?

Daniel had coined the term *I Got Mine-ism* to describe when ex-cult members ignore the harm the cult caused others because they had a net positive experience. The term would be picked up by other therapists and cult de-programmers.

I didn't think I was doing that. But I also didn't think one negated the other. We ended up arguing aggressively. I got angry at him. Not because he was condemning OneTaste, but because I didn't want to believe that my last two years had been a waste. I couldn't accept the Sucker's Payoff.

"Yes, of course, OneTaste did some bad things," I said, "but maybe it was worth it for the growth in the end?"

"Yeah well," he grumbled, "*Enlightenment leaves no scars.*"

I met Theresa in Ditmas Park. She still lived in the intentional community house, but was moving soon. She had made a lot of money recently.

"When I met you, I was focused on going deep into the spirit realm," she said. "The following year I decided I had to figure out money because for so long I had been afraid of it."

She switched from teaching esoteric sex and hypnosis stuff to executive coaching. She had made over a quarter of a million dollars last year— over five times her previous income.

Her secret? Do everything the opposite of what she learned at OneTaste.

"I just don't trust anything I got from OT. I know there was good stuff in there, but it's tied to too much darkness. So I cut myself off from that energy."

She had been celibate for over a year. No OMing, GOing, anything. She said Fear Inventory was one of the worst things you can do. It was a way OneTaste controlled people by keeping them focused on their fears.

"Don't you still have desires?" I asked.

She was wearing a pant suit, not her previous flowing goddess wear. She looked good.

"Yes of course," she said. "But no thank you."

In mid-December, an email went out to the New York OM Community email list with the subject, "Farewell For Now, It has been Quite the Ride." It was from Winter.

She wrote that she was leaving OneTaste and the OM Community. She said she was "grateful to the practice of OM" and would "cherish the many friendships" she made. But she now had a series of health issues and didn't like the direction of the company. In a very authentic way, she called out OneTaste for being "out of alignment." I was proud of her. She was the first OneTaste casualty to fire back publicly. Unfortunately, her heartfelt message was weakened by poor grammar and many spelling errors. She once again spoke from her old voice, not the one Rachel implanted into her.

She came to visit me a couple weeks later.

"I just wanted to say," she said with teary eyes, "I realized I became a totally different person. I'm really sorry."

When Rachel took her on as a protege, she was honored. She did everything Rachel suggested, believing it was her path to growth. For her that meant doing sales and having sex with different men— often that was the same thing.

When she felt worn out, she was told she needed to have more sex. She was assigned to sleep with random guys from Tinder. It was part of her "Aversion Practice." This was on top of sleeping with men on the staff, and potential sales in the OM Community. Rachel instructed her on how to communicate with Arjun— playing with his heart strings under the guise that she was helping him grow as a man. Winter thought she was OneTaste's new golden child. But once Arjun finally bought into OneTaste New York, they discarded her.

"They used me to get Arjun's money," she said. "Once he put in his money, they didn't need me anymore."

As Arjun was exalted as a "Priest of Orgasm," Winter was demoted. They flipped the script where Arjun was encouraged to sleep with many women. When Winter felt hurt and jealous, and increasingly crazy, she was ordered to do more menial work. Rachel made dog-training noises whenever Winter tried to speak up. The night before Thanksgiving,

Rachel "felt the stroke" that Team New York should spend the day with Team San Francisco. They flew out in the middle of the night while Winter was asleep. She woke the next morning to an empty Bunker, not understanding why she was alone.

Then came the Nicole Daedone Intensive. Arjun had paid forty thousand for both of them. But the night before, Winter was told that she was "off" and had to do some preliminary work and wouldn't be allowed to attend. They kept her in San Francisco while everyone else spent the two weeks in the retreat center. During the retreat, they married Arjun to another longtime staff member. Unlike his "marriage" to Winter, this time it was done legally. It was part of a mass wedding including three other couples. Marriage was seen as the new "edgy thing" to do in OneTaste. It was very often between a wealthy OMer to a OneTaste staff member.

"I hate him. I hate him so much," Winter said.

When the team got back to New York, Winter confronted Arjun and his new wife.

"She tried to stop me from talking to Arjun," Winter said. "So I punched her in the head."

We both laughed

"Wait, seriously?"

"Yeah. It felt great," said Winter. "Nicole texted me after, 'Are you Sicilian? You sound like me when you're angry'."

Winter gloated that Nicole had given her an *upstroke*. This was why Nicole had been untouchable for so long. Even her victims still looked up to her. Even her enemies still valued her attention and approval. But Nicole's biggest defense was revealed at the following CP8 Immersion.

Too many people had seen Winter's email blast for it to be ignored. So that weekend, at the CP8 Immersion, Nicole called Rachel up on stage, and publicly shamed Rachel for "causing harm." It was never explicitly stated, but everyone understood that Rachel was being blamed for Winter's breakdown. Many people said it was the first time they had ever seen Rachel as weak. It was like she became a little girl.

Winter smiled at the thought of Rachel being punished.

"But wait," I said, "doesn't Rachel get all her direction from Nicole? Nicole must have been telling Rachel how to stroke you. So Nicole punished Rachel for following the orders Nicole gave her."

"I hadn't thought of that."

You didn't climb the OneTaste power pyramid. You were added to the bottom to make it taller.

Rachel was never going to succeed Nicole. Rachel was Nicole's executor, her scapegoat. Rachel had a daughter's devotion to Nicole and would act on any directive mother gave her. And anytime things went wrong, she would absorb all the blame. With Rachel as her shield, Nicole could orchestrate any kind of abuse and never get her hands dirty.

Tomorrow was a new year.

I decided to host a little New Year's party in my new apartment. I invited a few OMers who were also "halfway in" OneTaste—these were the only people I felt I could relate to.

Talia and Greg arrived early to OM before the party. They went to Talia's old bedroom while I cooked some steaks. Her vocalizations put me at ease. For two years I hadn't gone a single day without hearing a woman in Orgasm.

The last few weeks had been strange. I couldn't believe it was "normal" to live in a little box by myself, in a building of other boxes of other isolated people. I could go back, I thought. I could prostrate myself, and admit I was wrong, go through a little penitence, and become a Priest of Orgasm.

Or I could write the book.

Neil Strauss had said, "You might remember what you did, but you won't remember how you felt."

I was already unsure of how I felt. I could write the parable that Nicole wanted, but that didn't feel right. I got in touch with Naomi Wolf who encouraged me to write a hard-hitting expose. But that didn't feel right either.

I flipped a steak. Talia let out a guttural, "unngh." Greg must have hit the spot.

"You are so in the middle, that you're neither liked, nor a powerful man," Nicole had said.

I also had superstitious fear that I'd lose my Orgasm and Nicole would cast a spell on me if I betrayed her. I didn't fully believe it, but denying that possibility meant denying my positive "magical" experiences.

Talia's moans got higher and louder, from contralto to alto to soprano...

BANG!

Everything went black. My ears were ringing. I faintly heard Talia's dog barking, as if she was far away. My vision returned to see I was five feet back from the stove. The dog became louder. I realized she was right next to me, frantic. My throat was stinging, and my left hand had a piercing pain. I opened my fist. There was a hot piece of shrapnel, burning a welt into my palm.

I stumbled to the kitchen sink and ran it under cold water. It looked like a fastener or a bolt covering. The dog switched to howling. Talia came out of the bedroom with her pants off.

"What was that?"

"I don't know. I was cooking... gunshot sound... my hand..."

"Oh my god!" she said pointing to my throat.

I went to the bathroom mirror. There was a bright pink gash on my throat, a perfect vertical slice, as if done with a scalpel. It formed an ellipse, like a sideways eye or...

"It's a pussy!" Greg said.

"Greg! This is serious!" Talia said.

"Let's Facetime my dad," Greg said. "He's a plastic surgeon. He used to be a gynocologist but he hated it. He always says, 'I used to look at the worst vaginas, now I make the best breasts.'"

"Greg!"

I sat on the toilet while Greg FaceTimed his dad. His dad recommended we go to the ER. He wished us a Happy New Year then said some things in Hebrew before hanging up.

"Ok, let's go to the ER," Talia said.

"No. No no no. I don't have health insurance."

"You have to listen to Greg's dad. He's a doctor."

"This is Tanisha. She's a doctor."

"What?"

"It's not even bleeding. Just get me a band-aid," I said rising to my feet. "I can walk this off. Watch me."

I had to stop at the door frame to catch my breath. My arms felt tingly. Dots were forming in my periphery. Talia's lips were moving but I couldn't make out any words. My vision tunneled on the stove. Someone should turn that off, I thought.

Everything went black.

I returned to consciousness to see a bunch of faces looking down at me. It was my entire party. I was lying on the kitchen floor.

"Hi Ruwan," a teary-eyed woman said. It was Sally.

"Oh hey. I made steaks."

Sally laughed through some tears.

"Greg caught you just before you hit the floor," Talia said.

"Thanks Greg."

"You got it buddy."

The whole party had showed up right after I passed out.

"We also have sweet potatoes and baklava..." I said.

Everyone stared at me.

"Okay, I'll go to the fucking hospital."

My party escorted me around Fort Greene Park to Brooklyn Hospital Center. As a party of OMers, no one seemed phased by this change of plans. RCR, *Rapidly Changing Reality*.

"It's so interesting that it hit you right in the throat chakra," Sally said. "That's your communication center. It's like someone is trying to silence you."

Greg went with me into the ER room. While waiting on the table, we snapped a selfie and posted it to Facebook with the caption, "Kitchen exploded. Shrapnel cut my throat. All so I could hang in the ER with Greg."

It immediately got a comment from Nicole: "Oh my god are you okay? Thank you Greg for taking care of him."

Something in my chest contracted. My heart started racing. Did she cast a spell to silence me? If I believed that, then I'd never feel safe.

The ER doctor walked in scribbling on a chart. He was a young American-born Desi with a SoCal accent. Greg kidded him about being stuck working New Year's Eve. The doctor said it's not that bad. After midnight it was just tending to people who got too drunk.

"So what happened?" he asked.

I showed him the piece of shrapnel. "I'm pretty sure it's the covering of the bolt that connects the pan to the panhandle. It must have gotten too hot and exploded. It shot at my throat then landed in my hand somehow."

"I've never heard of that before," he said with absolutely no expression. I wondered what Dr. Tanisha was up to these days.

He scribbled on the chart. He shined a pen light on my laceration and looked closer. "You're lucky it only went skin deep. If it pierced your trachea, you'd be in the morgue right now."

Greg was grinning. I knew he wanted to point out the cut's resemblance to the female anatomy.

"We're going to need to do an x-ray," the doctor said. "It looks clean, but sometimes foreign bodies will get stuck in the wound and cause serious problems later. Once we know it's clear, I'll stitch you back up."

"Will it leave a scar?" I asked.

He clicked off his penlight and thought for a moment.

"Depends on how you treat it."

AfterTaste

Federal court is a lot like a TurnON.

There's an intro talk to "get everyone's voice in the room" (opening remarks). Then one at a time people come up on the HotSeat (witness stand), where they get asked extremely personal, vulnerable, and well-thought-out questions to illicit a certain response. There's a lead facilitator (judge) who cuts people off when they are offstroke. There are even two teams of Saboteurs (attorneys), vying for control of the consensus reality who end the event with attempts to change people's realities (closing arguments).

In June 2023, the FBI indicted Nicole Daedone and Rachel Cherwitz on "conspiracy to commit forced labor." This was after a 2018 expose by Bloomberg News, and a 2022 Netflix documentary *Orgasm, Inc.,* along with much other copycat coverage of OneTaste as a cult.

I was quoted or appeared in every piece of media covering OneTaste. Going back to 2015, one year after I left, I began speaking on podcasts about my experience. Initially, I emphasized the positive aspects. Even with my seeming clarity, I found it hard to ever really criticize Nicole. I could see most of OneTaste's manipulations but still couldn't help seeing Nic's halo. Naomi Wolf suggested that I had Stockholm Syndrome.

I was still committed to writing the book I had planned on with Nicole, but it went through many phases on the way to becoming the one you are reading. At first, I wanted to highlight the paranormal aspects. I really wanted "muggles" to see what was so cool about this weird community. I wanted to believe in magic. I wanted to prove to myself that all this was worth it.

I struggled to make sense of reality.

The hardest part of returning to the "real world" was the realization that there was no such thing. At least not the way I had previously thought. *Reality is a set of agreements.* Every group had its own "reality tunnel" — a set of memes, beliefs, and assumptions about reality that weren't proven, but were confirmed by others in their group. Normie society was just another cult—a big disorganized one. I missed the time when my world was small and certain.

I had a hard time connecting with "muggles." I didn't know who the mayor of New York was, despite being here the past two years. I didn't get any pop culture references. Unless we were talking about sex or mysteries of the human experience, I didn't know what to say.

So the only social interaction where I felt normal was in dating. But after awhile, even that faded. With no community to confirm myself, I began doubting all my thoughts and behaviors. I went back to being awkward, but a new kind of awkward where I was painfully conscious of my awkwardness.

"People keep their Orgasm for about six months after they leave OneTaste," Rachel said.

Sally left around the same time as me, and we ended up in a relationship. We clung to each other as the only two who really understood what the other experienced. But our trauma bond led to replaying "compression" patterns. Our attempts to love each other resulted in hurt. We split after six months and I fell into a deep depression. I came down with an inexplicable eczema on my eyelids which meant for periods of time I couldn't open my eyes.

It felt symbolic of something.

The only job I was able to hold onto was driving a cab. I enjoyed talking to the random passengers. It felt like doing HotSeats.

One evening, I drove a middle-aged woman from LaGuardia to her mansion in Connecticut. I felt a pressure in her and asked her about it. She burst into tears. Her husband had just died. Over four hours of traffic, I let her unload. I asked some questions. But mostly I just felt her. When we got to her place, she hugged me and gave me a hundred-dollar tip.

"You should really be a therapist," she said.

Some of my ex-clients from OneTaste reached out to work with me again. OneTaste had been getting weirder and more demanding. It became increasingly uncomfortable for the "masculine-minded." Ken, Jane, and even Rob had quit. The only people allowed to stay were those willing to submit completely.

Once in awhile, I still attended the New York OM Circle. I did it to try to "keep my Orgasm." I did it to feel "normal" in the otherwise strange world of muggle New York. Since I was no longer a Saboteur liability, the staff was friendly to me. Rachel always gave me a hug. Arjun had become male leader of New York. He and his assigned wife were a power couple in the community. I had to admit, Orgasm looked good on him.

In this time, I still recommended friends and acquaintances to try OMing. I just gave them a warning.

"Their front-end product is really good. Just make sure you don't get stuck," I said to many.

Sometime after enrolling in CP10, Talia asked me if it was a good idea to work for OneTaste. After all, I was largely responsible for her being there. I told her what I honestly believed at the time, that as a Left Hand Path it was going to put you through the ringer, and you'll either survive and thrive, or get fucked up. But it was probably a net positive if you only did it for a couple years.

I should not have told her that.

Less than a year later I met Talia for dinner. She had just left. She had been on a fast-track through Orgasm: CP10, employment, NDI, Nicole-sanctioned marriage. As a young, hot member of the staff, she had been paired with a wealthy tech guy, who coincidentally was friends with my old client, Leo. She convinced him to pay for NDI and a new program, "Membership" where for fifty thousand a year, you get access to all OneTaste courses. At NDI, they convinced him to propose, and they were legally married in a group wedding. After milking the sanctioned couple for both currencies, she and her husband were able to leave. Their relationship didn't last long.

She was traumatized. She was broken. I never recommended anyone to check out OMing again.

I did, however, feel a duty to speak the truth on all of it. Most people wanted to pick out one shade of the truth. Some asserted that OneTaste was a vehicle of healing and Enlightenment. Most others said, "it's a cult and cults are bad."

I always felt both perspectives were lazy and untrue ways to abstract reality. If anything, my observations on OneTaste shine a light on the deeper truths of human nature—that ethics, will, and consciousness are not easily put in moral "Good vs. Evil" boxes.

Per general semantics, most people confuse the very abstract word, "good."

"Good" can refer to competence. OneTaste was very good in this sense, at changing people. Nicole was a genius manipulator. She was very good at it.

"Good" can also refer to morality. Morally, OneTaste did many not good things, regardless of intention.

These two definitions of "good" are independent and not at all mutually exclusive. Anyone who can't see how a "good" thing can be bad, is semantically confused.

But hey, it happens to the best of us.

Arjun stayed in OneTaste for a little over a year after me. I caught up with him in LA, some months after he left with "guns a-blazing," as he put it. Nicole wanted to get more money out of him, so she invited him for a "special experience" where the two of them would do a heroic dose of LSD together.

"I don't know if there was any LSD in Nic's cup," he said. "But there definitely was in mine."

Throughout the eight-hour trip, Nicole verbally stroked him to get him to give One-Taste more money. He almost did. But during the come down he snapped out of it. Thankfully, he tied himself to the mast before answering the Sirens' call. Before buying the New York affiliate, he had a lawyer sneak a clause in his contract that he could get his entire investment back when he decided to leave.

Winter also got paid. She told a lawyer about her experience through tears and asked, "so do I actually have a case here?" His jaw dropped. This would be a slam dunk—forced labor, pandering, emotional abuse. His only concern was if she'd be emotionally stable enough to appear in court. They settled out of court for three hundred fifty thousand. Winter bought land in Montana.

I saw her only once after that— We caught up in New York for lunch. She was in town for some expensive mastermind for women who owned marketing agencies. She seemed to be thriving. I asked her, with all that happened, was it worth it to have developed such confidence?

"Hell no," she said.

I never saw her again.

Over the years, I did my best to separate the gold from the dirt of my experience. I began coaching full time, trying to use the OneTaste skills but without the manipulation. I moved to Asia.

In 2018, Priscilla invited a reporter from Bloomberg News to cover OneTaste as a ground-breaking female-led company with a fascinating take on work culture. This reporter, Ellen Huet, happened to be acquainted with Talia's ex-husband from the San Fran tech scene. She got enough of the real scoop to turn it into an expose.

I was happy to contribute information to the article. I felt she was the first journalist to care about the nuances beyond superficial praise or condemnation. But I didn't think much would come from it. I had been quoted in several such articles, and nothing resulted.

But this expose shook everything.

Shortly after the article broke, OneTaste imploded. Like in the Morellino when we accidentally met non-OM residents while in our underwear, it was like the outside world got a real look at what was going on in OM land.

My mother called me frantically the next day. OneTaste had hired a private investigator to leave harassing voicemails on my parents' cellphones. He did the same to others who were quoted in the Bloomberg article. Intimidation tactic. My neurotic mother was afraid Nicole was going to put a hit on me. Nicole was Sicilian and liked to tell everyone about it, after all.

Shortly after, OneTaste announced they were closing all their centers. I got an email that the New York OM Center in Soho would be having a closing party.

I didn't ever intend for OneTaste to go out of business. I just wanted to tell the full nuanced truth that most weren't telling. But OneTaste had made me an enemy by harassing my folks.

I happened to be in New York visiting them, so I decided to show up. I brought Daniel with me. We stood in the center of the room and chatted with a few peripheral OMers who we knew from the good old days. There was a gaggle of young men wearing necklaces signifying that they graduated from CP10. They made grimacing faces at us. Elma and some other staff I knew walked the long way around the room to avoid us. I smiled at them anyway.

Everything is a communication.

Later that week, I received a visit from the FBI. They waited for my parents to go to work before they knocked on the door. We sat at my parents' kitchen table and had coffee while one probed me with questions, and the other jotted down notes. They were looking to find evidence of prostitution or employment crimes. I told them it was a grey area regarding free will. No one in OneTaste was ever physically forced. Instead, they modified our will so that we *wanted* to do what they wanted.

I thought about explaining Bottoming. But the agents didn't seem to care for my analysis.

Before I left town, Daniel and I had dinner with Om Rupani at his home. We discussed the latest OneTaste gossip. Nicole had sold her shares in OneTaste to a pair of trust fund kids. Rumors circulated around the ex-OneTaste community that Nicole was scoping out Bali as a new base because Indonesia doesn't extradite to the United States.

"That breaks my heart," Om said. "She doesn't deserve to go out like that."

We discussed and debated OneTaste ethics.

"Nicole's shadow was to keep alpha males out," Om said. "She had to be the topmost Top. I was able to top her because I saw through her bullshit... Nicole and OneTaste is like a Queen and her court. The Queen has all her Ladies-in-Waiting. The Queen needs to look out for her ladies, so she allows certain men to dance with her ladies. If she didn't, the ladies would revolt. But she doesn't let in all men, only the ones that serve her agenda, or at least don't get in the way. So if you're a man and you want access to her ladies, you need to play by the rules of the court. Most men do, because she has the most Turned On ladies.

"Nicole said a lot of nonsense, but she had a few insights that really rang true. One was, 'A woman will try to buy you at the lowest price she can get.' She and Regena were some of the best hustlers to ever come out of Morehouse. Nicole hustled the best of them. And that was the education we all got. In Nicole's field, you learned how to truly handle the Feminine. It's the most genuine education. You learned the real truths, the ones that most people can't teach you because they don't want to accept them. You learned that someone could see into your soul and still be morally corrupt. Previously, you thought anyone who could see your soul must be a pure being. But that isn't true."

Daniel brought up a Word document that had been circulating around the ex-One-Taste community. Allegedly, it was was written by Ray Vetterlein, Nicole's personal instructor in the stroking arts, a contemporary of Vic Baranco.

The document detailed a plan to create a sort of community-driven business that taught about sexuality and communication, and also hooked people for huge amounts of money. It detailed the strategies that would make this new company a success— such as by enrolling young, hot, impressionable women because they would be able to recruit everyone else.

To whom it was addressed wasn't clear. But it wasn't written for Nicole. Much was written *about* Nicole. It described how Nicole was the ideal leader for such a movement because she was beautiful, articulate, and had a magnetism greater than most people could dream of. It also said that Nicole would crave all that attention because she was unconsciously traumatized from being sexually abused by her father.

"That's some deep karma," Om said. "And if the FBI pursues, Nicole could be headed for the same fate... I don't know if these allegations of her past are true, but just imagine they are... And then that little girl grows up to be *the* Nicole Daedone... that charismatic, that sexy, that confident... who has the power to influence how many people so deeply... Ruwan, just think of the life you live, the life we all live. Your karma is deeply intertwined with Nicole. You get to travel the world and women ask you to touch their bodies. You might have a book deal and a TV show, on top of the lifestyle you're already living. If it wasn't for Nicole and her past, her father, maybe none of that would have happened. So tell me, who owes whom?"

"But you can't say she isn't to blame," Daniel cut in.

"I didn't say anything about blame," Om said. "I see only karma. Karmic lines are simply causes and effects. Our lives are like these long cords. And they get woven together and knotted with different people along the way. The three of us have some sort of intertwined karma, otherwise we wouldn't be sitting here. Why are the two of you sitting here and not some other two? The three of us, in different ways, became intertwined with Nicole. How many others? For most, being hooked by Nicole is the most meaningful thing they have ever done."

Some months later I got a call from Om Rupani. We never spoke on the phone so I figured it was about something that didn't want a paper trail. OneTaste had invited him to *The Land,* a retreat center property that OneTaste now used as their headquarters. It was purchased for them by a member of the Wrigley family.

"I just had dinner with Nicole," he said. "She's very concerned about what you'll put in your book. If there's anything you want from her, now's the time to ask."

I thought for a moment of what sum I'd be willing to sell out for. But I decided that abandoning this book would be abandoning myself.

In 2019, I was contacted by a production company who wanted to make a documentary about OneTaste. I thought they were going for a full nuanced analysis. *Wild Wild Country,* the docuseries on Osho's Ragneeshi cult had recently come out. I thought they'd make something like that. I sat with them for over ten hours of interviews.

Orgasm, Inc. turned out to be a one-speed documentary pushing a "look how weird this is" narrative. I don't know if that was the producers' intention all along, or if the legal pressure from OneTaste forced them to make last minute changes. Either way, the final cut was a weird collection of disjointed scenes that made it seem like OneTaste was me and a bunch of old guys.

Winter indirectly appeared in the documentary in an attempt to circumvent her NDA. The documentary had her sister read emails allegedly from her. They sounded fake to me—Winter never had the best grammar. They also claimed she was physically beaten and abused by her boyfriend. Arjun was way too physically frail to have done that. I wasn't sure why she had to lie. The truth was bad enough.

A lot of legal actions came downstream from the documentary. A former OMer who also used to work for Tony Robbins encouraged me to sue for corporate crime. She said a bunch of his ex-employees received huge payouts under similar "cult-like" circumstances. I was notified that a handful ex-OneTasters were bringing civil suits against OneTaste for "adult sex crimes." One of their lawyers told me I could join the suit. The statute of limitations would be up in November 2023. I declined. I felt it would be dishonorable. I just wanted to tell the story.

In June 2023, the FBI officially indicted Nicole Daedone and Rachel Cherwitz.

Meanwhile, OneTaste sued Winter for breaking her NDA. I received requests from OM friends who were still friendly with OneTaste to help them against Winter and testify for the defense in the FBI's criminal case. I agreed Winter had lied, but I wasn't going to help them further harm one of their victims. They subpoenaed me to provide all my messages with Winter and various other disgruntled OneTasters. I decided to pay the $150 court fine instead.

Later, some of the same pro-OneTasters passed on threats that I better contact John to help their defense or else OneTaste would have me extradited. I told them to shove it.

Other angrier ex-OneTasters, and the FBI, asked if I would testify for the prosecution in the criminal case. I also declined. I just wanted to tell the story.

But funny enough, I did end up in court anyway.

After a couple years of reschedulings and appeals, the case went to trial in May 2025. Coincidentally, I happened to be in New York visiting my parents. I had bought my flights when the trial was still scheduled for January, partly looking to avoid being in New York during the trial given the legal threats OneTaste was sending me. But given the divine coincidence, I had to go.

Also, Om Rupani said if I didn't go, I'd be a pussy. Point taken, Mr. Rupani.

I only got to be in court for one day. Not knowing court protocol, I accidentally sat on the "defense" side. Nicole, Rachel, and Nicole's lawyer all had raised eyebrows upon seeing me, but otherwise avoided eye contact. Paralegals from the prosecution whispered while looking my direction. I assumed they recognized me from the Netflix doc.

Judge Diane Gujarati opened with "housekeeping" before the jury entered. Her main point was regarding how OneTasters were communicating with those who had come to see the trial.

"No one should be the recipient of any unwanted interaction in this courtroom," she said. "Efforts to intimidate and/or to deter the presence of any member of the public or courthouse staff will not be tolerated."

The OneTaste loyalists did not help their case. They made angry faces at all the government witnesses. Reporters covering the trial noted the OneTasters dressed in white, praying with mala beads. Some even were doing yoga in the hallway.

They didn't even try to not seem like a cult.

I only got to see one person testify, a person who inspired one of the characters of this book. She described the Warehouse, how staff was sent to pleasure Reese Jones, how many OneTasters did sex work until the New York Times article and Nicole decided to clean up their image. She described the term "white rabbit"— a woman used to entice a man into OneTaste.

On cross examination, Nicole's attorney drilled her on how no one forced her to do the things she did. Everyone acted on their volition—this was the defense's main play. The witness explained, in the best way one could, that when in OneTaste you didn't really have a choice. They controlled your feelings. To disobey was to lose all your emotional bonds.

After the morning break, I was handed a subpoena to testify for the *defense.* I couldn't understand why. Did they want to highlight the positives I've said about them? Were they going to use me to discredit the media or other witnesses' testimony? Or maybe they just wanted to keep me out of court—Subpoenaed witnesses can't watch other witnesses testify.

I stayed for the rest of the testimony that day anyway. That week many others I knew testified for the prosecution including Ken Blackman, and Rob Kandell, who took an immunity deal.

All week, I wondered why the defense would subpoena me. It was from Rachel's lawyer specifically. Maybe she knew I had a soft spot for Rachel and would save her if I could. If there was anyone brainwashed at OneTaste, it was Rachel. I remembered how devoted I was to her when I was her mentee. Rachel must have been a hundred times more the devoted daughter to Nicole. She likely received the same or better deal as Rob to throw Nicole under the bus, but didn't take it. Maybe she even knew her role was always to be

Nicole's scapegoat. "Just following orders" is not a defense. But I know any harm Rachel took part in, she did out of genuine devotion to Nicole.

I showed up the following Monday in a suit ready to testify. Outside of the courthouse, OneTaste staffers all smiled at me hypnotically. I was ready to tell the whole truth regardless of which way it swayed the case.

Rachel did walk by me as I sat outside the courtroom. She flashed a familiar smile. I knew it was mostly a play, a Hail Mary to try to get me on their side. When your only tool is seduction, the whole world looks like a john. But at the same time, I couldn't help being reminded of that nostalgic love. The emotion was real, though I knew it had all sorts of strings attached.

Love is a complicated emotion.

But it ultimately was anti-climactic. Ironic. Rachel's lawyer told me she wasn't sure if she'd need me, but she'd let me know later. Maybe just to keep me out of the courtroom.

Many of my friends testified for the government, people I came to love deeply, though most I hadn't spoken with in years. Reading the court transcripts was reliving my youth. My loss of innocence. I was mentioned over twenty times throughout the trial, including events covered in this book.

Enlightenment leaves no scars, Daniel always said.

The scars were apparent in many of the witnesses. PTSD symptoms over a decade later.

On June 9, 2025, the jury came to the verdict. Nicole Daedone, guilty. Rachel Cherwitz, guilty. More surprising than the verdict, was that the judge remanded them, meaning they were to be taken into custody immediately, despite having been out on bail over a year.

Judge Gujarati said the defendants had failed to prove that they weren't a flight risk. Nicole had followers around the world who were clearly willing to hide her. Rachel had continued living with named co-conspirators— the rest of the Exec Team in an OM Residence.

Most assumed part of the judge's decision came from OneTaste's out of court behavior. They had hired a skeevy PR guy to run various articles slandering people who had spoken against OneTaste. I braced for one about me, but it never came. Either they were saving it for later or were hoping to bring me on their side. One piece was about the judge herself, calling her names, accusing her of bias, and showing the Brooklyn Court House with a swastika over it.

Not even Nicole's supporters could explain why a defendant would slander the judge overseeing their case. Nicole, OneTaste, lived in their own bubble. A false reality of their own creation.

The court's marshals allowed Nicole to take off her jewelry before being taken in. Rachel mouthed, "I love you," to her supporters in the gallery.

The sentencing was initially scheduled for September 2025, but was rescheduled upon appeals from the OneTaste lawyers. At this time,* the sentencing date is still pending.

It took over ten years to complete this book of my two years at OneTaste. In that sense, those two years really were the longest decade of my life. And truthfully, if I knew it was going to take so much of me, I would have never begun.

But as they say, the Left Hand Path is best never started, but once started it must be completed.

*This Advance Reader's Copy does not contain the the final sentencing
of Nicole Daedone and Rachel Cherwitz.
See the next page on how to get the updated version once sentencing is passed.

Get the updated version + bonuses

This is a limited edition of the book, pre-federal sentencing. It will be updated once sentencing is passed.

Put your email in at:

<u>orgsmbook.com/prerelease</u>

to receive an updated version + the following bonuses.

1. Advance copy of Ruwan's next book, *Anima: The Five Aspects of the Feminine Unconscious*

2. How To Brainwash Yourself (mini-course)

3. Ruwan's meditation library

If you enjoyed this book, please rate & review on
Amazon or Goodreads

More from Ruwan:

How to get in touch or stay updated:

   Instagram: **@ruwando**

   Other writing: **ruwando.substack.com**

   Courses & coaching: **ruwando.com**

Two more books coming soon!

     1. *Anima: The Five Aspects of Feminine Unconscious*

     2. *The Scorpion & The Frog: Defend Yourself Against Dangerous People By Understanding Their Nature*

(Follow on substack to be notified.)

www.ingramcontent.com/pod-product-compliance
Lightning Source LLC
Chambersburg PA
CBHW071454140726
47997CB00005B/1721